MILITARIZATION, INTERNAL REPRESSION AND SOCIAL WELFARE IN THE THIRD WORLD

MILITARIZATION, INTERNAL REPRESSION AND SOCIAL WELFARE IN THE THIRD WORLD

MILES D. WOLPIN

ST. MARTIN'S PRESS
New York

© 1986 Miles D. Wolpin
All rights reserved. For information, write:
St. Martin's Press, Inc., 175 Fifth Avenue, New York, NY 10010
Printed in Great Britain
First published in the United States of America in 1986
Library of Congress Cataloging in Publication Data

Wolpin, Miles D.
    Militarization, internal repression, and social
welfare in the Third World.

    Bibliography: p.
    1. Armies, Cost of. 2. Public welfare–Developing
countries. 3. Civil-military relations–Developing
countries. I. Title.
UA17.W65   1986   303.4′8   85-10843
ISBN 0-312-53233-4

Contents

Contents

Contents

Contents

Contents

Contents

Contents

Contents

To Nils Petter Gleditsch and Vigdis Mathisen
who have both in different ways
inspired this work.

Chapter 1

MILITARIZATION AND WELFARE ASPIRATIONS

As the decade of the eighties opened, Mexico's leading newspaper, Excelsior (Weekly Review, 24 March,
1980:4) warned its readers that "the rate of progress and development to improve the standard of
living in Third World countries has been reduced
drastically in the last decade, according to a
report by the World Bank published last Thursday in
Washington". Nine months later, while addressing a
hundred or so persons who with the Foreign Minister
of Norway had gathered on 11 December, 1980 to
honour him, Nobel Peace Prize winner Argentine human
rights activist Adolfo Perez Esquival implored "you
should try to prevent the sale of armaments to Latin
America because they are used to oppress the
people". While Perez Esquival was alluding to the
consequences of domestic militarism, the scope of
this analysis while encompassing repression is more
far-reaching. As Table 1 makes clear, underdeveloped
countries' economies are growing so modestly that
they are failing to narrow the lead of developed
countries. Thus designating them as "developing"
becomes increasingly problematic or even illusory.
Elsewhere, Sivard (1981:20) records that "in absolute terms, the gain since 1960 has been over ten
times more for developed countries, $3,600 in con-
stant dollars, as against $340 for developing". More
recently the UN Group of Governmental Experts on the
Relationship between Disarmament and Development
(UNSG, 1982:25) echoed this warning of

> the large and widening gap in standards of
> well-being between developed and developing
> countries. In 1975, the developing countries
> (excluding China) accounted for 52.3 per cent
> of world population but for only 16.8 per cent
> of world GNP. Put in another way, average per

1

capita income in the developing countries was
just 8.5 per cent of that in the developed economies. This disparity is far greater if the
comparison is confined to the poorest developing countries, those where per capita income in
1970 was less than $200. This group of coun-
tries accounts for 21.1 per cent of world population but a mere 1.6 per cent of world GNP.(1)

Put succinctly, to what degree can it be said that
the rise in living standards in the Third World has
been adversely affected over the past two decades by
the allocation of increasing resources to military
purposes?

The mere existence of armed forces does not itself
mean that a state is either militaristic or embarked
upon a course of militarization. While the latter
refers to a growing (Lumsden, 1980:358-9; Hveem and
Malnes, 1980:6) armaments capacity and allocations
of societal resources for military ends, militarism
has been most usefully distinguished from this process by Vagts (1967). In this view it pertains to
values, attitudes and practices which connote a bias
or preference for military means where they are un-
necessary from the standpoint of territorial defence.(2) Thus, although militaristic sentiment may
catalyse or even be an unintended consequence of
militarization, it is conceivable that where a society is externally threatened and unable to resolve
the conflict by non-military means that devotion of
greater resources to the armed forces would not be
inherently militarist. But this situation is relatively rare in the contemporary world. Hence the
ubiquitous synonymous employment of these two terms
mirror in stark terms an ominous dimension of the
reality in which we survive: thermonuclear terror,
global militarization and an ever more pervasive
tendency to equate "defence" with the diversion of
vitally needed socio-economic resources to military
ends which now extend to internal repression, state
management, external intervention, and alleged "de-
terrence" without a capacity for impending societal
devastation.

The breakdown of détente since 1978 has catalysed an
intensification of the East-West arms race. This is
not only reactive to relative superpower parity and
rivalry in the developing areas, but it constitutes
a direct impetus for arms exports and militarization
within the Third World. Thus the UN's "Third Decade

of Development" promises an even greater tempo in
diverting resources to armed forces than preceding
decades. By the late 1970s an economist (Whynes,
1979:33) could observe "these data indicate that
defence is the single most important item in average
world public expenditure". He records elsewhere (81)
that "the annual volume of arms imports has risen
over the past two decades - the increase has been
almost six-fold as compared to the four-fold growth
in Third World military expenditures". Similarly,
according to SIPRI (1980:8-13):

> In 1979 ... the value of arms exports was five
> times greater than in 1969, and twelve times
> greater than in 1959 ... Two thirds of the
> world armament trade are transfers to the Third
> World, a good part of which suffers from under-
> development, hunger and sickness.

Official government responsibility for arms exports
is highlighted by the fact that private commercial
transactions account for little more than (Askari
and Glover, 1977:10) 5% per cent of arms sales. If
in the decade of the 1970s, the United States accounted for almost two-fifths of the world's arms
exports and the Soviet Union virtually a third, we
can anticipate that their intensified rivalry in the
1980s may lead not only to increased exports but
quite possibly to a near duopoly over the global
arms trade. Murphy (1982) for example, notes that
"Washington is a major supplier to more than 120
countries, with sales that have gone from $4.9 bil-
lion in 1971 to over $20 billion this year, accord-
ing to Pentagon figures." This despite the fact that
24 of the 56 countries now producing major weapons
are in the Third World.

In terms of world military spending, between 1965
and 1979, the share of developing areas increased
from 6.3 to 15.3 per cent, though due to concealment
these figures are probably a gross understatement.
Thus well before the escalation of military spending
in the Afro-Asian "new nations", Janowitz (1964:18)
acknowledged that

> the cost of a military establishment are, in
> proportion to per capita income, high for a new
> nation. In particular, military expenditures
> take a large portion of the public budget. ...
> Of course, the official budget often markedly
> underrepresents military expenditures, which

3

can go unreported or be carried on civilian agency budgets.

Similarly with respect to Latin America, another scholar (Weaver, 1973:64-5) cautions:

> The budgets and the overall costs of maintaining a military establishment are extremely difficult to measure since without exception Latin American governments hide military appropriations in several budget categories (the Ministry of the Interior or Justice expenditure, for example, may conceal funds ostensibly programmed for military controlled 'public safety'); moreover, debt repayment and service charges on loans to military and counterinsurgent programs, or for equipment, are usually not included in the formal accounts of the armed forces.

For these reasons, one Israeli scholar (Seliktar, 1980:341) completely rejects the utility of a statistical tradeoff analysis of his own country, arguing that

> According to an authoritative work on Israeli economy, even the overt figures for defense spending 'must be regarded as minimum estimates' (Halevi and Klino-Malul, 1968:193). Also since some defense expenditures appear under agriculture, transport or industry and some educational and welfare projects are financed through the defense budget, an analysis of tradeoffs between defense and selected social spending is not feasible.

Similarly, two Finnish scholars (Tuomi and Väyrynen, 1980:244) enter the caveat that "an estimation of the development costs of the Indonesian military establishment is complicated by the fact that the official defence budget covers only 40-50 per cent of the real expenses. The deficit is financed by the state-owned oil company, Pertamina, as well as by the companies - ranging from shipping lines to timber concessions - controlled by the regional military commands."

As far as imports are concerned, similar problems confront the analyst. Thus Tuomi and Väyrynen (1980:215) emphasize that:

International trade statistics do not report arms imports at all. It can be assumed that some military transfers are hidden in various SITC subcategories; on the other hand some countries totally exclude arms from their trade figures, to make their statistics look better.

And Gunder Frank (1979:5) adds the caveat that "in official trade statistics, arms are frequently camouflaged as ´transportation´ and other equipment". Furthermore, Sivard (1981:9) underscores the salient fact that:

Official records of arms transfers represent only the tip of the iceberg in the proliferation of weapons and technology throughout the world. Not included in arms trade data:
- Nuclear weapons.
- Gray area trade in equipment such as computers and electronic machinery with military applications.
- Licensing arrangements for production of everything from small arms to weapons of mass destruction.
- Exports of plutonium, uranium, and nuclear reactors.
- Thefts from government arsenals.
- The remainders of past wars, included the estimated $5 billion in guns, vehicles, riot-control gases, etc. left in Vietnam by US forces.
- Training by the arms-exporting nations of thousands of foreign military personnel yearly in the use of the latest weapons of war.
- Black market trade in restricted items.
- Acquisition of equipment and production manuals through bribery and espionage.
- Covert, officially-sanctioned movements of arms and supplies to guerrillas and insurrectionists.

Leitenberg (1976:112-13) underscores another dimension of this problem by demonstrating that US military aid - which accounts for a preponderance of non-OPEC arms transfers to the Third World - is grossly understated in that it fails to include several military related aid categories. And to compound our dilemma, Brzoska (1981:268-74) in a carefully reasoned methodological critique of ISS, SIPRI and ACDA military expenditure figures stresses that because the military expenditure category (Milex) is based upon exchange rates rather than domestic purchasing power parities, it considerably understates Third World military burdens. An earlier discussion of the latter comparability problem was published by SIPRI (1973). Data inconsistencies and related matters are also essayed by Neuman (1978:569-94) and by Leitenberg and Ball (1980:286-95).

Notwithstanding these difficulties and because as yet there has been no systematic analysis of the average understatement of military expenditures, I shall be forced to rely upon official ACDA figures. Even so the rise in military spending has been impressive. In terms of constant 1978 dollars (USACDA, 1979:27), the use of global societal resources for military ends escalated from 225 billion in 1960 to in excess of 450 in 1980. More than a hundred billion of this has been expended in the Third World with approximately three-quarters in non-Middle Eastern poverty stricken areas. Third World militarization is apparent in both a faster rise of expenditures as well as a greater increase in the size of armed forces than in the developed countries. Thus, USACDA (1979:27, 70) records for the 1968-77 decade indicate that the former's military expenditures in constant dollars escalated from 54 to 92 billion while among the latter the rise was from 305 to 319. With respect to men under arms, the developing countries went from 12.5 to 15.6 million while industrialized nations decreased theirs from 11.9 to 10.6. If we look at the past two decades, the trends are even more stark. Thus Sivard (1981:8) points out the salient fact that:

> Between 1960 and 1980, the regular forces in developing countries rose from 8.7 to 15.1 million men (chart 2). They now represent over 60 percent of the world total. In the same period, their military expenditures in constant dollars - although dwarfed by the budgets of the major powers - increased three-fold. The forces were growing not only in numbers but even more rapidly, in equipment and infrastructure.

Arms import as officially reported (Sivard, 1981:9, 16) totalled in excess of $122 billion for 1961-71 to developing countries.(3) And this drain accounts for an appreciable portion (Tuomi and Vàyrynen, 1980:217-21) of Third World external debt - currently well in excess of $650 billion. Some of the countries defaulting on external loans during the 1982-84 period are major arms importers.

While the developing nations are differentiated by language, ethnicity, religion and race, almost all are afflicted by extreme poverty at the mass level. This study will explore the degree to which mass living standards and political freedom have been directly affected by the level of military burdens and the rate of militarization which various Third World countries have experienced between the early 1960s and the late 1970s. Put differently, is there an inverse relationship between the use of resources for the military and various indicators of mass social betterment? The possible effects of alternative development strategies, civilian vs. military rule, varying levels of foreign aid, state extractive capability and economic development - along with the use of physical indicators of socio-political welfare including sexual equality - are features which differentiate this analysis from most others in the field.

Before turning to the data which are the basis for this book, I shall examine the findings of those who have analysed relationships between arms buildups, weapons transfers, war incidence and the human costs associated both with military and structural violence. Attention will then be directed at a number of recent conversion studies and "trade-off" analyses of the opportunity costs for military spending in both high and low income countries.(4) Albrecht (1978:86) has aptly characterized these as "reactionary", "reformist" and "radical". The first category, of which there are very few, seek to justify militarization as a source of employment and other spill-over benefits.(5) They are militaristic in the sense as Lumsden (1980:363) has put it, that they purport to "'legitimise' the expropriation of surplus produce for illegitimate macroparasitic purposes". Hveem and Malnes (1980:6) share a similar perspective: "Militarism is in our conceptualization the ideational counterpart of militarization, the former representing the military as ideas, beliefs and values in various forms and in several social strata." The mythologizing function of such superstructural beliefs is elucidated with precision by Eide (1980:308) who addresses military pretensions for a "nation-building" role:

Since economic development is a widely accepted

7

goal, this myth has significantly helped obtain acceptance of the quickly accelerating armaments in the Third World. (For social science contributions which have advanced the theory of modernisation, see Johnson, 1962, and Kennedy, 1974.)

Over the years, however, a process of intellectual liberation from these myths has slowly evolved. Peace research is the process of demystification, through hard empirical work and through further theoretical analysis. The claim is not that the myths are entirely wrong - in most cases, they have a core of truth - but in their general and vague contents they result in highly distorted perceptions which make disarmament difficult.(6)

In addition to assessing the "core of truth" in such "reactionary" studies, greater attention will be given to the findings of Albrecht's "liberal" reformists - whose research represents the preponderance of empirical work in this area. Many, however, eschew specific policy advocacy notwithstanding the implications of their findings that arms expenditures adversely affect mass living standards. Few indeed devote attention to the political obstacles to conversion. As Albrecht (1978:100) has stressed, "the most formidable problem, in view of the elaborated studies - the political one - is scarcely dealt with in detail." Political aspects are addressed in class or systemic terms by the very small number of "radicals" who have done empirical work. What distinguishes this last school is that it

assesses the continuing arms race not so much in terms of decay and maldevelopment of bureaucracies and enterprises but more as a systemic outcome of capitalist development. In recent developments of this school of thought, only a minority considers capitalism as vitally dependent upon military activities. Others maintain that the existing symbiosis between the arms industry and the economy is a more contingent development and not the sole possible path for late capitalism. Military expenditures form, in the view of all the radicals, the most decisive barrier against social reform.

On this latter point the "radicals" are in apparent accord with the "reformists". But their critique is not limited to resource diversion as an impediment to financing welfare measures. The function of the armed forces in underdeveloped areas, they argue (Albrecht <u>et al</u>., 1974; Kaldor, 1978:64-8), is to maintain the structure of neo-colonial dependency in the periphery, i.e. surplus appropriation and transfer to core countries.(7) Tuomi and Vàyrynen (1980: 246) see this role as being reinforced because local initiatives to produce modern and especially complex weapons systems often require dependent linkages in the form of licensing, specialists and/or ownership by transnational corporations.

Chapter 2

WAR, ARMS TRANSFERS AND STRUCTURAL VIOLENCE

Prior to the 1960s with few exceptions most peace research was either legalistic or employed what Moll (1980) refers to as "arms using" models. The latter focus upon the probability, incidence and occasionally the human costs of war. Thus, for example, Singer and Small's (1972:374-5) systematic analysis of such conflicts between 1816 and 1965 yielded the following among its conclusions:

> there were 50 interstate wars and 43 imperial and colonial wars, leading directly to the death of over 27 million military personnel, exclusive of civilians. There was some sort of international war underway in all but 24 of the 150 years covered, consuming over 4500 nation months of active combat; with 144 nations having been in the system at one time or another, and its size ranging from 23 to 124, this is 5.2 percent of the total nation months available.

> The number of wars, the battle deaths, and the nation months have fluctuated considerably over time, with the 'average' decade seeing 6.2 wars, over 300 nation months of war, and almost 2 million battle deaths.

> the initiators 'win' in 70 percent of the interstate wars, and they sustain fewer battle deaths than their 'victims' in nearly 80 percent of the cases.

Singer's Correlates of War Project also found that high rates of militarization during or in situations of international tension were associated with a greater probability of war. And this is even more

10

likely when relative parity characterizes major pro-
tagonists. Singer (1981:11) reports that "while only
13% of all major power militarized disputes since
1816 escalated to war, that figure rose to 20% when
the parties were approximately equal in military
terms, and to 75% if such parity was combined with
rapid military buildup during the three years prior
to the dispute". This as well as increased alliance
tightness and induced polarization as sources of increased probability of war (Eberwein, 1981:31) are
especially relevant to the 1980s, as is the rising
proportion of civilian casualties in the twentieth
century. Hence, while 27 million military personnel
died in wars between 1816 and 1965, total twentieth
century fatalities until 1965 were in excess of 110
million (Stein, 1978:1).(8)

Of greater relevance to the direct effects upon developing areas is the analysis of post-Second World
War military conflicts by Kende (1973:73-82). He
found positive correlations between military expenditures and arms imports on one hand, and war on the
other. With respect to this relationship, Whynes
(1979:91) underscores its strength:

> When examining the aggregate figures ... we
> find a really striking similarity between their
> trends, especially those in wars and arms im-
> ports ... Kende's intuitive conclusion is sup-
> ported by regression analysis - the relation-
> ship between war and imports gives a coeffi-
> cient of correlation of 0.821, and this figure
> increases slightly if imports are lagged by one
> year.(9)

The "wars were predominantly domestic rather than
international". Most occurred within the Third World
and this became increasingly the case as the 20-year
post-Second World War period under scrutiny progres-
sed. Similarly, the average duration of internal
wars tended to lengthen, and this in turn was most
likely to occur when there was foreign intervention.
The United States was the most ubiquitous foreign
participant in such conflicts.

Sivard's (1981:8) more recent report is broadly consistent with Kende's analysis. Approximately 95 per
cent of "the 125 or more conflicts which have occurred in the world since World War II" have been in
the Third World. "In most cases foreign forces have
been involved, western powers accounting for 79 per-

11

cent of the intervention, communist for 6 percent, other developing nations for the remainder." The linkages between foreign involvement, conflict intensification and high military spending are given salience by a study (UNSG, 1982:87) of

> 36 developing countries with a growth rate ranging between 0.1 per cent and 9.9 per cent and military spending as part of their national budget varying between 5 to 20 percent, concludes that all of them have been actively involved in one or more of at least three types of security crises: (i) adversary relationship with neighbors; (ii) hostile groups threatening organized insurgency and secession; (iii) adverse strategic environment reflecting the conflicting major power interests extraneous to the immediate national security concerns of the developing countries themselves. At least 20 out of the 36 countries in the sample made hostile pairs; as many as 30 had faced secessionist and insurgency situations; almost two thirds of those experiencing one or more of the above-mentioned situations showed ascertainable evidence of the original conflict being intensified or extended owing to external involvement.

Although he does not scrutinize foreign involvement, Kennedy's (1974:158) analysis of Third World military expenditures revealing "a strong relationship between military hostilities and the size of the allocation" is consistent with the study abstracted in the above textual quotation.(10)

Consonant with foregoing global studies is Fitch's (1979:369) conclusion that the US Military Assistance Program to Latin America "generally leads to increased budgetary demands by the armed forces and to heightened frustrations where economic constraints prevent satisfaction of these demands". He goes on to cite Schmitter's statistical findings (1973:135-6) indicating that:

> U.S. military grants, credit assisted sales, and surplus sales generally have the net marginal effect of raising national defense expenditures above the level anticipated by the total size or relative level (of development) of a nation's economy.

Almost a decade earlier Hanson (1965:20-37) had argued US military aid to the region was used primari-
ly for repressive internal purposes rather than external defence. And a few years later (1968:84) he
buttressed this thesis citing testimony by the
Pentagon's Director of Military Assistance before a
congressional committee in which the latter denied
that any Latin American country needed larger forces
or "a lot of major items of hardware" even from the
standpoint of countering "the insurgency threat".(11)
What the transfer of weapons did, according to
Hanson, was to promote militarism and divert resources from pressing socio-economic development needs.
Wolpin (1973) and Murphy (1982) identify intelli-
gence activities as a function of efforts by US
military attachës to promote arms exports. Randle
(1980:96-97) cites a study by Lars Schoultz which
while not dealing explicitly with military regimes,
nevertheless found

> that the U.S. gives more economic and military
> aid to repressive regimes in Latin America than
> to others which are not so repressive. It found
> that there was a positive correlation between
> the level of U.S. aid and the violation of
> human rights, with the correlation for military
> aid being stronger than for foreign aid in
> general.

That this also retarded development is indirectly
implied by Avery's (1978:121-42) finding for the
1961-70 period of a very pronounced negative statistical relationship between growth of GNP and increased arms imports for Latin America. Related to
these patterns in a global context is Randle's
(1980:84) observation that "weapons and associated
equipment may account for up to one third of the
cost of all imports to the Third World".

The Middle East which "received 60 per cent of all
Third World (arms) imports between 1961-1980" is
perhaps an even better example of the frequently
spurious nature of "security" rationales. South
Editor Altaf Gauhar (1982:11) cogently stresses that
while the

> phenomenal growth of arms and military expen-
> ditures in the developing countries is usually
> justified on political and strategic grounds
> ... the obvious correlation between the wealth
> of a country and its propensity (or compulsion)

13

to spend that wealth on arms is often ignored. To put it bluntly: political and strategic conditions remaining the same, a country coming into wealth tends to (or is made to) apply its sudden riches to military purposes. Conversely, if the resources of a country do not significantly increase, the curve of its military expenditure, whatever its basic level, and despite occasional large-scale injection of funds to meet active military threats, remains relatively inflexible. It is suggested that a marked and sudden rise in military expenditure does not necessarily reflect increased security needs: it is often related to the increase in the wealth of a nation. If a country has the money, arms merchants would find and, if necessary, "create" the requisite security climate to induce or compel it to undertake higher military expenditures and higher arms imports. Indeed, the arms merchants "create" not only the requisite security climate to suit their marketing strategy, they also play hard to get. Nations coming into wealth are seen begging for arms while reluctant sellers explain how difficult it is for them to part with sophisticated weapons: the regional balance will be upset, there will be an uproar in the Senate, Congressman X will lose his shirt etc.

To illustrate, take the Middle East which saw a sharp increase in its income due to a rise in oil prices in the seventies. The value of major weapons imported in the region was US $196 million in 1961. By 1980 the value had risen to a staggering US $5,414 million, registering an increase of - hold on - over 2,762 per cent! The five year moving average shot up from US $327 million to US $4,312 million. Can one explain this massive increase, to which there was no parallel in any other part of the world during the period, except in terms of the oil-wealth which the manufacturers of military weapons decided to appropriate? Admittedly tensions were created, even crises unleashed, but they were part of the West's high-pressure arms marketing strategy. Two decades of profligate arms spending did not resolve any dispute in the region, nor did any country acquire a greater sense of security. All that happened was that oil was converted into guns.

Even if Gauhar's thesis is slightly overdrawn and undue significance attached to the influence of arms merchants, his argument is in an important sense persuasive and warrants careful attention. This conclusion is reinforced by the adverse socio-economic domestic effects found by Hansen (1972) and Gottheil (1974) - both discussed subsequently in Chapter 4.

These regionally focused studies highlight the significance of Kende's (1973) and Pierre's (1979) work which both treat the global consequences of arms transfers. Thus in his review of the latter, Kozyrez (1980:124-5) quotes the following summary from the introduction:

> Among the negative consequences of the arms transfers to 'unstable areas', they note, in particular, the exacerbated political tensions and armed conflicts, the escalating arms race, and exhaustion of scarce economic resources that it would be more rational to use for economic development and improving people's welfare. Moreover, repressive regimes use the weapons they receive to violate human rights, and arms transactions embroil their participants in special relations that may involve the supplier in local conflicts. (p. 4)

He concludes by noting that "The book provides an indicative description of the regimes that buy American weapons. It says, for instance, that the US government 'maintained close military ties and arranged large scale deals to transfer arms to different governments violating ... human rights flagrantly, for instance, resorting to tortures of political prisoners'."(12) (p.147) American culpability for Third World military repression (Wolpin, 1973; Chomsky and Herman, 1979; Herman, 1982) may also be indirectly inferred from Sivard's (1981:8-9) report that while the USSR trained 43,000 military personnel from developing areas between 1955 and 1979, for the US alone the number from the 1950-80 period was in excess of 411,000. "Approximately three-fourths of those trained by the superpowers came from countries now under military domination." Sivard notes that "half of all the developing countries" in her survey - 54 - were controlled or dominated by the military and that fully "41 have been cited for violating basic human rights to safety under the law". Her assessment of the trend toward military rule may be somewhat conservative. Reporting on a

15

global "Quality of Life" study by Richard Estes published in 1983 by Praeger, Fred Farris (1982:7) notes that "The number of poor countries with either military control or military influence in the background ... has increased from 33 in 1972 to 65 in 1978." Although Estes correctly - as we shall see in Chapter 7 - attributes the "widening socio-economic gap between the North and South to this phenomenon, it is equally true that when military regimes engage in warfare, the duration of such conflicts has been found (Midlarski and Thomas, 1975, as cited in Eberwein, 1981:37) to be longer for military dominant regimes.

A less obvious underlying dimension of arms transfers is that along with training (Wolpin, 1973) they are integral to structuring Third World armies according to the prevalent political norms, organizational patterns, and sophisticated weaponry of industrialized capitalist donors. Thus Kaldor (1978: 70) maintains:

> The industrial armies, like their progenitors in the metropolis, are rarely used directly, except in external war against a competing ruling class with a similar form of force. When direct repression is necessary, they revert to the methods of the pre-industrial armies, or to the use of simple "intermediate technology" weapons, designed in the metropolis especially for the purpose. As in the metropolis, the true significance of the weapons system concept is political; it creates a commitment to industrialization and, more particularly, to a model of industrialization that is decadent by the standard of the most advanced industrial societies. The primary function of the industrial army is not so much combat as political intervention. It is through the military coup that the army preserves the system. The major weapons may have prestige significance and they may be used in external war and, on occasion, domestically. (Tanks and aircraft have proved effective as instruments of terror.) But, first and foremost, they orientate the soldier toward a particular political tendency.

While there may be an element of technological determinism at work here, the question of appropriate military technology and the political implications of external dependence are both important and inter-

linked. So for that matter are the consequences of
weapons imports, their local production and unbal-
anced development as well as deepening external
political, economic and technological dependence.
Thus, the UN Group of Governmental Experts on the
Relationship between Disarmament and Development
(UNSG, 1982:86-7) has warned that:

> A high degree of vulnerability to political and
> cultural penetration accompanying arms pur-
> chases is discerned in a study of data covering
> 70 developing countries during the period 1960-
> 1975. Such penetration is characterized by the
> emergence of export enclaves, patterns of un-
> even development, divergent returns to labour
> in different sectors of the economy and margi-
> nalization of substantial segments of the
> labour force creating social tension and poli-
> tical unrest. The study hypothesizes that an
> increase in marginalization of the labour force
> manifests itself both in a decline or stagna-
> tion of living standards and an increase in the
> number of unemployed.

> Attributing a culture to the military sector
> which diffuses values of militarization, a case
> study of three developing countries concludes
> that not many newly independent countries have
> succeeded in evolving an indigenous military
> sector. The traditions, training, linkages and
> equipment supply-lines of developing countries'
> military establishments can frequently lead to
> their alienation from their own societies, to
> political interventionism and to excessive,
> non-productive demands being placed on national
> economies. Significantly, even among developing
> countries which have set up their own arms-pro-
> ducing sectors, dependence on excessive arms
> import has remained, _inter alia_, because of the
> military's constant pressure to keep abreast of
> the most sophisticated innovations possible.
> This conclusion is borne out by the fact that
> the setting-up of an indigenous arms-producing
> sector has not necessarily reduced the need for
> importing arms by some of the weapon-manufac-
> turing developing countries. The list of the
> 15 arms producers, among the developing coun-
> tries also contains nine of the 20 major arms
> importers.

The almost inevitable dependence on imported

technology may largely negate the effects of self-reliance advocated by many developing countries as the critical determinant for domestic manufacture of arms. If the policy of self-reliance forms a part of a strategy to challenge centre-periphery relations then one of its main objects has to be a breaking of the existing patterns of technological dependence. But military technology, directly or indirectly obtained, has rather limited potentials for innovation. It tends to adopt, rather than adapt itself to, its climate of operation. Innovative capacity is the hardest thing in the world to transfer. Technology can be transferred because the very definition of technology implies transferability in some degree depending on the receptivity of a different culture; but innovative capacity is more culture dependent. Even in the developed societies, many innovations fail because in the end they do not quite "fit". This problem is compounded when innovations in a society at one cultural and material level are attempted for duplication for the benefit of another society at quite a different level. Even from a purely national security approach, dependence on foreign technology components and critical spares may cause new problems: in the case of an actual conflict their continued supply may not be guaranteed; the co-operation of supportive foreign personnel may not be ensured; the technology may not be up-to-date.(13)

Yet even less "up-to-date" equipment may have similar effects. Thus:

According to American estimates it takes an inventory of 70,000 spare parts to keep a squadron of F-4 Phantoms operational under wartime conditions. The import of this type of weapon system thus leads to continued dependence on spare parts. The importing countries are very seldom capable for overhaul and repair; the result is the purchase of such services from the supplying country and company. The necessary facilities like repair halls, test apparata and so on will have to be constructed. Arms importers will also have to prepare themselves for the retooling of their expensive weapons several times during the life-time of the weapon, because of the technological changes. If they do not do this, their weapons get old in 5-10 years because their performance lags behind new developments. Particularly developments in military electronics cause this situation.

The authors (Tuomi and Vayrynen, 1980:223) preface the above admonition by underscoring the pivotal issue of Third World countries'

war machines which do not correspond to their level of development. Besides, the basic idea of many weapons of industrial countries is to decrease the role of men and increase the role of weapons - a conception which contradicts the situation in many developing countries which have large human resources but a small number of technically educated personnel.

They also take pains to emphasize (237-50) that local production of sophisticated weapons and even simple ones in countries lacking a coherent industrial structure "restructures" rather than eliminates external dependency. Thus "by trying to eliminate dependencies embodied in the arms purchases and developing a self-sufficient arms industry, a new set of dependencies is in fact created. This is not to imply that such countries should unilaterally disarm." The question of alternative defence strategy will be scrutinized in Chapter 8.

Before turning to the opportunity cost or trade-off analyses, it might be useful to set the foregoing studies in perspective from the standpoint of repression-based "structural" as well as military violence inflicted upon civilians in the developing areas. Thus, as Table 2 brings into sharp relief, although most of post-Second World War victims of both domestic and international war have been in the Third World, the human costs of these traditional forms of violence are dwarfed by the casualties of "structural" violence. The latter is defined by Kohler (1978:8) as

a term used in contemporary peace research and is to be distinguished from armed violence. While armed violence is violence exerted by persons against persons with the use of arms, structural violence is violence exerted by situations, institutions, social, political, and economic structures. Thus, when a person dies because he/she has no access to food, the effect is violent as far as that person is concerned, yet there is no individual actor who could be identified as the source of this violence. It is the system of food production and distribution that is to blame. The violence is thus exerted by an anonymous 'structure'. The measurement of the number of persons killed through structural violence uses statistics of life expectancy. By comparing the life expectancy of affluent regions with that of poor regions, one can estimate how many persons died in a poor region on account of poverty and poverty-related conditions (e.g. lack of doctors, clean water, food, etc.), which can be interpreted as 'structural violence'.

Even if one concedes the need for "defence" capabilities of some sort - a question I shall return to in the last chapter - it seems reasonable to conclude that a large if indeterminate proportion of Western training and aid as well as the $100 billion expended by non-radical Third World countries upon the military has been responsible for the devastating human costs associated with this structural violence. What the latter encompasses in somewhat broader relief at the outset of the 1980s has been vividly portrayed by Sivard (1981:20):

> The numbers stand in long rows, like tombstones, silent documents to lives lost:
> - 870,000,000 adults who cannot read and write
> - 500,000,000 people who have no jobs or are less than fully employed
> - 130,000,000 children who are unable to attend primary school
> - 450,000,000 people who suffer from hunger or malnutrition
> - 12,000,000 babies who die every year before their first birthday
> - 42,000,000 people who are blind or nearly so
> - 2,000,000,000 people who do not have safe water to drink
> - 250,000,000 people who live in urban slums or shantytowns

Even higher figures in some categories are given by the World Bank which (UNSG, 1982:11) estimates "that there are now 570 million people who are malnourished, 800 million who are illiterate, 1500 million who have little or no access to medical services, 250 million who do not go to school".

And not unexpectedly, the highest incidence (Weede, 1981:650-1; Powell, 1982) of deaths from political violence occurs in underdeveloped nations. Repressiveness, in turn, is strongly correlated (Bollen, 1983) with the degree of "dependency". Consonant with this perspective is Ball's (1981) work analysing the range of beneficiaries when military intervention occurs - civilian upper classes, foreign interests, opportunistic officers and the military's institutional interests. Excluded for the most part are the popular mass sectors who tend to be victimized by domestic militarism. The armed forces often play a direct role (Wolpin, 1981) in violently repressing leftist movements for structural change. This occurs both in civilian as well as the rising proportion of states which are under non-reformist military domination.(14)

Structural violence is indirectly reinforced by the immediate diversion of economic resources on a vast and rising scale from the productive economy to what is aptly defined by Melman (1974:62-3) as a "parasitic" sector.

> Productive growth means goods and services that either are part of the level of living or can be used for further production of whatever kind. Hence, they are by these tests economic- ally useful. Parasitic growth includes goods and services that are not economically useful either for the level of living or for further production.

> Military goods and services are economically parasitic. This differentiation is fundamental. When it is applied it is possible to perceive and diagnose a series of consequences that flow from military economy. In the absence of the differentiation between production and parasitic growth, the activity of military economy appears as simply an extension or a part of the ordinary civilian economy.

While a few of the studies to which I shall now turn may be classified as "reactionary" in the sense that they stress beneficial secondary effects of military spending, the preponderance of them as will be seen tend to substantiate or are at least consistent with

Melman's thesis - one reaffirmed more recently by Whynes (1979) - that most if not all contemporary militarization has been parasitic upon civilian mass sector socio-economic needs and aspirations.

Chapter 3

MILITARIZATION AND OPPORTUNITY COSTS:
THE INDUSTRIALIZED NATIONS

In one sense it may be inappropriate to treat the
effects of militarization in developed countries as
relevant to a study of its consequences for the
Third World. The former are by definition vastly
more prosperous. Destitution hardly exists. What
makes them interesting for comparative purposes is
first that they set an example as the most militarized countries in the world. As Albrecht (1978:67)
notes in his discussion of alternative indicators:

> common sense would suggest that the absolute
> level of military spending is a better measure
> of militarisation, and that, on this measure,
> Western Europe is much more heavily militarized
> than the Middle East. The computation of mili-
> tary spending as a percentage of GNP is much
> favoured by Western sources, for it suggests
> that there is nothing unreasonable in rich
> countries spending more on armed forces than
> poor countries.

Even if in relative terms they do not spend a larger
percentage of GNP than developing countries, a small
fraction of the world community accounted for expenditures on the order of $400 billion (constant) in
1981. Since about 4.5 per cent of (Sivard, 1981:16)
the developed countries' GNP is used for military
purposes while 0.3 per cent is allocated to foreign
aid, release of even a portion of these funds would
provide greater potential resources for relieving
Third World destitution and thus diminishing structural violence. An equally strong argument for their
inclusion is that despite relative affluence, welfare is far from uniformly shared internally. Impressive lower class sectors are anything but affluent. There are housing, employment, educational

and in some countries such as Britain and the United States major unmet health and urban renewal needs at the mass level.

Furthermore, the opportunity cost studies to which I now turn reveal trade-offs that are strikingly similar to those examined in the next chapter for developing countries. Finally the developed countries are the source of most Third World arms imports and a prime if not exclusive impetus for their patterns of militarization, internal repression and consequential structural violence. Klare (1982) cogently argues that Reagan's militarism has added a new qualitative dimension to world militarization because of a commitment not only to restrict Soviet influence but to expunge it entirely from the South, Eastern Europe and possibly within the USSR itself. Hence, effective resistance to externally supported militarism and intervention in the South will be exceedingly difficult - as the experience of Chile, Angola, South Yemen, Nicaragua and others suggests - in the absence of parallel movements to alter the competitive militarizing systemic environment in the North.

One of the earliest and most widely cited comparisons of both Western market economies and Warsaw Pact countries was carried out by Pryor (1968:85-127). Civil government expenditures as well as possible trade-offs with GNP categories were examined for 1956-62 - admittedly a very brief period. An interesting datum was that military expenditures as a ratio of GNP were unrelated to per capita as opposed to total GNP. As in the previously mentioned case of Latin American arms imports (Avery, 1978) and Gauhar's thesis on the Middle East, expenditure levels are "positively related to the total national product" and this statistically significant correlation is even more pronounced for Western than Warsaw Pact nations. Interpreting these and closely related armed forces manpower patterns, Pryor recalls

> it has been propounded that the key variable in determining the size of 'defensive armies' is the length of the frontier, while other variables play an important role in determining the size of 'offensive armies' including the absolute size of the population and the GNP per capita.
>
> ... in both years (1956, 1962) the number of

military personnel is significantly and positively related to population; however, in
neither year is there a statistically significant relation with area, and indeed, even the
sign of the calculated coefficient is different
than expected. Since the area of a country and
the length of its frontier are roughly related,
the ´defence army´ hypothesis can be rejected.

He concludes his analysis of the magnitudes of military outlays by noting "Theories that relate defence
expenditures to the level of economic development,
the economic system, or other factors are rejected
when tested against the data of this study." Pryor
hypothesizes "that the primary causes are political".

In so far as opportunity cost trade-offs were concerned, the only Warsaw Pact countries where statistically significant relationships appeared were the
USSR and Czechoslovakia. His time series analysis
revealed that in the former military expenditure increases adversely affected private consumption while
in the latter negative correlations appeared for
both this as well as civilian governmental expenditures. For the Western nations, Pryor´s longitudinal analysis revealed that:

Among market economies in countries such as
Austria, Denmark, Ireland, the Netherlands, or
Norway, where defence expenditures are a relatively small proportion of the GNP, there are
no statistically significant substitution relations between defence and any of the GNP end-
use aggregates. Here changes in defence expenditures are of relatively small magnitude and
are absorbed in different sectors in different
periods, so that no consistent substitution
pattern can be found. In countries where defence expenditures are relatively more important, such as Canada, Greece, West Germany, the
UK, and the USA, defence expenditures have a
statistically significant substitution relationship with current governmental civilian expenditures (excluding transfers) although in
almost every case the elasticity of substitution (the percentage change in governmental
civilian expenditures accompanying a 1 per cent
change in defense expenditures) is less than
0.1 per cent. This means that once transfer
payments are removed, defence expenditures do

have a significant substitution relationship with other types of government expenditures, although the magnitude of this substitution is very small. It is impossible to generalize about the results of the substitution experiments on other GNP end-use aggregates. In some countries, such as Greece or Canada, there is no statistically significant substitution relationship with any other sector. In some countries, such as the United States, there is a statistically significant substitution only with domestic investment, while in other countries such as France and West Germany this substitution relationship appears between defence and foreign investment.

Elsewhere, Smith (1977:71) identifies a number of factors which may explain such differences.(15)

What might be labelled "tradeoff diversity" also characterized Pryor's cross-sectional analysis. Here he found:

In West Europe in 1962 statistically significant (0.05 level) substitution relations with defence exist only for investment (gross fixed investment plus inventories) ... In 1956, however, such substitution relations with defence do not occur for investment or, for that matter, private consumption, but rather for current government civilian expenditures, including transfers.

In general substitution occurred for civilian government expenditures only when the military expenditure ratio to GNP was high, and even then the relationship was not particularly strong. Despite these findings of limited and varying substitution effects, it seems clear that the costs of military expenditure increases were in fact imposed upon one or another sector of the societies in question.

Analogous relationships are postulated for the Soviet Union by Becker (1981:1-2, 18-19, 29, 60-74). After noting that the rapid military buildup since the early 1960s has been accompanied by declining economic growth rates, he stresses the assumption underlying his study, "that reduction of military spending would yield resources badly needed for civilian development". The foregoing is premised on both statements by Khrushchev as well as several

tradeoff simulations and estimates.(16) One of the
latter, a study by Cohn (1973:153-4)

> estimated the effect of defense separately on
> investment, consumption, and major components
> of each. He found (a) that 'Soviet defense ex-
> penditures have adversely affected Soviet eco-
> nomic growth,' (b) 'strong evidence of inverse
> movements between defense expenditures and
> those for both capital investment and private
> consumption,' and (c) 'even closer relation-
> ships' between weapons procurement and producer
> durables production.

The second pertinent study cited by Becker was a
more recent CIA (1977:19) estimate

> that the sum of direct and indirect military
> uses absorbs about one-third of the Soviet out-
> put of machine building and metalworking, one-
> fifth of that of metallurgy, and one-sixth of
> the production of both chemicals and energy.

While Becker anticipates that further rises in military spending are likely to have "severe" effects
upon "the economy and society", his generally pes-
simistic analysis – drawing upon hypothetical econometric models (Calmfors and Rylander, 1976:383-93;
Bergendorff and Strangert, 1976:418; Bond and
Levine, 1981) – stresses the cruciality of productivity increases and sufficient lead time for any reductions in military burdens to have significant
payoffs for civilian economic sectors. A number of
additional studies referred to by the UN Group of
Experts Report (UNSG, 1982:75-6) stress the economic
benefits that would accrue to a number of CMEA countries if military expenditures were reduced.

Somewhat stronger but essentially analogous findings
were reported by Russett (1970:127-73) for the US,
Canada, France and Great Britain. His multiple repression analysis of US defence expenditures as a
ratio of GNP between 1939 and 1968 indicated that
private consumption was the major tradeoff cost:
"changes in defense expenditures account for 84 per
cent of the variance in total consumption, and the
regression coefficient is a relatively high -.42."
The second most pronounced effect occurred with
respect to investment (fixed capital formation) with
72 per cent of the variance explained and a -.29
regression coefficient. Significantly, residential

construction took "the greatest proportionate damage". Also adversely affected was the balance of payments. While the relationship with federal civil expenditures was weaker, he notes that these declined "from 4.3. per cent of GNP in 1939 to about 2.5 per cent in the middle and late 1960s". Within this category, educational expenditures were the most severely affected - particularly when military expenditure upswings occurred. Although somewhat weaker relationships affected the health sector, he stresses

> the pattern of health and hospitals is almost identical to that for education - some longterm growth but great cutbacks in periods of heavy military need and only slow recovery thereafter.

Russett's conclusion is indeed prophetic in light of the militarization embarked upon by Carter in 1978 and carried to unprecedented peace time levels by the militarist Reagan administration: "It seems fair to conclude from these data that America's most expensive wars have severely hampered the nation in its attempt to build a healthier and better educated citizenry."

With respect to Great Britain, Russett examined an even longer period beginning in 1890 ane extending to the mid-1960s. The relationship was slightly weaker than the American case. Yet what appeared "most striking" to him was "the negative relationship between defense and personal consumption, just as in the United States". While imports increased during 1946-66 as a consequence of rising military spending, exports suffered even more:

> The other very strong relationship is between defense and exports, with 40 percent of the variation in the latter accounted for by the former. Furthermore, the regression coefficient is high, indicating a decline in exports equal to about one-sixth of any increment in defense expenditure.

In so far as civil expenditures were concerned, only education was adversely affected and this was limited to periods of war when military expenditures were above 37 per cent of the GNP. Yet he also found that "from the mid-1950s onward every decrease in defense expenditures made possible a fully equiva-

lent increase in civil consumption expenditures in
the public sector".

Russett's post-Second World War comparison of
Canada, France and Great Britain was consitent with
Pryor's findings in that "there was no single pattern for the impact of military spending". Investment was adversely affected in both France and
Britain by high levels of military spending and was
especially benefited by reductions. In Canada, on
the other hand, there was "a very direct conflict
between defense and personal consumption", while
"the decline from 8 percent to below 4 percent of
Canadian resources devoted to defense since 1953 has
been matched by a fully equivalent transfer of resources into the health and education sectors".
Similarly, for "France and Britain it is quite apparent that defense expenditures have been negatively correlated with government spending for civilian needs."

Less striking findings were reported by Caputo
(1975) in his analysis which was restricted to budgetary tradeoffs with education and health between
1950 and 1970 for Sweden, Australia, Britain and the
United States. At high levels of military spending,
education but not health was adversely affected,
while neither appeared to benefit from lower military outlays. Health and military expenditures were
"positively related regardless of the prevalent economic conditions". Interestingly, he concludes that
"except in periods of low national income, health
and education tend to be policy alternatives ... it
appears that decisionmakers trade one for the other
except in situations where the national income is
below average." Obviously his findings cannot be
wholly reconciled with those of Russett's in so far
as negative impact upon health is concerned, although Russett's inverse relationships were less
pronounced for health than for education.

Russett's study did not encompass the escalation of
military expenditures during the Vietnam War. Hence
Peroff and Warren's (1978:21-39) time series analysis of the relationship between arms spending and
both private as well as public health expenditures
in the United States for the 1929-74 is particularly
valuable. Their findings

> give more weight to the hypothesis of a trade-
> off (the position of Russett and Wilensky) than

to the hypothesis of no tradeoff (the position of Eckstein, Gouldner, Rimlinger). A peacetime tradeoff exists between federal health and defence <u>appropriation requests</u> and it increased slightly during the Vietnam War. The evidence points to no tradeoff, however, in <u>federal allocation</u> or <u>final federal expenditures</u> on these two goods during war or peace. The largest tradeoff exists between <u>total</u> health and defence expenditures: during the Vietnam War, this tradeoff was 7.4 per cent while it was 5.1 per cent in all other years. The analysis reveals no tradeoff between health research and defence at any stage of the federal budgetary process (except for a very small substitution in appropriation requests during the Korean War). Lastly, a tradeoff exists between the private health sector and defence only in terms of capital investment in health.

More generally their "findings imply that when a policy begins to constitute a 'significant' share of the budgetary pie, that policy becomes more politically salient and sensitive to defence spending". Hence, with respect to the actual incidence of war:

The size of the tradeoff does oscillate according to periods of peace and war, although not as frequently or by as much as expected. The greatest war-induced effect occurred in the total health-defence tradeoffs during the Vietnam War. For the most part, however, the analysis suggests that wars do not cause much greater losses in health spending. The lack of great variation between periods of peace and war may be due to the fact that the defence share of the budget has not always been that much smaller in non-war years, especially during the Cold War era of the 1950s.

Finally, while they employed the Cochrane-Orcutt estimation technique to avoid auto-correlated error, there was one serious difficulty which this otherwise highly sophisticated methodological analysis was unable to surmount. Peroff and Warren conclude with a caveat - one of great contemporary relevance - that "There is no way to measure monies not spent or programmes not introduced in health or other domestic areas because anticipated costs are seen as insupportable given existing and future defence spending. As this is also an important potential tradeoff our analysis has probably underestimated the actual impact of defence on health-related activities."

More consonant, however, with the work of Pryor and particularly Russett is that by Smith (1977:61-76) who draws clearly radical conclusions from his findings. The relatively uniform patterns discerned also distinguish his cross-sectional analysis of 15 advanced capitalist nations between 1953 and 1973. Noting in comparison with the pre-Second World War period that "military expenditure has absorbed a far higher share of output throughout the post-war period than in the past", Smith emphasizes that in 1975 alone the advanced capitalist nations allocated about $155 billion to "military preparations". Countering other radicals, he maintains that such expenditures were both unnecessary to avoid domestic crisis and in fact at high levels tended to weaken the system. Not only was military spending found to be negatively correlated with per capita GNP growth, but according to Smith:

> The empirical evidence ... suggests that military expenditure imposes a substantial burden. Among the advanced capitalist nations high military expenditure is associated with much lower investment, lower growth and higher rates of unemployment.

Similarly, Lindroos (1980:115) summarizes some of the conclusions of a widely cited study by the Labour Party Defence Study Group (LPDSG, 1977:43-4) on the OECD area which found that:

> where the rate of armaments is high (in particular in Britain and the United States), the countries invest least, and in them, the annual growth rate is the slowest; on the contrary, countries where defence expenditures are small (in particular Japan) there have been considerable resources for investments. The only exception among the Western countries seems to be France where both investments and growth have increased swiftly despite a high level of arms expenditure.(17)

Such consequences square completely with the findings of Melman (1979:364-5) who like Russett and many others stresses that because of its capital intensive character military spending creates less employment than civil expenditures or personal consumption. And if it is financed wholly by taxes which are no more than mildly progressive, military procurement may actually increase unemployment. Further, because of the cost-plus oligopolistic structure of the military-industrial complex and its "parasitical" character, "defence" spending is highly inflationary.(18) Melman is by no means alone in stressing these deleterious consequences. Lindroos (1980:119) reports that the UN Expert Group (UNSG, 1978:41-2)

> that studied the economic and social consequences of the arms race noted, however, that the impact of the arms build-up on inflation is not insignificant. First of all, the arms race spurs inflation as it creates demand, but does not simultaneously increase the production of consumer goods. Secondly, the armaments industry does not curb the rise of labour and other production costs as well as other industries, as it is capital- and technology-intensive and as the rise of costs in this area can easily be passed on to the consumer. A third factor promoting inflation, according to the United Nations expert group, is that the arms build-up deprives civilian production of a considerable amount of funds for research and development and thus hampers the long-term growth of productivity in this sector, making it also more vulnerable to inflationary pressures.

The same report (UNSG, 1978:40-8) emphasizes the harmful effects of diverting scientific, technical and skilled manpower while observing that there have been fewer civilian "spinoffs" from military research than the contrary. With respect to this, Tuomi and Väyrynen (1980:239) make the following salient points:

> the military applications have grown so specialized that they have very little useful applications in civilian life. The estimates on the share of military inventions applicable in the civilian sphere appear to vary between 20 and 35 per cent.
>
> ... a more potent reason is the disproportionate allocation of resources to the military R&D, which prevents the development of science- and technology-related components in the

civilian industry. This is in fact detrimental in the long run even for the military industry because its technology base is much more dependent on a healthy civilian technology than vice versa.

... in spite of patents and other forms of monopolies, civilian technology is disseminated more freely through commercial channels than military technology, which is effectively guarded by secrecy and vested bureaucratic interests. This tends to hamper the spread of military innovations into the civilian field. A related explanation would also be valid for the Soviet Union, in which interaction between research centers and the industrial system, in terms of the application of science-related innovations, is considered to be rather slight.

Their view is cogently endorsed by a more recent report (UNSG, 1982:73-4) by the UN Group of Governmental Experts on the Relationship between Disarmament and Development which stresses that:

Many econometric investigations have pointed out that technological progress, in its broadest sense, is the major source of economic growth. Research and development outlays are the impetus for this process. In Chapter III it is estimated, that some 20 per cent of the highly qualified technical and scientific research personnel is working in military-related R and D projects. In several other parts of this report, the arms race is described as a dynamic technological process. Therefore, it is quite understandable that, in common understanding, military research and development is seen as an important stimulant for economic growth and development. Nevertheless, this opinion is misleading. There are several basic errors in this way of reasoning. In the first place, noboyd can deny that military R and D has a positive spin-off in some civilian sectors, such as the field of nuclear energy and space technology. But the opposite is also valid. Many technological breakthroughs in the civilian sectors also have a positive spin-off in the military sector. Several important technological developments have nothing to do with military research. Some of the studies commissioned by the Group provide quantitative and qualitative arguments to suggest that, in reality, civilian research is more effective for economic growth than military research.(19)

This point is further underscored by the finding that on the basis of "different macro-economic models for different sets of countries, several studies commissioned by the Group suggest a high correlation between military expenditures and low rates of growth". Arms as opposed to civil expenditures also reduce the effectiveness of expansionary policies during recessions, contribute to trade imbalances and deterioration in the terms of trade for importers, result in lower rates of overall investment as well as slower growth of the economy. Thus the same UN Report (UNSG, 1982:72-3) warns that:

> With regard to capital formation, reduced military expenditures will have a positive impact on economic growth. For the most part, military expenditures do not contribute to production of capital goods and so do not increase the capacity of an economy. But they still compete for investible resources. Moreover, military procurement competes with civilian investment because both are generally directed at roughly the same industries, e.g., metallurgy, chemicals, and energy. An expansion of the demand for military procurement will thus tend to be associated with a relatively lower share for investment by causing supply bottle-necks that constrain investment. The extent to which reduced military expenditures will affect economic growth will depend, of course, on the way in which the released resources are used.

In preceding paragraphs the same report stressed a more indirect source of lower economic growth - productivity enhancing R&D:

> Besides directly competing with investment, military spending may indirectly affect economic growth in the civilian sector by constraining the growth rate of productivity, which depends heavily on research and development (R and D) expenditures. There is sufficient empirical and historical evidence to demonstrate that the civilian spin-off effects of military R and D in the past have been considerably exaggerated because, with a few exceptions, notably in electronics and to a lesser extent

in aerospace, the gap between civil and military technology is rather wide and, in some cases, is growing wider still. Moreover, the considerable time lag required to secure the civilian spin-offs from military technology is a significant constraint in situations where low productivity returns demand immediate inputs into research and development into the civilian sectors. Historical comparisons of the non-military or economically relevant R and D effort of the major industrialized countries yield a pattern of economic performance indicating that, in terms of expenditure and employment of professional manpower per unit of GNP, in the mid-to-late 1960s the intensity of non-military R and D was highest in Japan, with the United States lagging significantly behind both that country and the major Western European countries. A relative decline in capital productivity in the civilian sector, owing to insufficient R and D activities, has, as a result, caused a diversion of capital from the civil to the military sector.

While the sources of America's economic decline are undoubtedly multifarious, as the world's largest military spender it does seem that the consequential diversion of vast and growing scientific/economic resources may be an important dimension of the problem. Such consequences are intensified by deficit financing, while tax funding has greater negative employment effects. These analyses do not ignore the disproportionately harmful effects of inflation upon lower-class sectors.(20) Secondary effects flow (Dumas, 1981) from diversion of scientific manpower, deterioration of export capabilities of civilian industries, subsequent currency devaluation, etc.

The implications of the foregoing are vividly delineated for the United States by a number of projective opportunity costs analyses. Thus, Dr Roger Bezdek, an economist at the Energy Resource and Development Administration, has calculated the direct job effect from spending $1,000,000 in each of the indicated activities. His results are set out in Table 3. In a similar vein, Marion Anderson (1975) has estimated the net employment effect associated with the classes of economic activity forgone owing to military spending. Her estimate of the negative employment impact of military spending shows an annual average (1968-72) of 844,000 jobs forgone.

In addition to the above-mentioned analyses cited by Melman (1979), Lindroos (1980:115-17) refers to several official studies that posit similar outcomes. Thus, one by the US Department of Labor (USDL:1972) estimated that "every billion dollars invested in the armaments industry creates 76,000 jobs whereas if invested in civilian projects, the same amount of money would create, on the average over 100,000 jobs". The same agency (USDL:1976) estimated "that to channel a billion dollars into private consumption through tax cuts would create 112,000 new jobs". And according to US Congressman Les Aspin (1976:1), "one billion dollars for the armaments industry creates 35,000 jobs while for the same sum 76,000 jobs could be created in the construction sector, 100,000 in education (teachers) and 132,000 in public administration". Finally, Albrecht (1978a:32) contends "that in 1977 one billion dollars created 48,800 new jobs in the armaments industry whereas the same amount of investment would have secured employment for twice this number of people in the civilian industry or in public administration". The previously cited UN Group of Experts' Report (UNSG, 1982:81-3) cites several studies which also include the USSR:

> Several studies about the post-war economic reconstruction experience in the Soviet Union and Eastern Europe have confirmed that the reconversion of war-related military efforts into civilian sectors have in most cases surpassed the employment levels in the pre-war period. In the Soviet Union, for example, the industrial manpower in 1950 had increased by 3 million as compared to 1940: over the same period, employment in engineering increased by 250,000, in construction by 1,542,000, transport by 657,000, communication by 64,000. The total number of people employed in Soviet offices and factories in 1950 was 7.7 million more than in 1940. Retrospective analyses of the post-war Soviet economy generally look back with approval on the period 1946-1950 when a decrease in defence expenditure by 42.6 per cent released 42.7 per cent additional funds for economic rehabilitation and development and another 27.6 per cent for social rehabilitation measures. During 1946, the output of consumer goods increased by 8 per cent, food-stuffs by 12 per cent, and domestic goods 3.3 times.

... For the economies confronting unemployment, some pioneer investigations carried out mostly in the United States suggest that as a creator of jobs, military expenditure may be among the least efficient types of spending. A study of the forgone employment opportunities accompanying accelerated military spending has noted that as many as 26 manufacturing industries in the United States suffered a job loss of 5,000 or more each owing to their growing non-competitiveness during the period 1964-1972, which coincided with increasing United States involvement in the Viet Nam War. Another analysis of the years 1968-1972 indicates that the net annual job loss nation-wide when the United States military budget averaged about $80 billion, was about 840,000 jobs: the net job gain in a few states being accompanied by net job losses in many others, including some of the most populous states. Contrasting the job opportunities associated with the programme to develop the B-1 strategic bomber and a programme of tax reduction or public housing of equivalent magnitude, a study bu the Chase Econometrics Associates has concluded that, over a 10-year period, the B-1 programme would generate lesser employment primarily because of its heavy reliance on the manufacturing sector, whose employment requirements are relatively low. Similar results are yielded by another study which contrasts the net output and employment effects of comparable increases in the military budget on one hand and on the other, public expenditure on programmes like health, education, public assistance and environmental protection.

The job creating differential between spending $1 billion on the military sector and the same amount on public service employment has been estimated to be roughly about 51,000 jobs in a major industrialized country like the United States. This can be attributed partly to the fact that, in the societies with a sophisticated military sector, non-personnel military expenditure is generally concentrated in the capital- and technology-intensive fields of industry which tend to become labour-intensive only at the final assembly stage.

Summarizing in more general terms, the Group of

Experts refers to a report prepared for it which "suggests that an average of two working places could be created in the civil branches of national economy at the expense of one in the military sector".(21)

These and related non-employment costs of high military burdens are highlighted in a series of recent analyses by Kaldor (1981), Anderson (1982), Cortright and Stone (1982), Mosley (1982), and DeGrasse (1982). The last two deal with both the US and other industrial states. Of particular significance are DeGrasse's conclusions on the differential impact of 1960-79 military burdens for 13 leading advanced capitalist states: Sweden, Denmark, Canada, Austria, Norway, West Germany, United Kingdom, the Netherlands, Italy, Belgium, United States, France and Japan. As Table 4 indicates, theres is a statistically significant inverse correlation between relative military burdens and GDP growth, productivity growth, and investment. Weaker negative associations appear for private consumption and civil government expenditures.

Indirect effects of militarization should also be at least mentioned. The weakening of leftist social reform forces in the West and especially in the US since the onset of the Cold War has not only attenuated the constraints upon rightist and military-industrial proponents of rising military burdens, but at the same time consumer protection from corporate and governmetal toxification of the human environment has also been minimal despite some temporary gains in the late 1960s and early 1970s. Paradoxically this has led (Rimland and Larson, 1981) to a marked deterioration in the emotional stability and intellectual capabilities since the early 1960s of the civilian manpower pool upon which the US military draws its enlistees, and inferentially to a weakening of military capabilities.(22)

In France, on the other hand, the strength of both organized and potential leftist constituencies constrained militaristic political sectors until recently. Thus, an American security analyst (Kolodziej, 1982:193-4) laments:

> Since the events of May 1968, military spending has been subordinated to domestic social and economic expenditures ... It has taken almost a decade to increase the proportion of spending

> to previous levels ... Despite these dire (se-
> curity) threats, the internal social and eco-
> nomic claims on the budget continue to be suf-
> ficiently compelling to check increases in de-
> fense expenditures even for French nuclear
> forces.

While he is cognizant of the welfare tradeoff costs
to military claims, Kolodziej's militaristic conceptualization of "security" obscures its socio-economic or cultural bases. To this question and to crucial political dimensions of the militarization vs.
social welfare/development conflict, I shall return
in the concluding chapter.

What warrants reiteration here is the clear and present danger - ironic in a sense - that overall impact of pronounced militarization - most salient in
the United States - may be to weaken rather than to
increase security. Thus Robert S. McNamara, outgoing
World Bank President and former Secretary of
Defense, recently (Kansas City Times, 8 August 1980)
prophetically warned "To the extent that military
expenditures severely reduce the resources available
for other essential sectors and social services -
and fuels the futile and reactive arms race - excessive military spending can erode security rather
than enhance it." Although not cited by McNamara,
Szymanski's (1973:1-14) test of Baran and Sweezy's
stagnation thesis some years early is generally
supportive of the former Defense Secretary's appre-
hensions. Szymanski examined both employment and
economic growth as functions of military spending
for the 18 wealthiest capitalist nations between
1950 and 1968. His major finding was that:

> When we examine the relation of total nonmili-
> tary expenditure to stagnation, we find an even
> more pronounced positive correlation between
> level of expenditure and rates of growth than
> we found with overall government spending (Tab-
> le 5). The effect of nonmilitary expenditure
> appears to be the opposite of military expendi-
> ture. While the latter generally helps produce
> stagnation, the former alleviates it.

It is crucial to underscore that this negative relationship between military spending and growth was
confined to six of the most technologically advanced
capitalist powers - the US, Britain, France, West
Germany, Italy, and Japan. They accounted for the

overall inverse relationship since smaller economies benefited "slightly" from such expenditures. Similarly, while Szymanski concluded that military expenditures tended to absorb more unemployment than others, he also found that:

> In countries with low nonmilitary expenditure, those with the greatest military expenditure have the highest unemployment rather than the lowest. This last fact, together with the similar results for the six biggest capitalist countries, casts further doubt on the thesis that military spending necessarily reduces unemployment.

Smith carries this line of argument further and in the process disposes of the claim by some radicals that high military spending is essential to avoid systemic collapse with a cogent summation of his findings:

> While military expenditure has been a substantial component of demand in some capitalist nations, in particular the US, one cannot make the inference that the need to maintain demand was the cause of the high military expenditure. Other capitalist states maintained demand without equivalent levels of military expenditure, and in fact states with high military expenditure had higher than average unemployment. The alternative approach is that the functions of military expenditure were not primarily to maintain demand, and that its economic consequences which, in fact, undermined the system it was intended to support. This has already been suggested by the balance-of-payments arguments and the negative correlation between the share of military expenditure and growth rate.

In fact he correctly maintains that capitalists are enmeshed in a contradictory situation. They prefer prosperity yet also need some employment slack to safeguard profits by disciplining labour.

But this, even less than the influence of the military-industrial complex, is insufficient to fully explain militarization in the US or other advanced capitalist nations. In addition to the important role of the military-industrial complex, other significant factors include bureaucratic politics, the need for an internal repressive potential, inter-capitalist rivalries and above all (Halliday, 1983) an increasingly costly determination to suppress Third World national liberation movements. They of course threaten access to raw materials under conditions that perpetuate what Emmanuel (1972) has termed "unequal exchange". The militarization process itself consumes according to Hveem and Malnes (1980: i) approximately 5 per cent of energy resources and between 5 and 20 per cent of other minerals. Hence the arms race leades to a competition for more scarce resources resulting in more conflict, consequential militarization and consumption of more raw materials by advanced capitalist nations. Integral to these imperatives are arms transfers, more than 200 armed interventions by the US alone since the Second World War (Blechman and Kaplan, 1978), military training and base agreements or de facto alliances, proxy forces and accelerated militarization of the Third World. Mindful that this self-reinforcing process has intensified in the early 1980s, I now turn to a number of analyses dealing with trade-offs and substitution effects of high and rising military burdens in the "developing" countries.

Chapter 4

MILITARISM AND OPPORTUNITY COSTS: THE THIRD WORLD

Some of these studies are restricted to the Third World while others use a broader universe or example. I shall consider both types. The first generation of research assessed trends and patterns for the 1950s and 1960s. Here again we turn to Russett (1970:157-9) who regressed data on various tradeoff indicators for 120 nations in the World Handbook of Political and Social Indicators. His only important tradeoff was with consumption as a percentage of GNP, and military expenditures accounted for 17 per cent of the variance (significant at the .002 level). Like Charles Wolf Jr who found that "each political system absorbed the economic impact in a different way", Russett stresses:

> This failure to find strong relationships between defense and civil expenditures is really surprising ... If defense spending does not take a very large fraction of a nation's resources, there are indeed many different ways in which the slight burden can be carried ... We could only expect to find notable regularities in nations where the level of defense expenditures is high enough to force some painful choices. Since more than two-thirds of the world's nations spend less than 4 per cent of their GNP on defense, comparing their experiences is not especially likely to be fruitful.

A related problem of course which was pointed out in Chapter 1 is that many and perhaps most developing countries conceal military allocations under civil budgetary categories. Notwithstanding such obstacles, the rise in official military outlays during subsequent years for Third World countries has been sufficiently great to yield tradeoffs with civil expenditures. In 1977 according to USACDA (1979:27) Third World countries averaged 6 per cent of GNP and 30 per cent of their budgets on the armed forces. Before turning to the more recent analyses, two widely cited studies employing earlier data should be mentioned.

One of the most controversial of these was published by the late Emile Benoit (1973). His key discovery was that

> the average 1950-1965 defence burdens (defence as a percent of national product) of 44 countries was positively, not inversely, correlated with their growth rates over comparable time periods, i.e. the more they spent on defence, in relation to the size of their economies, the faster they grew - and vice versa.

Given the ubiquitous underutilization of labour as well as excess agro-industrial capacity in non-socialist Third World countries, it seems reasonable to conclude that any increase in aggregate demand would stimulate some economic growth. Economic development, however, presupposes a rise in investment, and Gottheil (1974:505-6) reports that when Robert Dorfman replicated the analysis with Benoit's data Dorfman found "no correlation between military outlays, investment, and international economic aid". Gunder Frank (1979) stresses that a rise in GNP does not imply an improvement in social welfare, and Whynes (1979:71) referring to Benoit, observes that "the statistical evidence is highly ambiguous". Brzoska and Wulf (1980) carry the critique further. First, they note that while some short run rise in economic activity may indeed have occurred, this is not tantamount to development. Second, a very small sample was used and Benoit's data sources were unidentified. What they then did was to replicate Benoit's study using USACDA data for 90 countries from 1960 through 1975. Their regression analysis yielded either no relationship or a negative one between the ratio of military expenditure to GNP and civilian GNP growth. The only exception was the OPEC group. Elsewhere Mary Kaldor (1978:73-4) also isolated a group of exceptions whose heavy military expenditures were accompanied by high economic growth. Again these were either oil rich or heavily dependent upon US aid - Israel, Libya, Saudi Arabia, Taiwan, Iran, South Korea, Thailand and Brazil. Indeed, Benoit conceded the relationship may have been spurious because of a strong correlation between foreign aid and growth for the same countries during the 1950-65 period. More recently, Ball (1983) takes issue with Benoit's restriction of aid to bilateral transfers and in other respects provides a devastating critique of his methodological assumptions.

Thus, it must be stressed that financing is always a critical factor. Short run military-led growth may well employ unused factors of production. But if mass sectors had not been taxed, their spending would generate greater employment, consumption and less inflation. External or internal debt financing is inflationary and postpones both employment and consumption costs imposed upon mass sectors. Thus, in the 1980s "austerity" is being enforced as Third World governments discover they have over-borrowed during the 1970s. Worse still, the UN Group of Governmental Experts (UNSG, 1982:83) warns that for the less developed economies facing severe unemployment problems, the job-loss effects of

> military spending may be more far-reaching in the long run because the sustained emphasis on technological sophistication in the military sector usually raises the qualifications required of its personnel, with the result that its demand for labour becomes increasingly selective and may largely bypass the general worker of the so-called hardcore unemployed.

And in so far as technological or other spinoffs are seen as a consequence of creating indigenous arms production facilities, Tuomi and Vàyrynen (1980:240) caution that such reasoning "is deceptive because the entire conception of spin-offs is inapplicable in most developing countries as they do not have a coherent industrial structure".

Benoit's study was followed within a year by Kennedy's (1974:158-74) work which actually focuses upon the entire range of military roles within developing countries. Before turning our attention to the tradeoff question, it might be useful to briefly summarize some of his other findings. First, military budgets during the 1960s tended to be markedly higher for Third World countries involved in "belligerency" than for others. Regimes involved in domestic or external armed conflict allocated 31 per cent of their budget on the average to military ends while more peaceful governments spent about 13 per cent. Second, military regimes as one would expect devoted a larger share of their budgets (21%) on the average to the armed forces than civilian ones (14%).

Military governments in Asia, sub-Saharan Africa, and Latin America allocated about double the percentage allocated by non-military governments on defence out of the state budgets.

Except in Latin America, Kennedy found military spending to be uncompetitive with health and educational expenditures. Only in Asia and to a lesser degree Latin America did civilian governments spend more on education and health than military regimes. It was about the same in Africa while in the Middle East the largely traditional monarchic civilian autocracies spent even less upon such welfare activities than did the military. A disproportionate number of radical military regimes, it should be added, were concentrated in this region - Iraq, Libya, Syria, Egypt, Algeria, Yemen. In global terms, however, civilian governments devoted slightly more (20% vs. 18%) to their welfare budgets. Even more pronounced negative relationships with welfare were reported by Morrison and Stevenson (1974:345-7) for military expenditures. In Asian and Latin American countries there was a moderate (-.30, -.27) inverse correlation with economic growth and a strong positive one with political instability (.56, .57). Weaker relationships (-.10, .28) were reported for Africa where many of the countries had only recently gained formal independence. Thus using the 1960-73 time frame, Ravenhill (1980:99-126) was unable to find statistically significant performance differences for African military and civilian governments. Yet he adds the caveat that "this type of research design, by aggregating the performance data for all 'military' regimes, obscures the substantial differences in performance between regimes classified within either the civilian or military groupings".

Although the comparative performance of civilian and military regimes is somewhat tangential to the focus of this study, since domestic militarism is one of the most important sources of militarization, it may be helpful to mention the conclusions of several other analysts. With respect to Latin America, Needler (1966) found a decline in the proportion of

coups which were reformist and low in violence between 1935 and 1965. Tannahill's (1976:233-44)
policy analysis of ten South American countries
between 1948 and 1967 revealed that the military did
slightly better in such areas as economic growth,
manufacturing production, exports and inflation,
while civilians were marginally superior with respect to indirect taxation. His overall conclusion
was that:

> The major difference in the performance of mil-
> itary and civilian governments, however, is a
> political one. On every indicator of political
> responsiveness to demands for reform - govern-
> ment sanctions, social welfare spending and
> direct taxes - the military as rulers opt for
> more conservative or more repressive policies
> than do their civilian counterparts. We must
> concur with Nordlinger, then, that military
> rulers are commonly unconcerned with the reali-
> zation of reform, and where there are civilian
> organizations pressing for such changes, the
> military purposefully oppose them.

Even more than Kennedy, Tannahill discovered a salient distinction in the vital area of social welfare
spending where approximately 23 per cent of civilian
budgets fell into this category while for the military regimes it was slightly in excess of 17 per
cent. Furthermore, this was the only policy differentiation that was statistically significant (.01).

The validity of Tannahill's findings is underscored
by Dickson's (1977:325-45) cross-national and longitudinal assessment of tradeoffs for the same countries during the 1961-70 decade. He concludes that:

> (1) military regimes appear to have been more
> fiscally conservative than civilian ones, and
> (2) civilian regimes appear to have been more
> developmentally oriented than military ones. In
> justification, military regimes were inclined
> to spend less and run lower deficits, even
> though they spent more on the military. They
> showed a lower rate of increase in the cost of
> living and maintained a stronger international
> liquidity position for the central bank. Civi-
> lian regimes, for their part, spent more, did
> more for education and effected higher savings
> and investment rates, although the military had
> an edge in electrical production.

Unfortunately, the only direct welfare or reform indicator employed by Dickson was public education expenditures. Yet using an earlier 1950-67 time frame, Schmitter (1973) found that military rule in Latin America was associated with higher regressiveness in tax structures. Although he also reported that frequent military intervention was associated with higher economic growth rates, Schmitter entered the caveat that: "We have shown, rather convincingly, that, in some penetrated societies as those of Latin America, exogenous variables - especially the level of commercial and financial dependence on the United States - do explain a wide range of outcomes, including the rate of gnp increase."

Other analysts who focused upon the Third World such as Nordlinger (1970), and McKinlay and Cohan (1976) conclude that the military regimes are not socially reformist for the most part while being highly repressive politically. Although Nordlinger found some evidence for higher economic growth by African military regimes, this was not attributed to inherent regime capabilities. The latter authors discerned in the socio-economic area that "the military regime systems do score consistently lower than the non-military regime systems". And while noting that the variations were not of sufficient magnitude to warrant statistical confidence, they reiterate that "what differences do exist place the military regimes in the weaker position".(1926:23) Sarkesian (1978: 9) reports on analogous yet more striking findings by Park and Abolfathi who

> analyze military involvement in domestic politics and its consequences for foreign and defense policies. Five indicators of military influence (M.I.) were operationalized and correlated with approximately sixty variables across 150 countries (ca. 1970). Among other things, Park and Abolfathi found that ´countries with a strong political rating of the military tend to spend a higher proportion of their governmental revenues for defense´. They also found that health and education expenditures tend to decrease as military influence increases.

The foregoing patterns and similar ones reported by Finer (1975:234-8) for an earlier period (1950-67) - again by differentiating degrees of military dominance - are even more striking than those by Jackman,

Nordlinger, McKinlay and Cohan who like Tannahill use a _formal_ or nominal criterion to distinguish military from civilian rule.(24) Whether or not a chief executive wears a uniform ignores the possibility that civilian designees may be subject to military veto as it does other policy areas subject to praetorian intimidation.(25) Despite this methodological reservation, the research is less consonant with the expectations of those who imputed a modernizing role to military "nation building" than it is with Heeger's (1977:247-8) conclusion that:

> The military decade (1965-1975) that has just ended in Africa and Asia has been highly disillusioning. Contrary to most scholars' earlier depiction of the military as a highly modern force, able to transfer its organizational and technological skills to the art of governing, most military regimes have hindered the development of their countries. Explanations for their incapacity abound. Military organization is now seen as incapable of dealing with the more elusive problems of development; the military is seen as preoccupied with its own class interests; military rulers are described as so antipolitical as to frustrate their efforts to gain popular support.

A similar conclusion for most developing countries is articulated by Ball (1983:81) who notes "It is increasingly accepted that for these countries high rates of economic growth, investment and employment are inversely related to high levels of military expenditure." She assesses the effects of militarization upon economic development as being more "negative" than positive. These comparative findings limiting military dominance and high armed forces expenditures with repression and socio-economic conservatism - a small minority of socially reformist military regimes partially excepted - will become more ubiquitous in the 1980s as the Reagan administration gives its active support to the spread of counterrevolutionary militarism in the Third World.

Before concluding this chapter, several analyses of highly militarized regimes which in varying was reinforce this thesis will be summarized. One reformist military regime - Nasser's Egypt - was the object of a case study by Hansen (1972) who correlated "increases in military expenditures to the stagnation of the share of growth expenditure for Egypt during the Yemen Wars".

Poor social welfare and economic performance for Nigeria under military rule is amply documented by Olorunsola (1977) and Chikwendu (1977). Analogous patterns for the Greek military regime a decade ago were reported by Danopoulos and Patel (1980:197-9) who emphasize: "Statistics show that during the years of military rule the rate of increase for defence expenditure was two to three times higher than the rate of increase for Social Welfare Programmes such as education and health." The overall socioeconomic effects of the colonels' policies were adverse for the working classes as well as the national economy:

> The average yearly rate of growth in agricultural production dropped from 4.9 per cent in the period 1960-66 to about 2.5 per cent during 1967-72. This figure is less than half of the regime's 5.2 per cent target. This decline of the rate of increase in agricultural production cannot be attributed to unfavourable climatic conditions, rather it was due to the reduction of state support for agricultural development.

> This overall retardation of agricultural and industrial development was also associated with a deterioration in the balance of payments, due to marked reduction in the growth of earnings from the export of goods in certain areas and the sharp increase in importation of goods and services. In the 1967-73 period total imports almost quadrupled. There was also a significant rise in overall public deficit and significant tax reduction and exemption for some wealthy groups. The cost of living in 1973 went up by 30.6 per cent. In the same year the wholesale price index increased by 48.3 per cent while wages went up by only 12 per cent.

These findings underscored Danapoulos and Patel's conclusion - one consonant with those of most scholars who have investigated other instances of non-leftist military rule - that "in the case of Greece, military professionalism was inadequate to bring about economic growth and social reform". Parallel conclusions were reported for Israel by Seliktar (1980:339-55), who "found that the extent of the gun-butter tradeoff is very considerable, both in terms of direct cuts in social and welfare spending and the less direct losses in opportunity costs". Although not military dominant to the extent that Greece was, Israel was similar to Athens and many of its Middle Eastern neighbours by virtue of her high military burdens and their rate of growth which are the highest in the area.

In the preceding paragraph, I have summarized research on particular countries characterized by heavy military burdens. Gottheil (1974:510-12) analyzed forgone economic output for Israel along with a group of Arab states with high armed forces budgets. Although he employed a number of assumptions which might not be perfectly applicable to conversion, his basic contention seems politically well taken: if there were a major reduction of military budgetary allocations the consequence would be a marked rise in consumption and economic growth within the civilian sector. A similar conclusion was reached by Askari and Glover (1977:59) for all developing countries:

> The compounded effect of lost GDP in 1973 due to the resources diverted for military purposes from 1953 to 1973 was calculated to be roughly $102.6 billion in constant 2970 U.S. dollars; in 1973 dollars this was equivalent to a loss of nearly 26 percent of aggregate GNP of all developing countries in 1973. Even with an extremely conservative estimate, the loss would be around 12 percent of aggregate GNP. This loss is an average for all developing countries. Individual countries were affected much more; in some cases, such as Jordan, the loss was more than the country's entire GDP for 1973.

Elsewhere (52) they note that military expenditures have both exceeded combined foreign aid and net investment, and increased at double the rate of the latter.(26)

Almost as impressive are the patterns revealed in a comparative analysis by Dabelko and McCormick (1977: 149-51) of budgetary substitution effects between military, health, and educational expenditures reported by 75 countries in various parts of the world between 1950 and 1972. Their regression analysis was consistent with the opportunity cost thesis although the coefficients tended to be weak - yet this was less the case for education than health. When they controlled for regime type - polyarchic, centrist and military which they called "personalist" - their most pronounced substitution effects were revealed in the case of military regimes: "it is safe to conclude that military spending in personalist regimes has had the harshest impact on spending for education and health". Opportunity costs were only marginally affected by economic development levels, although these tended to increase for education among the more developed countries while they declined for the least developed which may have been impacted more by foreign aid programmes.

Whynes (1979) using a sample of about 20 Third World nations found like Benoit that in the area of economic growth there was a strong correlation with defence spending. Thus, "the evidence of this chapter does suggest that the defence sector will generate some growth of its own accord". Although he does not examine specific social welfare tradeoffs, Whynes denotes much of his book to the thesis that "the defence sector absorbs an enormous quantity of resources", "which might have an alternative use in the civil sector". Like Albrecht et al. (1974) and Wulf (1979), the author underscores that both arms imports and local weapons production often aggravate balance of payments deficits and in the smaller economies seldom have multiplier or spillover effects. Analysing coups and military expenditures between 1963 and 1971, Whynes finds that in every case there was a post-coup rise in military expenditures. An earlier and longer term association between military intervention and enlarged budgetary shares was also reported by Thompson (1973:20-3) who discerned for the 1946-66 period "that years in which military coups occurred were more likely to coincide with years in which relative defense expenditures increased, not decreased". While this may well have at least partially reflected abortive attempts by incumbent governments to buy off intramilitary support for conspirators, Thompson warns against causal assumptions. Nevertheless, he stresses that "more generally, it would appear that there is a tendency for relative defense expenditures to rise in the years after a coup, especially after successful coups". The same holds for subsequent increases in arms imports and "weapons stocks". These patterns of course are consonant with previously mentioned findings by Kennedy, Finer, Park and Abolfathi which together may be reconciled without difficulty with the earlier stated proposition that militarism promotes militarization. Whynes echoes this by contending, along with others as we have seen, that internal repression is a major factor in rising Third World military expenditures, and like Kende warns that "the costs of defence spending are not purely economic. As the UN has made clear, increases in spending merely serve to enhance the instability of international politics by increasing social tensions between nations." These consequences were considered in Chapter 2.

The penultimate analysis to be essayed here is by Cusack (1981) who criticizes studies limited to six or ten years both because they fail to take account of the possibility of autocorrelated error and ignore long term substitution effects. Employing the Cochrane-Orcutt iterative estimation technique to adjust for short term autocorrelated error, Cuscak analysed tradeoffs between 1960 and 1977 in 32 "market economies" within both the industrialized and developing world. In the short term he found no significant tradeoffs for 17 countries and little uniformity elsewhere: in six it was with civil government expenditures, in another six it was with investment and in the final three it was with personal consumption. A much stronger relationship was discovered over the long run, but again there was no uniform pattern. The most that could be said was that civil government expenditures predominated in a relative sense as the major tradeoff:

> In more than half of all instances, a 'significant' substitutability relationship appears to exist between it and defense spending. Slightly less than a third of the cases reveal evidence of such a relationship between consumption and defense. Less than one fourth of the cases evince a pattern of long term substitutability between investment and defense.

He found that countries with rising defence burdens finance them out of civil government expenditures and private consumption, while both investment and civil government expenditures tend to benefit when defence burdens decline.

The last study to be considered here is the UN Group of Governmental Experts on the Relationship between Disarmament and Development. Highlighting in a systematic manner the potential benefits of demilitarization (UNSG, 1982:85), the Report summarizes several recent comparative and case studies by Lance Taylor, Bruce Russett and David Sylvan, and Jacques Fontanel that stress:

(a) increases in military spending as a share of the GDP are associated with reductions in the rate of economic growth. A sample of 69 countries, in the period 1950-1970, shows that increased military spending tends to be related to lower investment and a greater tax burden. Similar results are yielded by another study of 70 developing countries, which concludes that any positive result in spin-off or modernization is either marginal or its narrow economic utility is tempered by its social and political implications.

(b) The negative effect of military spending on the formation of fixed capital, consumption in real terms and inflationary trends may not be materially different for the developed and the less developed countries. A comparative study of one developed and one developing country concludes that any short-term increases in total consumption resulting from increases in the total wages paid after additions in military spending are followed by noticeable decreases in the long term because the growth rate has been appreciably reduced.

Only a few of the tradeoff studies considered in this chapter are assessed by the Group of Experts who in the main derive their findings from such specially commissioned studies as those referred to above.(27) Further, on the basis of several of these, the Group concluded "it appears that the multiplier effect of military spending is somewhat lower than civilian spending".(28) Their overall conclusions are that "on the basis of the reports commissioned by the Group, that military expenditures have definite negative effects on economic and social development".

Since all military expenditures are, essentially, government expenditures, a reduction in these expenditures may, on the one hand, promote government consumption and investment for over-all economic and social development. On the other hand, as a result of tax reductions, private consumption and investment may also be promoted. This tenet is in sharp contrast to the view, held in some quarters, that increased military expenditures have positive effects on economic growth and employment and, thus, on economic and social development, although the extent of these may vary according to the stage of development of the countries concerned, and the period of analysis. The conceptual error in this latter line of reasoning is that it does not make a comparison with a situation in which the resources now used in the military sector are used for alternative civilian production.

The findings of the studies commissioned by the Group strongly suggest that, irrespective of their current levels of development, all societies engaged in a steadily high or increasing military effort are pre-empting resources which could and would, otherwise, have been utilized for socially productive ends. These studies also support the existing evidence that any short-term economic benefits accompanying the military activities of societies with unutilized or under-utilized resources are likely to be negated by their long-term effects on economic growth. The fact that historically higher rates of economic growth and high levels of military spending have co-existed in the past, in some countries, does not provide evidence of a positive relationship between the two: if there was a relationship, the causation was possibly reversed, with high defence spending being possible because of high growth.(29)

This of course is consonant with Altaf Gauhar's thesis concerning high petroleum earnings being transformed into weapons imports which I presented in Chapter 2. It is also underscored by Tuomi and Vàyrynen (1980:245) who caution that "the causal relationship is often interpreted in a misleading manner. Instead of resulting in higher growth rates of the economy the increase in military capability itself is made possible by economic expansion."

Like those restricted to industrialized nations, most of the studies referred to in this section provide impressive support for Russett's (1970:133) assumption "that defense spending has come at the expense of something else". Beyond this the patterns were diverse due to internal political forces and more technical factors.(30) In many instances the tradeoffs appeared to be more pronounced with private consumption and investment than with civil government expenditures unless military burdens were relatively high. Yet even the sacrifice of investment which is essential to future productivity bodes ill for development aspirations, while all of the tradeoffs and the concomitant growth of repressive militarism serve to perpetuate the structural violence endemic to these areas.

Chapter 5

THIRD WORLD MILITARY BURDENS AND PHYSICAL WELFARE

In the preceding chapters of this work the costs of
militarization have often been identified as falling
somewhat more underlined{directly} in the economic than in the
social welfare area. Justification for placing greater emphasis on welfare indicators need not rest
alone upon such factors as the widespread aspirations for enhanced mass living standards or a norma-
tive aversion to the staggering human costs of
structural violence. Even from the narrower perspective of economic development, social progress is, as
Askari and Glover (1977:54) stress, intrinsic to the
process:

> Development is not limited to economic mea-
> sures; it includes other areas, one of which is
> social development. In many ways, economic and
> social development are functions of each other;
> continued progress in either field depends upon
> concurrent gains in the other. In the develop-
> ment literature, expenditures in education and
> public health, for example, are labeled social
> overhead capital.

This perspective is also shared by the UN Group of
Governmental Experts on the Relationship of Disarmament to Development (UNSG, 1982:71):

> Development ... implies not only the existence
> of economic growth but also changes in the
> structure of demand, supply and income distri-
> bution patterns, changes in socio-political
> institutions and the improvement of material
> welfare.

These considerations explain the paramount focus of
my own analysis - particularly with respect to Third

World countries - upon social indicators of well-being.

A second reason is the obvious one that far from being an end in itself, economic growth - and economies themselves - are universally valued by citizens as a means to enhanced socio-cultural and material welfare. Brazilian Gen. Medici's 1971 quip "our economy is in good shape, but the people aren't", underscores this point!

Another problem that is ignored in most tradeoff comparisons pertains to use of educational, health or other budgetary expenditures as valid indicators of welfare. Considerable diversion of funds to administrative costs including salaries and corruption as well as differential efficiency suggest that financial expenditure indicators may be poor measures of actual welfare outputs, let alone outcomes. Public policy analyses in the US (Hofferbert, 1974) for example have failed to reveal correlations between expenditure differences by states in specific welfare areas and administrative performance unless the magnitude was very large. Such findings are particularly relevant to the Third World whose bureaucracies are even less efficient or professional and far more politicized than in the US. For these reasons I have selected and relied upon a series of largely physical indicators of socio-economic welfare.(31) My universe of countries is limited to slightly over 100 in the "low income" or underdeveloped category whose per capita GNP in the mid-1960s (1966) was below $1,600. Furthermore, nations with fewer than 300,000 persons in 1960 were also excluded.(32)

In addition to examining direct associations between relative military burdens and various welfare indicators over time employing where appropriate factor analysis, I shall also systematically control for conditions or situations which may limit the impact of resource transfers to the military. These controls include foreign aid, national wealth, differential state extractive capacities, levels of internal repression, alternative development strategies, and military vs. civilian rule.(33) My preoccupation of course is with the relationship between late 1960s military burdens - financial as well as manpower - and (1) late 1970s physical welfare; (2) change in such welfare indicators between 1970 and the late 1970s. A second primary relationship scrutinized is between the rise in various military

burdens during 1960-78 and the same dependent variables. The SPSS (computer) programme employing eta
coefficients for breakdowns of means is used as are
Pearson product movement coefficients for regression
analysis of other variables. Because of the paucity
of socioeconomic and political data for many recently independent and even some old "new nations" for
the early 1960s, this analysis will be limited for
most variables to the late 1960s and 1970s. Again,
non- financial (that is, budgetary) or "outcome" indicators will be used in such areas as school enrolment ratios, progress toward sexual equality, literacy, life expectancy, food availability, employment, etc. Although these have also been selected
because they appear as the most direct or valid
measurable indicators of mass welfare, all are provided by governments whose images are thereby affected. Hence the reliability of such data is problematic at best. Countries which did not provide data
are excluded from both breakdown and correlation
tables. Yet even when data are reported, there is no
way to control for differential candour. If we assume that countries with the poorest record are most
likely to favourably colour the data, the overall
effect is to exaggerate social progress for the developing countries as a group. Further, if the heavy
militizers or military regimes were the worst performers and therefore most disposed to alter such
data, the analysis itself, as I have recognized
earlier, would be biased against finding the hypothesized relationships. And such bias would be intensified if the heavy militizers also had the
greatest propensity to conceal and understate expenditures for the armed forces. This common practice
was remarked upon at the beginning of this work by
Janowitz, Weaver and Gunder Frank among others. Thus
even when militarization is found to be inversely
associated with welfare improvement, the strength of
the relationship may appear to be weaker than in
fact is the case.

Such a caveat - admittedly conjectural - is less
pertinent when one analyses indicators of political
welfare, for example, freedom. Systematic and periodic external assessments are available from independent organizations such as Amnesty International
for identifying cases where during the 1973-9 period
torture, political executions and disappearances
occurred. I have also used Raymond Gastil's periodic
"Comparative Surveys of Freedom" and the pre-Reagan
State Department's Country Reports on Human Rights
Practices. While all of these are systematic, there

is a clear if mild bias in the last favouring countries toward which the us desires good relations.
For this reason, when AI indicates a more serious
denial as more than an isolated occurrence, it has
been determinative. Consequential classification or
specific countries appears in Appendix F.

A final caveat pertains to the use of statistical
procedures. The Eta and Pearson significance tests
are premised upon normal distributions associated
with sampling probability theory. Their relevance is
qualified by the fact that we are using a population
representing the univers of countries rather than a
sample. Hence the differences appear, they are real
and cannot by definition be attributed to sampling
error. Hence, undue importance should not be attached to the failure to conform with statistically
acceptable confidence levels which here are really
measures of dispersion. The latter of course are
important however in assessing the meaningfulness of
differences.

My first hypothesis is that high military burdens in
the late 1960s are inversely associated with physical indicators of welfare in the late 1970s. Pearson
product moment correlations for selected military
burden indicators appear in Table 5. Interestingly
the only negative association is with US Trainees
(1950-76) as a percentage of 1977 Armed Forces
(USTAFS), which is also negatively correlated (-.24
significant at .05 level) with 1967 Military Spending as a percentage of Central Government Expenditures (MIXCGE67). Of these variables just two -
armed forces ratio and military expenditures as a
percentage of GNP - accounted for 68 per cent of the
total initial statistical variance. An extracted
factor explaining the largest amount of cumulative
variance - 51 per cent - will be called the Military
Burden factor (MILSPFAC).(34)

In Table 6 are regression coefficients for child
mortality and nine other key physical welfare variables. All but two were both strong and significant
at the .05 level. Again one factor was extracted
(PHYSICAL), which accounted for more than 55 per
cent of the cumulative variance with a standard
deviation of 1.01.(35) PHYSICAL in turn was positively correlated with the Military Burden factor
(MILSPFAC) yielding a regression coefficient of r
.33 (p .05, n 36). Yet the latter did correlate
negatively with the women in labour force factor

(WOMENFAC) with r -.48 (p .001, n 39). And it might
be added, the armed forces ratio (AFSIZE67) significantly correlated r .78 (p .05, n 7) with child mortality (CHILDM78).

Before turning to our controls, it might be worth
mentioning that military regimes during the 1960-7
period exhibited somewhat higher mean scores on
MILSPFAC than did civilian ones.(36) A strong negative coefficient -.44 (p .01, n 36) characterized
the relationship between US training (USTAFS9 and
the physical welfare (PHYSICAL) factor for all regimes. Mean scores for the physical welfare factor
do not differ significantly for civilian and military ruled societies during the 1960s. The latter
notwithstanding are markedly inferior with respect
to female participation in the labour force, primary
school enrolment ratios, child labour, pupil-teacher
ratios in primary education and protein consumption.(37)

When we turn to the most recent period (1965-78) for
which more complete data are available, a number of
relationships are particularly salient. Using our
most sensitive indicator (MXGNP68) for early military expenditure burdens, Table 7 reveals that they
do not differ significantly for regimes which were
civilian as opposed to military led. Yet a marked
contrast appears when systems are classified by development strategy.(38) The subclassification of
civilian and military regimes by development strategy in Table 8 demonstrates that while state socialist countries were characterized by the heaviest
mean military burdens, among the state capitalist
regimes, relative military expenditures were much
greater for military ruled societies. Most of the
forgoing regimes are of course targets (Wolpin,
1981) of US hostility and destabilization policies.
No significant difference appears on this score between the two "open door" variants. US training impact was far more pronounced according to Table 9
for open door regimes than those with other development strategies. Within the state capitalist category it was somewhat greater for military governments, though the amount of explained variance however is quite small.

When we turn to regime performance on two of our
most sensitive welfare indicators - child mortality
and women in the labour force - Table 10 reveals
that both types of open door regimes are moderately

inferior to state capitalist ones on child mortality. On women in the labour force there is no significant difference for these two regime types as the
deviation from the mean here is considerable. My
most striking discovery, however, is the performance
of the state socialist systems which did so well -
especially on child mortality - despite the previously mentioned heavy relative military spending - a
consequence of their hostile geopolitical environment.

While this contributes to explaining why a positive
association was found between the Military Spending
factor and our Physical Welfare factor, more can be
discerned by subjecting the relationships considered
above to other political as well as a number of economic controls.(39) In Table 12 the two aid indicators (AIDPER75 and EPDGNP78) which were selected as
controls appear with the remaining aid variables.
Multiple regression coefficients for these with the
other aid variables are r .57 (R^2 .33, p = .05) and
r .47 (R^2 = .22, p .002).

Tables 13 and 14 depict relationships between the
military burden and welfare factors when we control
for countries above and below the median on each of
the foreign aid variables. My conclusion is that
this makes little difference. It is possible of
course that if we limited our controls to the highest and lowest quartiles that differences would appear. But there are too few cases with data to explore this possibility. It does appear, however,
that countries above the median on AIDPER75 had
lower average 1977 military expenditures in millions
of constant dollars (127.6) than those below
(544.6). This was also true for 1968 military spending (50.0 vs. 282.3). Converse relationships appear,
however, when the median for EPDGNP78 is used. No
relationship appears, for AIDPER75 median positions
and the 1968 armed forces ratio means although the
latter is twice as high (4.2 vs. 2.3) for countries
above the median on EPDGNP78.

The next question is whether the extent and consequences of differential military burdens is affected
by how extensive government roles and extractive
capability are relative to the economy. Here controls are introduced for public consumption as a
percentage of 1978 GDP (PUCGDP78) and government
expenditures as a percentage of 1970 GDP (GVTGDP70).
The latter is moderately correlated with 1976 public

revenues per capita (r.36, p.001, n 82) and strongly correlated with 1960 GVTGDP (r.83, p.0005, n 52). As one might expect, countries above the median on either of these controls are much heavier relative military burdens (MILSPFAC). Yet Table 15 indicates that the deviation for those above the median tends to be high.

When we control for GVTGDP70, however, Table 16 reveals that for those above the median only one significant coefficient appears - a strongly negative one for US training impact and physical welfare. While this disappears for those below the median, an even stronger inverse association appears between the military burden factor and the women in the labour force factor. For those above the median on PUCGDP78, we find strong negative relationships in Table 17 for the military burden factor and women in the labour force as well as between US training factor and physical welfare. For those below, however, while the latter appear, there are also pronounced negative associations between US training and military burden factors as well as a positive one between the latter and physical welfare! This last finding and the lack of uniformity prevent us from drawing firm conclusions, though most of the relationships are in the hypothesized direction, especially for USTAFFAC and countries above the respective medians.

Somewhat more clear-cut differences appear when we control for economic development. In Table 18 we dichotomize manufacturing as a percentage of GDP (MFGDP70) which in turn is correlated (r.56, p.005, n 67) strongly with 1963 per capita national income - (NAIPER63). For those above the median only the physical welfare and women in the labour force factors yield a significant regression coefficient (r.54, p.005, n 27). Yet for the less industrialized, we again find, as with those below the median on public consumption, a strong positive correlation between the military burden and physical welfare factors, though the number of cases is admittedly small and there is an even stronger negative correlation with the women in the labour force factor. In the least developed countries then, high military burdens in the late 1960s do not appear to be associated with low physical welfare levels in the mid to late 1970s.

When we return to average annual 1960-70 GDP growth

rates (CGDP70) as a control, Table 19 suggests that
while there is a moderate inverse relationship between the military burden factor and women in the
labour force for higher growth rate countries, with
respect to those below the median we again find a
strong positive association r.61 (p.005, n 18) between military burdens and the physical welfare factor.(40) Similarly, a negative one for US training
factor (USTAFFAC) r.53 (p.05, n 18) and physical
welfare. Since we saw in Table 9 that US training
impact was most pronounced for open door or monopoly
capitalist regimes, this particular development
strategy - reinforced by such training (Wolpin,
1973) may contribute to explaining the negative association between the US training factor (USTAFFAC)
and physical welfare throughout this data analysis.
Thus for countries following this development strategy there (1965-78) is an inverse -.45 coefficient
(p.005, n 34) for USTAFFAC and PHYSICAL, while no
significant correlation characterizes this relationship for other development strategies. For military
regimes during the same period, the relationship is
slightly stronger (r-.48, p.05, n 20), while for
civilian governments its significance is problematic
(r-.35,   p.09, n 17).

This underscores the importance of political differences. It may therefore be pertinent to control for
associational and expressive freedom, or more succinctly political democracy. In Table 20, I have
dichotomized countries above and below the median
(.87) using a 1961-7 press freedom (PRESS67) index
(+4.0 to -4.0) from Taylor and Hudson (1972). The
only significant coefficients are for the less-free
countries where the military burden factor is negatively (r-.66, p.001, n 20) associated with the women in the labour force factor but positively (r.52,
p.01, n 20) correlated with the physical welfare
factor. A more comprehensive ordinal scale of political and civil rights by Gastil (1973) is used in
Table 21. Here for the less-free countries above the
median (5.50), a number of significant relationships
appear. Military burdens are negatively associated
(r-.58, p.01, n 16) with the women in the labour
force factor, yet positively correlated (r.55, p.05,
n 16) with the physical welfare factor. US training
impact (USTAFFAC) is again inversely associated
(r-.56, p.05, n 16) with physical welfare. For the
more free below median category, however, no significant relationships appear other than an inverse
one (r-.44, p.05, n 27) between the US training and

military burden factors.

Finally, we turn to the relationship between the military burden and US training factors on one hand, and the change which occurred in the particular wel-fare variables from 1970 until the late 1970s. My second hypothesis is that if military burdens were heavy, we should expect a less pronounced rate of welfare improvement than where they were light.

Here we shall focus upon what seem to me to be 14 key welfare improvement or change indicators:

CHÀPER: Children in the Labour Force (1970-5)
PROPER: Protein Consumption Per Capita (1970-6)
WOMLF: Women in the Labour Force (1970-7)
PTRPED: Pupil-Teacher Ratios in Primary Education
          (1970-7)
FPRSCH: Female Primary School Enrolment Ratios
          (1970-7)
CALPER: Caloric Consumption Per Capita (1970-7)
LITRCY: Literacy Rate (1970-8)
CHILDM: Child Mortality Rate (1970-8)
LIFEXB: Life Expectancy at Birth (1970-8)
CFOODP78: Change in Food Production (1970-8)
FOODIN78: Food Price Inflation (1970-8)
INFLAA78: General Price Inflation (1970-8)
INFL6078: General Price Inflation (1960-78)
EMPLOY78: Change in General Employment Level (1970-8)

In Table 22 the regression coefficients for the wel-fare change variables appear. It is apparent that re-lationships among a majority, though not all, fail to be strong or significant at the .05 level.(41) Conse-quently, because eigenvalues were less than 1.0, a positive matrix for factor analysis was unfeasible. As for our military burden and training factors, MILSPAC was inversely related to CHLPER (r-.39, p.003, n 49), while USTAFFAC yielded a regression coefficient of .26 (p.05, n 41) with FPRSCH and r-.28 (p.05, n.37) with CFOODP78. However, when controls were introduced, more significant associations were evident.

Thus when we control for 1973-5 per capita aid (AIDPER75), even in the more heavily aided countries, military burdens are inversely associated (r-.55) with per capita calorie intake, although for those below the median there is an even stronger relation-ship (r.80) with child mortality, while US training factor is inversely associated (r-.46) with change in female employment. The two favourable correlations in Table 23 for countries above the median indicate that high per capita aid may offset some of the consequences of heavy military burdens. Employing another type of and longer-term aid indicator (EPDGDP78) in Table 24, we find that welfare is adversely affected both above as well as below the median. Thus, except at high levels in per capita terms perhaps, "aid" itself does not seem to have a general impact upon the military burden/welfare change relationship. This is understandable as many external loans have simply refinanced earlier ones, ensured emission of profits by transnationals, and maintained international liquidity of friendly governments that otherwise would confront a crisis and possibly fall. That little benefits the mass sectors has been adequately documented by Teresa Hayter (1971) and Cheryl Payer (1975). And as we shall see in the next chapter (Table 44), countries on per capita aid were precisely those having the highest rate of increase in military expenditures!

It is unsurprising then that somewhat more clear-cut results are associated with high vs. low economic growth rates during the immediately preceding years. Thus, in Table 25 we see that all of the predicted relationships appear for countries below the median. The efficacy of impressive economic performance as a neutralizer for any adverse military burden impact may also be inferred from Table 26 where the less industrialized and lower per capita income countries account for almost all of the negative relationships - calories per capita, proteins per capita and food production. Only on child mortality is there a strong relationship with military burdens for the more developed category.

This conclusion is reinforced when we turn to governmental extractive capability (GVTGDP70) in Table 27. Here all of the adverse military burden effects, with an exceptionally strong coefficient for child mortality, are experienced by countries below the median. On the other hand, differences in 1978 public consumption as a percentage of GDP in Table 28 do not appear to have any effect. Moreover the three relationships are not adverse especially for training.

Our two political freedom controls in Tables 29 and 30 indicate that the degree of civil liberties and associational freedom is irrelevant to the effect of military burdens upon welfare. Yet a very strong positive coefficient with child mortality appears for the less free in the latter table. Even so, there are few significant relationships and most run in a contrary direction. The same holds for Table 31's regime type controls where, however, for civilian governments high military burdens are moderately associated with high rates of inflation. As for the two development orientations in Table 32, no clear pattern can be identified for the change indicators. At best it seems that in open door regimes high military burdens may exacerbate the unemployment problem. Cases with data for the state capitalist and socialist categories are too few for meaningful coefficients.

As implied in the foregoing discussion, no overall patterns were identified for either late 1960s military burden and late 1970s welfare or between the former and welfare improvement during the 1970s. In fact, relatively few variables exhibited significant relationships. At most it can be said that some of these were in the hypothesized direction and this tendency was slightly more pronounced on welfare factors and improvement indicators for less industrialized, less heavily injected with foreign aid, less on extractive capability, more economically stagnant and those following open door development strategies. Beyond that we can add that military burdens appear higher and WOMENFAC coefficients more negative for military regimes. Equally salient is that US training impact tends to be negatively associated with the physical welfare factor generally as well as for open door, les free, military and civilian regimes.

Among the more unexpected discoveries was the strong negative association between the military burden factor and WOMENFAC - a relationship that was particularly surprising for countries with superior economic growth records. Equally astonishing was the strong positive coefficients between MILSPFAC and PHYSICAL for the "less free" countries. In part this may be attributed to the impressive welfare performance on WOMLF and CHILDM by the state socialist countries - despite their heavy military burdens.

Chapter 6

THIRD WORLD MILITARIZATION AND PHYSICAL WELFARE

In this chapter I turn to the secular <u>rise</u> in military burdens. Between 1960 and 1980 the percentage of global military expenditures attributed to the Third World (SIPRI, 1981:169) has grown from 4.5 to 16. As we saw in Chapter 1, this reflected in part a 300 per cent increase in military spending (constant dollars), notwithstanding an official decline of military budgetary shares in many developing nations. Even so the threefold increase in military expenditures to more than $100 billion was substantial, constituted a diversion of resources that might have alleviated mass destitution and was accompanied by a doubling of combined paramilitary and regular armed forces. This 100 per cent expansion of armed forces in the South was as we saw in Chapter 2 associated with sharply escalating weapons imports as well as sanctioning of torture, executions and disappearances along with a steady rise in the number of military dominated states.

In the following pages we shall examine the extent to which <u>increases</u> in military financial and manpower allocations are negatively associated with the same welfare factors and change variables considered in Chapter 5. To be more precise I shall begin with our third hypothesis - that financial militarization as well as armed forces expansion are inversely related to both WOMENFAC and PHYSICAL. Before doing so or applying our set of controls, it might be useful to identify relationships for the selected militarization indicators which are delineated in Table 33.(42) The high coefficient for CAF70 and AFSIZE suggests that the most rapid force expansion occurred during the 1960s. Yet much of the military expenditure increase seems to have occurred since the late 1960s, probably reflecting rising costs of increasingly sophisticated imported weapons systems.(43)

One factor was extracted from these militarization variables which will be called the militarization expenditure factor (MXCGFAC), hereafter at times referred to simply as the ME factor. It accounts for 43 per cent of the cumulative variance for our four indicators of military expenditure change.(44) In addition, three indicators of armed forces expansion - CAF70, AFSIZE, and CAFR6779 - will be regressed separately as independent variables. This will enable us to assess the "impact" of armed forces expansion for different periods within the two decades under scrutiny.

In Table 34, we see the relationships among both the ME factor as well as the armed forces expansion variables and the welfare factors employed in Chapter 5. The ME factor is moderately related to armed forces ration expansion over the last twelve years and somewhat more strongly to armed forces growth over the entire period. To a lesser degree than USTAFFAC, both the ME factor as well as AFSIZE are negatively associated with the physical welfare factor. Hence it seems that countries which were low on welfare at the end of the 1970s experienced moderately greater militarization in both financial and physical terms than did those which had higher mass living standards. Yet, as Table 35 demonstrates when several of these militarization indicators were correlated with the welfare change variables for the 1970s, only one significant adverse association appeared while nine benign ones may be noted. Furthermore, three-quarters of the possible associations lacked significance.

Turning to our controls, we begin with 1965-78 development strategy. In Table 36, the breakdown reveals but one significant pattern - lower militarization rates by state socialist regimes, though because of the large deviation we can even here only have confidence in MXCGFAC and AFSIZE. For the other two orientations there are no significant differences. The same holds because of the deviation for all three development strategies over the entire period, although Table 37 does suggest a lower rate of expansion for state socialist armed forces during the 1960s. And the same may be said for change in armed forces' ratios in the 1970s, again only if one overlooks the large standard deviations in Table. 38

When we turn to both regime type and development strategy for the entire 1960-78 period in Table 39, it is clear that within the open door category no significant difference distinguishes civilian from military led governments. On the other hand the former's mean values for our ME factor are markedly lower and are twice as large as the standard deviations. Even so there is only an 80 per cent confidence level. This increases modestly for the 1965-78 period where the pattern is replicated in Table 40. Furthermore, while customary 95 per cent confidence is lacking, it does seem that marked demilitarization differentiates the state socialist orientation from others. In this and Table 41 which follows, it appears that high militarization is salient for state capitalist civilian regimes. Yet the standard deviations give us more confidence in the markedly lower mean on AFSIZE for the state socialist category. With respect to CAF70, the standard deviations are too high for all categories to warrant any confidence, and this holds as well for CAFR6779.

We shall now look at what relationships appear between associational freedom and economic control variables on one hand, and the four militarization indicators on the other. Two patterns are manifested by Table 42. First, there is a modest relationship between the ME factor and external indebtedness as a percentage of GNP. Second, we find a more pronounced negative association between economic development (manufacturing, per capita income and armed forces expansion).

With respect to associational freedom and militarization, two measures of the former - PRESS67 and FREEDM79 - are dichotomized in Table 43.Unfortunately, none of the differences between the mean values for MXCGFAC, CAF70, AFSIZE or CAFR6779 were significant or even came close to the .05 level of confidence.(45) Notwithstanding this it does seem that armed forces expansion during the 1960s was somewhat more pronounced for countries that were less free in both the 1960s and late 1970s. But not too much importance should be attached to this since the more-free countries in 1979 had far higher rates of armed forces expansion in the 1960s. Yet during that period it was precisely the less free on PRESS67 which experienced the greatest expansion. In all cases, however, the standard deviations are high. Nor was the armed forces expansion paralleled by changes in armed forces ratios. With one exception

a paucity of significant differences also characterizes countries above and below the median on our two
aid indicators - AIDPER75 and EPDGNP78. In Table 44
we note that the mean value on the ME factor was
considerably higher for those above than below the
median on 1973-5 per capita aid (AIDPER75) and further that its significance was .06 which is close to
the acceptable level. This, however, was not the
case with respect to armed forces expansion where
there were no differences that approached acceptable
levels of confidence.

The lack of any significant differences also characterizes our indicators of extractive capability
(GVTGDP70) and governmental involvement in the economy (PUCGDP78). One almost significant relationship
for the latter and 1961-77 armed forces expansion
(AFSIZE) does appear in Table 45. Nations with extensive governmental involvement seem to have more
rapidly increased their armed forces though the deviation is considerable.

When we focus upon economic growth rates and industrialization, several significant associations are
manifest. First, the breakdown in Table 46 demonstrates that those above the median on economic expansion in the 1960s (CGDP70) had a positive mean
value for the ME factor in the 1970s whereas a substantially lower and negative ME mean characterized
the more stagnant economies. Prior economic growth,
then, as Gauhar argued in Chapter 2 with respect to
petroleum, appears to have at least facilitated a
subsequent higher upsurge in military spending. The
lack of significant differences for breakdowns of
the armed forces expansion indicators (CAF70,
AFSIZE and CAFR6779) and CGDP70 allows us to infer
that much of the expenditure escalation went for
generally imported equipment rather than to increasing the size of armed forces. On the other hand it
seems that armed forces expansion during the entire
1961-77 period was greatest for those countries below the median on industrialization/economic development (MFGDP70) in Table 46. Both of the differences referred to in this paragraph are significant
at the .05 level.

At this point I shall focus upon mass welfare relationships that are germane to our third and fourth
hypotheses: if countries opt for high financial
militarization and armed forces expansion, their
social welfare improvement and late 1970s status

will be inferior to those devoting less resources to
the military. In Table 47, militarization and welfare change relationships are set forth along with
the two welfare factors considered in Chapter 5. A
substantial majority of the correlations lack significance. And with one exception the remaining nine
which are significant are inconsistent with the
hypothesis. Yet, as we saw near the beginning of
this chapter, there is a moderate negative correlation between the physical welfare factor and two of
the militarization indicators. Hence militarization
tended to be greater for countries which both at the
close of the 1970s and in the early 1960s exhibited
lower indices of social welfare. Although super-
ficially it would seem that improvement on a minority of welfare change variables might be attributed
to high military spending, it should be recalled
that in Table 44 we saw that a positive mean value
for militarization expenditures characterized only
those countries above the median on 1973-5 per
capita aid. Some "aid" thus may have "got through",
then, in the sense of reaching impoverished sectors.
Four of the eight positive changes were related to
education - a target of many aid efforts.

This interpretation is strengthened when we intro-
duce our first control. Thus in Table 48 I dichotomize 1973-5 aid per capita (AIDPER75). For the above
median category, there are nine significant and
generally strong correlations at variance with my
hypothesis while only two - 1960-78 inflation and
child labour - are consistent. The picture changes,
however, when we turn to the below median category.
While it must be conceded that no significant relationships appear for the majority of pairs, of those
that do only three are at odds with my hypothesis
while five are consonant. And two of the most crucial welfare indicators are linked to 1961-77 armed
forces expansion - child mortality and caloric intake. This difference also appears with respect to
PHYSICAL and especially WOMENFAC for the armed forces expansion indicators. Thus, in the short run,
heavy per capita aid would sem to account for some
of the welfare improvements sustained despite high
militarization.

When another aid indicator is used - 1978 external
public debt as a percentage of GNP (EPDGNP78) - a
less pronounced pattern of differentiation appears.
Again more inconsistent relationships are found in

Table 49 above median category. But here we do not encounter more than two out of six significant correlations that are consistent with our hypothesis even in the below median category. Further, only one is significant for PHYSICAL while in the above median category two armed forces expansion indicators have significant positive coefficients with WOMENFAC.

Other important political controls include the three development strategies and civilian vs. military rule. In Table 50 we discover that for the 1960-78 period (DEVSTR78), the open door orientation yields but eight significant welfare change coefficients of which only two – child labour and caloric intake – are consistent with the militarization hypothesis as are two of the four PHYSICAL coefficients including MXCGFAC. The state capitalist and state socialist orientations are omitted because of an insufficient number of cases. For civilian regimes the open door pattern is replicated although there is more inconsistency on the two welfare factors. Thus seven out of the eight significant coefficients are not in the hypothesized direction. For military ruled governments in Table 51, however, a more balanced pattern emerges. Of the 13 significant relationships, six – protein per capita (on both AFSIZE and CAFR6779), calories per capita (on these as well as CAF70), employment – are by and large strong and in the hypothesized direction. This is also true for three of the four PHYSICAL coefficients.

When we employ our more contemporary development strategies (DVST6578), we again encounter a relatively balanced directional patter yet somewhat fewer significant regression coefficients. Although Table 52 also indicates performance relationships including WOMENFAC that are substantially more inconsistent with the militarization hypothesis for the state capitalist orientation, without scattergram inspection the coefficients for literacy, protein intake and especially child mortality remain problematic. Again there were too few cases to include the state socialist model. With respect to civilin vs. military rule (CVML6578), we see in Table 53 that again military regime performance is less inconsistent with our militarization hypothesis than is civilian government. In the latter 8 out of 9 regression coefficients that were significant were inconsistent while a slight majority of 7 to 6 were consonant for military ruled societies.

Next we turn to our two controls for associational freedom. Those above the median on 1967 press freedom (PRESS67) manifested only half of the twelve significant regression coefficients that were consistent with our militarization hypothesis. Yet among the less free, Table 54 reveals that only two of fifteen were consistent. A similar if slightly less pronounced pattern characterizes FREEDM73. Table 55 indicates that for the less-free group, only 4 of 15 significant coefficients are consistent while the corresponding ratio is 5/11 for the more-free category. On both measures a vast preponderance of the significant relationships for the "less free" are adverse to our hypothesis though the ratio is virtually even for the "more-free" group of countries!

With respect to extractive capability (GVTGDP70), it appears in Table 56 that this control also has a decided impact. For those above the median all but 3 of 16 significant correlations were inconsistent with the militarization hypothesis, while for those in the below median category, only 3 out of 9 were. Similarly, we see in Table 57 that for countries below the median on public consumption (PUCGDP78), a majority of 11 out of 17 significant regression coefficients were consistent with the hypothesis. A marked contrast exists for the above median category where only 5 out of 7 significant correlations were similarly consonant. Thus our hypothesis is more applicable to countries with relatively low public consumption and government involvement in the economy.

As for economic growth during the 1960s (CGDP70), we see in Table 58 that the ratios of consistent significant regression coefficients are 6/21 and 3/7 for the above and below median categories. Hence there is some really persuasive support for the belief that high prior economic growth can offset the pejorative effects of militarization. Yet even within the high growth category both our ME factor as well as AFSIZE exhibited very strong (r.52, r.67) coefficients with child mortality increase. More interesting perhaps is the relative unimportance of economic development/industrialization (MFGDP70) to the hypothesized relationship.

Clearly Table 59 delineates very few significant relationships. The greater number of inconsistent ones, 4/7, occur in the above mean category while both consistent and inconsistent 2/2 are balanced below the median.

What conclusions can be drawn from the data delineated above? First it seems that militarization rates were unaffected by respect for civil liberties and associational freedom. Countries which were more free in this regard exhibited as much propensity to militarize as the less free. Similarly, neither state involvement in the economy nor public consumption levels affected the propensity to militarize. The same holds for civilian as opposed to military governments within the "open door" category. It is true that the former were characterized by a lower mean ME factor value. But the most pronounced difference pertains to the state capitalist orientation. Although there may be some questions as far as significance is concerned, this represents the only development orientation associated with what might be called demilitarization - reducing the rate of growth in resources (MXCGFAC, AFSIZE) devoted to the military sector. High per capita aid and EPDGNP78 were also linked to higher mean values for the ME factor while below median position was not. Equally consistent with Gauhar's thesis was the salient contrast for this indicator when we looked at high vs. low prior economic growth during the 1960s. The latter paralleled the above-mentioned state socialist group while the former were analogous to the high per capita aid militarizers. Since this was not equally true for armed forces expansion, much of the rising military expenditure probably was used to finance imports.

Other findings were that armed forces expansion was more pronounced for the below median group on industrialization which also tended to have the smaller military establishments in the early 1960s, as it was for civilian state socialist regimes during the 1965-78 period. Finally we found relationships between armed forces expansion in the 1960s with that over the entire period (AFSIZE), and a moderate one between the latter and our ME factor (MXCGFAC).

When, however, we turn to the relationship of militarization (MXCGFAC, AFSIZE) - which was moderately correlated with low physical welfare both in 1960 and at the end of the 1970s - we discover that in general it was not inversely associated with physical welfare improvement rates during the 1970-8 period.(46) Not only were significant relationships limited to a minority of between a tenth and a quarter of possible ones (and naturally this applies also to the controls), but when they appeared in most, if not all, instances a majority were incon-sistent with my hypotheses that militarization is negatively associated with welfare and its improvement.

A majority of significant coefficients were consistent with the hypotheses only for the following: (1) below median per capita aid; (2) below median on government spending as a percentage of GDP; (3) below median on public consumption. This in conjunction with patterns of less inconsistency for below median countries on prior economic growth and low industrialization leads to the tentative conclusion that militarization is in the short run most injurious to mass welfare and its enhancement in the "Fourth World" - the poorest, most stagnant and least heavily aided economies. State activity in these countries also tends to be most restricted and least effective.

If, then, our hypotheses were most inconsistent with the existence of superior economic resources and performance, it is altogether unremarkable to find them also at variance with the performance of state capitalist systems where the state not only dominates the dynamic sectors of the economy but actively endeavours to promote agrarian, educational and other reforms. And this applies with equal force to the "less free" category of countries. Somewhat less though pronounced inconsistency also characterized civilian regimes, and more dubiously those of an open door orientation. Ironically the only regime type where a (admittedly bare) majority of significant coefficients were consonant with my hypotheses was the military variant which we saw also evidenced high mean scores on our militarization expenditure (ME) factor.

Chapter 7

REPRESSION, DEVELOPMENT STRATEGIES AND PHYSICAL
WELFARE IN THE THIRD WORLD

In preceding chapters we saw that while military
burdens tended to be higher for military and state
socialist regimes, only the former exhibited sharply
rising relative military expenditures and that in
general "more free" countries manifested parallel
militarization propensities to their "less free"
counterparts. Here we shall look more closely and
systematically at the incidence of repression as
well as its relationship to both militarization and
welfare performance. We have already seen too that
"less free" countries tend if anything to outperform
the "more free" category. And if the military regimes had been excluded, the gap would have been
even greater. Furthermore, Third World elites commonly allege that Western civil libertarianism is
culturally alien and therefore inappropriate, or
abused by opposition elements and consequently a
luxury that must be dispensed with because of the
exigencies associated with the struggle to overcome
underdevelopment and/or imperialism (for example,
Nicaragua).

I shall begin by exploring possible linkages between
military burdens and their increase on one hand and
the most severe manifestations of repression - torture, political executions and disappearances. Based
upon Amnesty International's 1975 and 1979 annual
reports, all such occurrences where more than isolated acts will be subsumed under the rubric of "torture" in this discussion.

Only two of the mean differences - both for 1975 -
in Table 60 approach customary confidence levels.
Military burdens (MILSPFAC) were higher for countries engaging in torture but their armed forces
ratio increase (CAFR6779) was considerably lower. In

76

both years the US training factor (USTAFFAC) was lower for the torture category though infinitesimally so in the latter. If we take all of the military burden and militarization indicators, we find that on four out of six, the torture category in 1975 scores lower. For 1979, they are evenly balanced. Thus, it cannot be concluded that high military burdens and militarization are associated with such practices. At most there is a weak pattern of greater financial military burdens and a higher rise in them among the torture prone while more pronounced armed forces expansion occurred among countries where such acts did not occur.

Ironically, a similar tendency appears when we dichotomize countries into "more" and "less free" employing the Gastil rankings for 1973 and 1982. In either of the years do the differences and standard deviations allow us to approach customary confidence levels. Notwithstanding this we find a pattern identical with one exception to that for the torture variable. Here, however, US training impact is greater for the less-free category. Otherwise the median group with higher financial military burdens and increase thereof tends to be the less free while those characterized by greater armed forces expansion are the more free. And Table 61 indicates that this holds regardless of the year selected. On four of the indicators mean differences are quite small while on almost all the dispersion is fairly impressive.

The greater growth of armed forces among the more free category increases the manpower resources of military establishments which can enhance the prospects for successful seizures of state control - a trend during the 1960-80 period. Yet when civilians are polarized, weakly organized and unarmed, even small detachments may be sufficient to depose some of these regimes. In Chapters 2 and particularly 4, findings by McKinlay and Cohan, Tannahill, Needler, Sivard and others on repression and military rule were commented upon.

While all military regimes are not equally repressive and obviously some of a civilian stripe (for example, Saudi Arabia, Philippines) are highly so, the previously mentioned findings and general consensus of civil-military analysts is that on balance their systems tend to be more repressive than those dominated by civilians. This view is strengthened by the breakdowns which appear in Table 62. Although the deviation is again too large to attain customary confidence levels, the patterns are suggestive.

The same may be said for MILSPFAC and the US training impact (USTAFS) where military governments score higher although as Table 63 reveals not only considerable deviance but also that USTAFS is higher for military regimes only during the more recent 1965-78 period. The pattern however is again suggestive and less ambiguous than that for the militarization indicators. With respect to the latter, Table 64 shows that while during the latter period armed forces expansion (CAFR6779) was greater for civilian governments, military regimes were so characterized in the 1960s (CAF70) as well as over the entire span of years (AFSIZE). The large deviations however underscore the tentative rather than conclusive nature of these relationships. This general pattern however is not wholly consistent with the findings of Park and Abolfathi, Kennedy, Finer and others in Chapter 4 with respect to higher military expenditures by military regimes. While the difference was minimal and the deviation impressive, civilians were slightly higher on the ME factor.

I now turn to the question of whether freedom is associated with superior welfare performance. We shall begin by looking at the same civilian military dichotomy even though it is but an indirect indicator of political liberty. On the PHYSICAL welfare factor there are no differences of any importance on the mean scores due to the large deviations. While Table 65 reveals the same for the women in the labour force factor (WOMENFAC), the military regimes appear on balance to be inferior. Turning to change in welfare performance during the 1970s, we see in Table 66, that the military governments were superior on changes in female primary school enrolment ratios, female secondary school enrolment ratios, pupil-teacher ratios in primary education, life expectancy and on another measures, 1960-78 inflation. Civilians did better on changes in child labour, proteins per capita, women in the labour force, calories per capita, changes in food production, food price inflation during the 1970s, general price inflation in the 1970s and rise in employment. While a majority of these indicators of welfare change favour civilians, in a preponderance of cases it must be emphasized the differences were exceedingly small. Further almost all the standard devia-

tions were large, thus qualifying the significance
of the observed differences.

When we measure respect for political and civil
rights more directly using Gastil's 1973 and 1982
"Comparative Surveys of Freedom", a more clear-cut
pattern is manifested. Thus in Table 67 we find virtually no difference on child labour and caloric intake while the more-free countries do better on increasing women in the labour force, the rise in
pupil-teacher ratios and growth of food production.
On the other hand the less free exhibit superior
improvement or less deterioration on a preponderant
majority of physical change indicators: literacy,
child mortality, protein intake, female primary
school enrolment ratios, female secondary school enrolment ratios, life expectancy, all three inflation
indicators as well as the growth of employment. Some
of these differences are significant at the .05
level, and most coefficients tend to be stronger
than for our civilian-military dichotomy. As for the
two factors, we see in Table 68 that the less free
have a higher mean value on the women in the labour
force factor (WOMENFAC) while with greater confidence the more free are higher on the PHYSICAL factor. These of course are based upon the end of the
period. Thus it would seem that the goal of sexual
equality is better served by "less-free" regimes
which appear also to have made more impressive progress over a broad range of physical change indicators.

Even if we restrict consideration to more- and less-
free systems in 1973 - which more precisely dove-
tails our welfare change period - the result is analogous. Thus on literacy and female secondary school
enrolment ratios - the only two indicators on which
our confidence level approaches .05 - the less free
are superior on both. When we add all those below
the .20 confidence level, the same category is
superior on six out of eight. Finally, if we take
the entire range of change variables, the less free
score better on eleven (literacy, female secondary
school enrolments, life expectancy, employment, all
three inflation indicators, female primary school
enrolment ratios, protein intake, child labour, and
child mortality) while the more free do so on the
remaining four (women in the labour force, pupil-
teacher ratios in primary education, caloric intake
and food production). On our two late 1970s factors,
the latter are superior on PHYSICAL and the former

on WOMENFAC. When we control only for the most extreme deprivations in Table 69, countries which did
not engage in torture, political executions or disappearances boast higher means on WOMENFAC in 1975
(but not 1979) but are markedly lower on PHYSICAL in
both years. Furthermore, two of the four differences
are significant at the p .05 level. Hence it is
clear that such conventional measures of political
freedom are if anything inversely associated with
welfare improvement. This finding is especially
important since my earlier scrutiny of military
dominant systems yielded more problematic conclusions than the Gastil-based dichotomy where a considerable number of relationships approached acceptable levels of significance and a few actually did
at the .05 level. Yet, as we shall see, even marginal civilian superiority can be reconciled with this
more clear-cut better performance by our "less-free"
category.

Hence, if military rule does not convincingly explain the extent to which less-free countries are
superior with respect to welfare change vis a vis
their more-free counterparts, what might? Using
FREEDM82, we find the former to be somewhat less
industrialized and moderately lower on per capita
income. Yet they did benefit from higher 1973-5 per
capita aid according to Table 70, although the deviance was considerable. When this is interpreted also
in light of the significant difference for EPDGNP78,
it seems that external assistance may be more than a
negligible determinant. The salience and impact of
aid may have been heightened for the less free by
their somewhat lower GDP growth rates during the
preceding decade. Thus higher MILSPFAC and ME factor
means within a context of lower economic development
and prior growth may have been offset to a modest
degree by heavy external financial as well as technical assistance injections.

Another political factor is the development strategy
pursued. Since most of the state capitalist and particularly the half-dozen or so state socialist regimes were classified by Gastil as being unfree (6
or 7) and thus within our less-free category, it may
be useful to examine what, if any, relationships appear when development orientation is treated as the
independent variable. In Table 71 we see that on the
four change indicators that are at or close to the
.05 confidence level, state socialist systems score
highest on reducing child labour and increasing

female secondary school enrolment ratios, while state capitalist regimes do so on the other two – increasing average protein intake and enhancing female primary school enrolment ratios. On the other hand, open door systems score the lowest on two and next to the lowest on two. If we add the remaining welfare change indicators (less two inflation indicators for which data is missing for the socialist cases but where in their absence the state capitalist do the best), on three the state capitalist do so while on only one do the open door regimes surpass all others. Further if the PHYSICAL and WOMENFAC late 1970s factors are considered, highest means in both instances go to the state capitalist development orientation. And they are significant at the .05 level. Finally, if relative performance on all of the above indicators is assigned 1 to 4 (high- low), the averages are: state socialist (1.9); state capitalist (2.3); open door (2.9); mixed (2.5). On this basis one may conjecture that even instability – shifting development strategies, i.e. "mixed" – is superior to the open door or monopoly capitalist orientation.

In this chapter we found that more repressive systems in general had heavier _financial_ military burdens and a greater increase while the more-free countries were characterized by greater armed expansion. In general, military regimes are not only higher on repression but also exhibited heavier military financial burdens, greater armed forces expansion, but a lower rise in military spending as well as slightly less welfare improvement than their civilian counterparts. US training impact was also somewhat higher for both military and less-free regimes (the latter including many of the former) but slightly lower for those engaging in torture and related practices in 1973–5. There was no difference on this, however, in 1976–9.

At the same time we saw that the less-free regimes in general demonstrated superior welfare performance. It does not seem that this is explained by such economic variables as prior economic growth rates, _per capita_ income or the degree of industrialization. Among the political variables which do seem relevant are higher foreign aid and especially the development strategy pursued. Superior orientations were state capitalism and particularly state socialism.(47) The findings of both Szymanski (1981) and Marquit (1983) also confirm the superiority of socialist developmental approaches.

Chapter 8

CONCLUSIONS: PATTERNS AND PROSPECTS

With rising unemployment, protectionism and East-West tensions afflicting the advanced economies of the North, one would like to see hope for world betterment fulfilled at least by the "new nations" of the Third World. Free of colonialism and almost universally committed to social progress and self-determination, these nations - some more than others - have in fact improved mass welfare and begun the process of industrialization during the past two decades.

The process has been slow, however, and both seldom publicized internal constraints as well as frequently denounced external obstacles account for a growing sense of malaise as the welfare gap actually widens with the advanced North. Furthermore, a decline in foreign aid, higher interest rates, stagnating export markets, and unsupportable debt burdens seem to imply greater austerity and authoritarianism for the peoples of the South in the 1980s and perhaps beyond.

My concern with the military does <u>not</u> stem from a conclusion that accelerating weapons imports, the spread of domestic militarism from perhaps 15 per cent to what is now a majority of non-communist Third World states, and undiminished militarization even for civilian ruled countries are <u>wholly</u> responsible for the contemporary development crisis. Furthermore, it must be conceded that armed forces have a legitimate, even honourable external defence function for all states so long as national sovereignty is more highly valued by the international community than world government. They may even be useful (Benoit, 1973; Kennedy, 1974; Neuman, 1978) for ancillary activities such as conscript education, vil-

lage health services and road construction. In Revolutionary Ethiopia, for example, Galperin and Platov
(1982:62) report

> the armed forces were formed on a fundamentally
> new class basis to defend the people' state. In
> peacetime the servicemen actively participate
> in rehabilitating and developing the economy in
> outlying regions of the country, help take in
> harvests, build bridges, roads and granaries,
> and join the national Literacy Campaign. Inten-
> sive ideological work is being carried out in
> military units ...

But for most armies that engage in infrastructural
and welfare activities, these tend to be peripheral
"symbolic" (Janowitz, 1964:77) or more ubiquitously
counterinsurgency functions which specialized civilian organizations could probably undertake at
greater cost efficiency.(48) Further, we have already seen that the size of military establishments
is unrelated to territory to be defended and in a
growing majority of cases better explained by internal repressive roles, available economic resources,
inducements by external sources of weapons, pres-
tige aspirations, and an absence of diplomatic
aversion to military confrontations. Thus Seliktar
(1980:344) offers us an almost prophetic Israeli
example of that country's Black Panthers who split
over the last mentioned issue and its tradeoff implications.

> While one wing has confined itself to a rela-
> tively mild criticism of the existing dispari-
> ties in allocating resources, the more radical
> wing has expanded its tradeoff criticism. A
> major point in its argument has been that the
> poor, disproportionately Sephadic sector of the
> society can leat afford the defense tradeoff.
> Taking this argument a step farther the radical
> Panthers have demanded that the government ne-
> gotiate a peace settlement with the Arabs and
> seek a meaningful solution to the Palestinian
> problem. Under the slogan 'if there is peace we
> can spend more money on tackling poverty in-
> stead of security', a number of Panther leaders
> met in 1975 with PLO representatives (Shama and
> Iris, 1970:230). Prior to the 1977 elections
> radical Black Panthers joined the pro-Arab Com-
> munist Party Rakah.

As in many other "national security" conflicts, there is usually a diplomatic option to seek peaceful solutions via compromise - thus reducing "legitimate" defence requirements. We may recall Gauhar's conclusion that despite the unprecedented escalation of Middle East arms expenditures, there has been no overall increase in "security". There may be a minimum necessary to "protect" domestic societal pursuit of welfare, but Kennedy (1974) notwithstanding, it would be absurd for analysts to assume that whatever rulers decide to spend in the name of "national security" is therefore empirically justified. The same may be said for "internal security" where political compromise can be opted for. Ironically, as Tuomi and Väyrynen (1980:230) warn, militarization even for external "defence" can create conditions for internal war:

> If, however, the army grows at the cost of the population, and armaments make it easy to apply military means to solve political and social contradictions, and finally, the army assumes social autonomy with no control whatsoever, repressing the population, then the "security" needs and development needs are in clear contradiction and deserve international attention as well. In each case the empirical judgements are problematic, but it should be borne in mind that the army and armaments should never be studied isolated from the general social, political, economic and cultural context.

And one may add, the environment of policy alternatives need not be regarded as invariable. Certainly the near meteoric rise in "gold plated" and other arms transfers to the Third World as well as their escalating military expenditures since the 1960s is well beyond minimal external defence requirements. They may serve growing internal repressive needs, and neo-colonial goals of strengthening client military elites (Albrecht et al., 1974).

The question then is really one of proportionality. Except for a small and declining number of Third World nations, military burdens are heavy and/or rising. Arms races, domestic militarism, regional and especially internal wars are ubiquitous. My contention is that such tendencies are excessive to the point of constituting a major if not exclusive impediment to mass welfare aspirations, economic development, political freedom and world peace.

Conclusions: Patterns and Prospects

While it has not yet been demonstrated that military
dominant regimes are necessarily more war prone than
others, Midlarski and Thomas have shown us that
their wars are of longer duration. Second, the work
of Kennedy, Finer, Park and Abolfathi, as well as
others discussed in previous chapters, indicate that
military dominated regimes as one would expect tend
to have higher military budgets than civilian counterparts. Third, Singer's findings - considered in
Chapter 2 - reveal a strong association between
militarization, tension and war. Kende stresses the
association between high arms imports, Western
intervention and internal war, as does Sivard in
some measure. Most war fatalities as well as those
from "structural violence" Kohler shows us occur in
the South. Hanson, Shoultz, Herman, Wolpin, Klare,
Chomsky and Pierre tangentially focus upon US aid
and support for rightist military repression - especially in Latin America though this might be extended to Asia and even parts of the Middle East as
well as Africa (for example, Zaire, Sudan).

Studies of military rule by Kennedy, Needler,
McKinley and Cohan, Dickson, Park and Abolfathi,
Gottheil, Heeger, Hansen, Dabelko and McCormick,
Danopoulos and Patel, Tannahill, Dickson, Morrison
and Stevenson, Olorunsola, Hansen, Chikwendu, Finer
and others considered in Chapters 3 and 4 variously
reveal not only greater repression but also lower
expenditures for education and less commonly health.
Some of these and other analyses stress forgone consumption, lower investment, adverse export effects
and lower overall growth. While a few analysts such
as the late Benoit - whose findings have been severely critiqued by Dorfman, Wulf and Brzoska -
Jackman, Kennedy, Neuman, and Ravenhill hold that
militarization and/or domestic militarism are
either unimportant or beneficial, the preponderance
of the tradeoff (for example, Finer, Cusack, Sylvan,
Taylor, Dabelko and McCormick, Cusack, Avery,
Russet, Askari and Glover, Gottheil, Park and
Abolfathi, Tannahill, McKinlay and Cohan, Morrison
and Stevenson) and case studies (for example,
Seliktar on Israel, Olorunsola and Chikwendu on
Nigeria, Fontanel on Morocco, Hansen on Egypt,
Melman, DeGrasse and Anderson on the US and
Danopoulos and Patel on Greece) conclude that socio-
political welfare and repression are adversely af-
fected by both military rule as well as heavy or
rising military burdens. According to Cusack, the

longer the lead time, the more pronounced the effects. And the specific substitution effects vary
from one polity to another, and over time. In some
cases it may be consumption, in others investment or
education. In all cases long run "national security"
is undermined for failure to maximize balanced
industrialization.(49)

Such diversity of impact was also a pattern which
Russett, Pryor, Mosley, Anderson, DeGrasse,
Szymanski, Peroff and Warren, and Smith discerned in
their tradeoff analyses of advanced capitalist
nations. The same was true for Becker's report and
Pryor's work on the USSR and other COMECON nations.
Similarly, the costs of militarization for all of
the North - East and West alike - varied over time
and were most clearly manifested as being extracted
from particular though varying civilian sectors at
high levels of military expenditure. The foregoing
along with Tuomi and Vàyrynen, Lindroos and the UN
Group of Experts underlined such pronounced negative
effects as reduced employment, investment, exports,
consumption, civilian technological growth, education and civil expenditures as well as higher inflation. In the Western countries, Smith stressed that
both employment and per capita growth suffered. Adverse effects upon productivity growth, investment
and GDP growth were highlighted by DeGrasse. Melman,
Anderson, Lindroos and others emphasized declining
export competitiveness, inflation, and higher alternative employment from civil expenditures. Yet the
effects of militarization in the North are not limited to such constraints upon improvements in mass
welfare and economic growth, but as we saw in the
case of the US, may indirectly encompass what
Rimland and Larson depict as deterioration in the
quality of the very manpower base upon which military capability is based. This and the deleterious
impact upon the economy suggest that high levels of
sustained militarization may over time yield less
rather than more defence security. Further, as we
have seen, such militarization in the South is promoted by military aid and training that reinforce
existing dependency relationships which simply assume a new form when nations in the South opt to
produce sophisticated weapons.

My own statistical analysis has indicated that no
clear pattern of inverse relationships exists between military burdens per se in the late 1960s and
welfare change during the succeeding decade, nor for

that matter with welfare levels toward the end of the 1970s. The military burden and militarization hypotheses were supported by some coefficients, while for a large majority no significant differences appeared, and in other instances the militarization/ welfare associations were positive. The latter were most pronounced for the more industrialized, more economically dynamic, and "less free"! Despite second heaviest military burdens (after military regimes), the socialists managed a better social welfare performance with respect to child mortality and the WOMEN factors. In addition it can be affirmed that military burdens were higher for military regimes while US training impact was most pronounced for them and the open door category. USTAFFAC was negatively related to the PHYSICAL welfare factor for the 1965-78 period for all regime types, as well as for those with more extensive state economic involvement, less public consumption and lower economic growth rates during the 1960s.

With respect to the welfare change indicators, our military burden (MILSPFAC) hypothesis was supported (with respect to significant coefficients) only for the less industrialized, lower growth rate and least economically active states. On the other hand, a majority of coefficients were positive between MILSPFAC and welfare change variables for more industrialized countries and those with higher prior growth rates. Neither external aid, nor civilian rule, public consumption or repressiveness for that matter seemed to affect the relationships when employed as controls.

As for the growth of financial and physical military burdens, a number of findings appear. First, militarization in the 1970s was highest for those countries which tended to be most socially impoverished and that possessed small militaries around 1960. Second, the repressive rather than defensive primary function of armies was suggested by the high regression coefficient (r.77) between 1961 population and the 1960-78 armed forces expansion (AFSIZE). The latter was strongly related to armed forces expansion during the 1960s and moderately associated with the ME factor. Third, militarization rates were strongly negative only for the 1965-78 state socialist development orientation. In general civilian open door governments, those with high public consumption and less industrialization tended toward more rapid armed forces expansion, while civilian

state capitalist and military open door governments
were characterized by higher rates of increase in
military expenditures. The differences in both cases
were quite modest. None appeared when controls were
employed for freedom or GVTGDP. More clear-cut and
significant differences denoted countries receiving
high per capita aid in the mid-1970s as well as
those benefiting from higher economic growth during
the preceding decade. These two categories exhibited
markedly higher growth of military expenditures
though they were not differentiated from below
median categories on armed forces expansion. Thus
the greater economic resources as Gauhar argues,
probably were absorbed by imports of new weapons
systems.

Shifting our attention to the PHYSICAL welfare factor, we encounter significant inverse associations
with MXCGFAC, AFSIZE along with one that is particularly strong for the US training factor (USTAFFAC).
On the other hand these same militarization factors
and variables were not correlated with physical welfare change in a majority of instances. Where significant coefficients appeared, only a minority were
consistent with the militarization hypothesis. Support for the militarization adverse welfare change
hypothesis occurred only with respect to countries
that were below the medians on government involvement in the economy (GVTGDP), public consumption,
and more weakly, military dominant systems (1965-
78).

Those which were most inconsistent with the hypothesis included the less free, this with high external aid, the economically dynamic during the
1960s, countries with high state economic involvement or extractive capability (GVTGDP) and public
consumption, the more industrialized, civilian and
state capitalist regimes, and more problematically
our open door category. For the last mentioned
group, however, this did not apply to the physical
welfare factors. Those underlined above were most
inconsistent with the hypotheses on both welfare
factors and change variables.

Finally we turned to repression. Although again
relationships were weak for the most part and seldom
significant, the "less free" category of countries
manifested somewhat higher financial burdens that
also exhibited a higher ME growth rate while as mentioned above their more free counterparts were

stronger on armed forces expansion. Military regimes
were not only more repressive but also demonstrated
higher military burdens but lower expenditure increases. On the other hand, their armed forces expansion surpassed civilians on two of the three indicators and they scored higher means on US training
impact. The latter, however, was lower for regimes
practising torture in 1975, but the difference was
almost completely attenuated by 1979 when there were
no differences on any of the military burden or
militarization indicators for the torture prone vs.
the torture free. In 1975, however, those engaging
in torture were higher on MILSPFAC but lower on
armed forces ratio increases than their more benign
counterparts.

Welfare factor scores and change were better for the
generally less repressive civilian regimes but the
difference was not pronounced. On the other hand a
much more marked contrast favoured the "less free"
over the "more free" category in both 1973-82.(50)
Since military hegemony could not explain this, two
other variables were examined. The less free were
higher on both foreign aid indicators. Furthermore,
they encompassed the state socialist systems which
along with, yet more than, those with a state capitalist orientation offered a demonstrably much better welfare performance on both factors and change
variables than their open door rivals.(51) Thus in
the final analysis we return to political determi-
nants.(52) This also explains why in many non-soci-
ally radical Third World regimes lower military burdens may simply be siphoned off into foreign bank
accounts, speculative investments, "luxury" imports,
other upper-class consumption, etc. Or in the more
euphemistic terminology of the UN Group of Experts
(UNSG, 1982:90): "For the developing countries, on
the whole, the short term consequences of reductions
on their military outlays may be less clear-cut. For
some of them, especially those with unutilized or
under-utilized resources, there may be other structural constraints on their development performance,
which means that military spending may not always be
in competition with other kinds of spending." Even
in the "more free" category, populist, reform and
socialist forces may be too weak or corrupt to force
welfare improvements, and/or in the alternative, the
systems may not for the most part be "free" enough
to sanction and assimilate such alternatives.

How are my patterns to be reconciled with those of

analysts previously considered? In the first place, I examined a more restricted - to physical welfare - range of dependent variables. Hence where many of them found substitution effects for investment, economic growth, consumption and exports, these were beyond the scope of my focus and may explain why significant tradeoffs were indicated for only a minority of our variables.(53) Second, their findings that tradeoffs varied for different countries and time periods were attributed to varying systemic parameters. And we did see that the introduction of controls often influenced the relational patterns. Third, their studies were restricted to budgetary expenditures where except at very high levels of military burdens, the substitution effects tended to be small. This in conjunction with my findings suggest that many of the costs of heavy and rising military burdens are immediately economic with their social effects postponed by rising external indebtedness and lowered economic growth rates that barely or fail to keep up with population growth. In the most impoverished countries, however, the social tradeoffs tend to be immediate.

One clearly consonant finding pertained to the dismal performance in the areas of both repression and welfare of military regimes. This confirms Heeger's pessimism concerning military rule, which is becoming more ubiquitous. Furthermore, domestic militarism as we saw results in heightened militarization. At best, this diverts resources that might have diminished structural repressiveness, internal war, arms transfers and further militarization which impedes the allocation of greater resources to mass welfare and development efforts. In such circumstances, Tuomi and Vàyrynen (1980:224) note that: "Paradoxically, this type of country acquires arms not despite poverty but precisely because of poverty."

This is not to say that militarization itself does not promote militarism - external and perhaps domestic. These consequences warrant further research. Nor that the mutually reinforcing process depicted above cannot be broken. But such considerations and the patterns elicited by my analysis in Chapters 5-7, lead us back to Albrecth's and Kaldor's concern with widely ignored yet crucial political factors. The almost universal assumption in "reformist" peace literature - the IPRA 1978 statement quoted in note 7 and tradoff studies of budgetary expenditures - is that health, education and other welfare spending necessarily will be enhanced by demilitarization. As we have seen, the welfare tradeoff may be postponed by aid or indirect short-run economic tradeoffs - investment, exports or consumption. Thus, in the absence of strong social democratic or more leftist movements with substantial policy impact, reductions in military birdens may, but will not necessarily, enhance mass welfare.(53) For example, if the Stroessner regime in Paraguay or that of Marcos in the Philippines reduced the armed forces budget, the benefits might well accrue for the most part to the dominant oligarchies. Furthermore, the armed forces in such systems have, along with security police and paramilitary forces, the important function of suppressing popular movements. Hence, what is needed politically in the Third World are hegemonic movements committed to mass welfare and from the standpoint of my findings in Chapter 7, a state capitalist or preferably socialist development strtategy.

This orientation would also be consonant with a minimal, labour intensive, highly mobile, decentralized and implicitly democratic defence strategy that is not politically and technologically dependent upon importation of "gold plated" or even slightly less complex heavy weapons systems which in any case seldom can be employed efficaciously. Elsewhere Wulf (1979) has cogently elaborated such an alternative "national security" doctrine that can be harmonized with a legitimate training and external defence role for the armed forces. In Table 72, Tuomi and Vàyrynen (1980:257) have extracted key components of Wulf's low cost "people's war" type of defensive security strategy which promotes maximal "self-reliance", reduction of rising external indebtedness and conservation of scarce resources to enhance social welfare. Considerable research needs to be done on the range of both experiences and possibilities for such alternative defence strategies. China, Nicaragua and Yugoslavia may approximate some of its parameters. Thus Pfaff (1982:6) reports that Yugoslav

> landing fields, potential paratroop drop zones and the coasts are under permanent surveillance. New radar gives or will give them coverage of the whole Eastern Mediterranean and the Black Sea. Their own ships are sheltered in caves cut into coastal mountains, and their aircraft in underground blast shelters. They have taken advice from the Swedes and the Swiss

on this.

There is a permanent, regularly exercised, national organization of popular defense, with tanks in factories, small arms stored in advertising agency cupboards and the back rooms of banks. More than a third of the population is actively enrolled.

The model is always that of the terrible guerrilla struggle against the Axis between 1941 and 1945. There is constant reference to the partisan experience. The Yugoslavs seem ready to do it again if they have to.

They have debated whether cities should be given up or defended, whatever the civilian cost, in an invasion. The decision is to fight for the cities, and if necessary to destroy whatever an enemy might use.

Further, a minority yet growing number of Third World officers (Wolpin, 1981a) are able to reconcile their professional responsibilities for national security with the imperatives of radical socio-economic change.

Ultimately, however, the political equation is constrained to an important but indeterminate degree by its external parameters. The intensified East-West rivalry and commercial motives are the major catalysts for militarization and growing political as well as economic dependence (Kaldor, 1978) as a consequence of escalating Third World arms imports. Further, NATO members and especially the United States (Wolpin, 1973; Chomsky and Herman, 1979; Klare, 1981; Herman, 1982) have provided most support for and/or imposed socially conservative, often military and/or terroristic, "open door" regimes in the South. And according to Klare (1982) and Herman (1982), Reagan has clearly distanced his administration from both his NATO "allies" and previous administrations by the rightist and militaristic fanaticism which reflects his Manichean world view. Hence, détente-oriented policy changes forced by resurgent peace, populist, ecological and left social democratic movements must occur in the North if demilitarization and prospects for appropriate military technology and development are to be maximized in the South.

Partially for this reason, I have incorporated analyses of militarization costs and tradeoffs in the
North. The findings on such costs are significantly
reinforced by those of Smith among Albrecht's
"radicals" as well as Lindroos, Melman, DeGrasse and
other "reformists" to the effect that heavy military
expenditures appear to either undermine or are at
least domestically inessential to the survival of
capitalist "prosperity" in the North. One might add,
to the extent they served in the past to ensure a
low cost flow of wealth to advanced capitalist
states which could "trickle-down" to the masses, the
situation today appears at best problematic. For the
direct and ancillary costs of neo-colonialism
(Wolpin, 1973; Klare, 1981; Herman, 1982) at the
mass level in the North now appear to exceed benefits that heretofore enhanced general prosperity.
Resistance to the old world economic order inspired
by growing nationalist and socialist movements as
well as the diffusion of such regimes in the Third
World has altered the world "correlation of forces".
This has drastically heightened the costs of infor-
mal empire to such an extent that only the transnational corporate owning upper classes (Sklar,
1980) clearly continue to accrue benefits. And if
currently incipient Third World bankruptcy becomes
generalized or a regional "proxy" confrontation
escalates to "tactical" nuclear warfare, even these
"benefits" may be sacrificed.

1. They also acknowledge that "Given the current concern over the adequacy of supplies of non-renewable raw material over the long term, a particularly disturbing dimension of this imbalance is that over the period 1971-5 the market and planned developed economies, representing less than one-quarter of the world's population accounted for 80 to 90 per cent of the annual global demand for such key minerals as iron ore, aluminium, copper, manganese and tin."(30) Elsewhere the Group of Governmental Experts (11-12) notes that "Between 1960 and 1980 the volume of resources devoted annually to military purposes increased by a factor of about 1.9; that is almost doubled." What this trend implies in terms of resources is indicated by their projections: "an annual rate of growth of 1 per cent in the value of resources devoted to armaments over the remainder of this century would probably be regarded as a triumph of restraint, but even in this case the cumulative value just of the additional resources devoted to military purposes - that is, resources in excess of those consumed if expenditure remained constant at $500,000 million annually - would be $1.1 trillion. At annual growth rates of 2 and 3 per cent - the former still modest by historical standards - the value of the additional resources denied the civilian sector would be equivalent to 28 per cent and 45 per cent respectively, of current world output. In this regard, it should be borne in mind that the prospect for the immediate future is one of acceleration in the rate of growth of global military expenditure."

2. Militarism, then, may be promoted by civilians as well as military officers. Similarly, the latter may

reject such a course in favour of what Vagts calls "the military way". This is the scientific application of existing and necessary resources to meeting external defence threats - nothing more. Soviet conceptualization, according to Lider (1980:179), draws what appears to be a similar distinction: "all states have military forces, but not all are militaristic. It is only when the governing exploiting class consciously increases armaments, armed forces and preparations for predatory wars, and also increases internal oppression, that one can speak about militarism".

3. "The international trade in arms is one of the most significant indicators of the ever-increasing global militarization. The value of world arms sales at current prices has now reached as high as $20 billion per annum. Of this, 70% goes in the direction from the industrialized countries to the less developed countries. During the first half of the 1970s, the average yearly increase in arms transfers to less developed countries was running at a rate of 15% per annum. The past five years - 1974 through 1978 - show an average yearly increase of 25%. The two dominant arms suppliers in the 1970s are the United States (39%) and the Soviet Union (32%) followed after a considerable gap by France (11%) and the UK (8%). The Middle East absorbed over half of the total arms supplies to the Third World ..." (Landgren-Backstrøm, 1979, abstract).

4. According to Dabelko and McCormick (1977:145-6), "the concept of opportunity costs refers to the benefits forgone by selecting one option at the expense of several other options. Assuming resources are scarce, if an individual selects policy A, he forgoes the benefits derived from policies B and C. Such a definition does not imply, however, that the notion of opportunity costs applies only to mutually exclusive situations. The concept equally applies to a situation where resources are allocated in preferential rank-orderings. This latter situation is most applicable to nations when considering their budgetary expenditures. The classic illustration of opportunity costs for governmental budgeting is the ´guns vs. butter´ dilemma. This dilemma depicts spending in military and social welfare areas as inversely related to one another. As military expenditures in a nation increase, the benefits of alternative preferences in social welfare areas must suffer." Such a situation presumes a fixed level and sectoral dis-

tribution of tax burdens as well as no change in deficit financing. Because of the variations in financial variables, equivalent budgetary tradeoffs seldom appear. Hence a number of the studies dealt with here which adopt a broader framework reveal tradeoffs in other welfare related areas such as private consumption, employment, investment, etc. With one exception, however, none attempt to measure "potential" opportunity costs for military expenditures which might and could have been employed in programmes that directly enhance civilian welfare.

Sivard (1979:18) epitomizes the customary treatment of "potential" costs: "The interconnections between military and social development are to be seen not only in the current competition for public budgets but also against the background of society's accumulated unmet needs. The most obvious price of the world's arms race, represented by trillions of dollars in taxes and public debt, is only a small fraction of the real costs. The real cost upon which no final price can be set - is in opportunities lost, the burden of material neglect, social alienation and upheaval, lives wasted in wretched poverty. The gap between what is and what should be cannot be bridged solely by a reordering of budget priorities. Even the unimaginable sum of $4,200 billion that was spent for military purposes since 1960, if wholly diverted to productive economic ends, would not have eliminated inflation, provided jobs for all, solved the energy crisis, and raised hundreds of millions out of poverty. But in innumerable ways, the constructive use of those vast resources could have made a significant difference, a difference not only in the course of economic-social development, but in enriched lives for multitudes of people."

5. This perspective has been articulated by Pye (1962), Johnson (1964), Janowitz (1964), Benoit (1973), Kennedy (1974), and using the Shah of Iran's regime as her idealized frame of reference, Neuman (1978). Yet even Janowitz who argues that officers in the large Third World armies are equipped with state management skills, nevertheless concedes (77) that "The economic function of the military includes its contribution to developing public works, roads, and engineering projects. Such projects can be found throughout most new nations, but, with some notable exceptions, their importance is more symbolic than economic." Elsewhere he stresses that perhaps their most important function is conscript socialization

in terms of equal treatment, literacy, citizenship training and the promotion of symbolic national identification. Even these presumed spinoffs may be questioned: Kaldor (1978:63-4) notes "Roads are built in remote areas where nobody wants to go; skills are often too sophisticated for civilian use." Hurewitz (1969) makes the point that the skills and infrastructure developed for the army may not be transferred at all. "In career armies, which account for two out of every three Middle Eastern armies, soldiers do not return to their villages. The use of airfields and communications may be exclusively confined to the military." Based upon the general poor performance of non-socialist Third World armies, one may question the efficacy of literacy and other alleged skill transfers.

6. Albrecht (1978:105) for example, argues that the benefits of new military technology "for general economic prosperity" are "dubious", and "The vast literature on technical progress created by military requirements can be put aside since there is no quantitative assessment on the aggregate impact or the real costs." More recently Lindroos (1980:116) argues that "there is no doubt that the inventions that have come about as a side-product of military technology could have been developed with considerably less cost if research resources had been directly made available for satisfying the needs of the people ... it can be said that military research and development is not useless for society, but it is, nevertheless, more inefficient than a direct concentration on research in civilian production." Similarly, Askari and Glover (1977:30) caution that "Military needs in developing countries sometimes make infrastructural improvements, such as airports and roads, necessary, but these are frequently located in places away from the civilian population, such as remote border areas, where the potential civil use is minimal. It is argued that importing weapons provide members of the armed forces training that is potentially useful in civilian life. This depends on the extent to which skills acquired in operating and maintaining weapons can be transferred easily to the civilian sector. The more sophisticated the weapons, the more specific the skills must be. In short, the contribution of military expenditures to economic development is at least highly debatable." Others who either pursue this line of reasoning or critique the military's purported modernizing function in the Third World include

Russett (1970:133-5), Finer (1975), Perlmutter
(1977), Olorunsola (1977), Adekson (1978), Melman
(1979), Wulf (1979) and a number of scholars whose
studies will be discussed subsequently.

7. While some Marxian structuralists - Hobsbawn
(1973), Block (1978), Farsoun and Carroll (1978),
Kaldor (1978), and less categorically Woddis (1977)
- concede that leftist military coups may catalyse
social change, they contend that this tends to be
impermanent and vulnerable to subversion by surviv-
ing capitalist institutions and linkages. A summary
statement of this perspective as elaborated by the
International Peace Research Association's Study
Group on Militarization (IPRA, 1978:175-6) follows:

"Militarization of the Third World is in the long
run incompatible with the promotion of participatory
democracy in political life. It diverts economic resources from the fulfillment of basic human needs,
material and otherwise, thereby increasing the dis-
crepancy between the poor and the rich world. Militarization, which is not geared to liberation, tends
to perpetuate or deepen social inequalities among
classes, ethnic groups, and races. Amongst the other
economic and social effects of militarization are
the following:

- Domestically generated economic surplus is diverted from mass distribution and consumption, and productive investment goes into military purposes;

- Foreign exchange is diverted from the import of
basic consumer necessities and equipment for production;

- External debt burdens tend to increase (except for
a small number of petroleum-producing countries).
Refinancing is customarily associated with the re-
quirement to adopt austerity policies, which further
reduce mass consumption and production accumulation.

- Inflationary tendencies are stimulated, and these
operate to depress the real earnings of wage labor;

- Regressive fiscal measures are enforced and sup-
pression of trade union activity is perpetrated in
order to create 'hospitable' investment conditions
for foreign capital.

    There is a preference for capital-intensive investment, thus hindering labor-intensive investments which would be essential for the maximum reduction of unemployment and underemployment. Most labor-intensive sectors, such as agriculture, experience a reduction in employment when they become integrated in the international economic order.

Thus, despite short-term rises in aggregate demand which militarization may stimulate, the overall impact for such regimes is fundamentally negative with respect to short- and especially long-term basic needs of the population. Differences can be observed in various parts of the world, depending on the orientation of the military. The short-term interests of the population are sometimes better promoted where the military pursue national or state capitalist policies. Although such regimes also divert surplus to the military establishment, increase external indebtedness, promote capital investment, and limit trade union activity, the armed forces have to varying degrees promoted temporary improvements in the satisfaction of basic needs for large sectors of the population in the following ways:

- agrarian reform;
- expansion of employment;
- retention of greater surplus for investment as a result of the expropriation of major industrial, financial, and commercial enterprises;
- rapid extension of educational opportunities and health facilities;
- constraining inflationary tendencies for mass necessities, and limiting the growth of regressive taxation;
- the use of units of armed forces for social and productive investment.

However, despite the benefits associated with some militarized state capitalist regimes, they remain oppressive and are almost invariably pressured into 'moderating' their egalitarian tendencies in order to subordinate themselves to the requirements of the global economic order. As long as militarization proceeds on the basis of an industrial-type army, the gap continues to widen - whether there is the typical 'open-door' regime or any version of a state capitalist government. Not one of these countries has succeeded in breaking with the 'old' international economic order or in mobilizing the productive energies of its population for a real self-reliant development. Whatever the short-term advantages that might at times occur through a military regime, evidence points heavily to a long-term situation of Third World militarization based on the adoption of industrial-type technology as being inconsistent with the fulfillment of basic human needs for the poorer part of the population ..."

8. In comparing the effects of the Second World War, the Korean and Vietnam Wars upon the US, Stein (1978:88) found a decline in societal cohesion "because an increasing number of individuals balk at making personal sacrifices". This was most pronounced for the two Third World interventionist campaigns. Other consequences were state centralization and a decline in lower class unemployment which purportedly enhanced social equality.

9. Lindroos (1980:77) adds that "The arms build-up of the developing countries has mainly taken place through arms imports. The arms exports from the industrialized countries into the Third World has since 1974 grown by an average of 25 per cent annually. One characteristic of the arms trade in the 1970s has been that the imports of the developing countries no longer limit themselves to what they can obtain from reserve stocks of the industrialized world, as was the case in the 1950s and 1960s. Today, also developing countries buy the latest products of arms technology. Furthermore, another main feature has been the concentration of arms exports into the crisis regions of the world."

10. Swadesh Rana, P.K. Namboodiri and R.R. Subramanian, "Reallocation of Military Resources from OECD to Primary Sectors of LDC's: Mutuality of Interests: A Third World Perspective". New Delhi: Institute for Defence Studies and Analyses.

11. "The Director of U.S. Military Assistance testified: 'I do not believe there is any country in Latin America that does not have adequate forces in size. They do need better training. They do need better communications, better ability. As far as hardware is concerned they do not need a lot of major items of hardware because of the insurgency threat. What they need is to employ their forces better, have better communications, be better trained, use what they have better'."

12. Chomsky and Herman (1979) provide a systematic specification of such linkages. Earlier analyses

Notes

which focus upon the sources of such relationships
include Wolpin (1973), and Albrecht et al. (1974:
173-4) who maintain that "In spite of considerable
changes in economic relations between capitalist
metropoles and dependent peripheries one fact remains: armaments and the military (whatever the
institutional setting might be) are indispensable
for the preservation of the metropole periphery
structure. The appearance and pattern of arms and
violence may have changed, basically, however, until
today it is the same process: their application is
an important determinant for the development of the
world wide capitalist system. Neither the replace-
ment of private armies by big colonial armies during
the 19th and beginning of the 20th century nor the
breakup of colonial armies and the reshaping into
and set-up of 'national' military apparatuses in
peripheral countries could change the fundamental
function of armaments and the military as far as
they are used in the periphery ...

The penetration of the present underdeveloped countries characterized by production sectors totally
dependent on and determined by outside powers was
only made possible by the use of arms, sometimes for
many decades. This applies especially to regions
with complex social structures and highly developed
productive forces. The process of increasing under-
development and dependence was carried out by means
of robbery, trade, extraction of resources, partial
industrialization to create markets for cheap consumer goods, outdated and already depreciated tech-
nologies, etc. The accumulation of these mechanisms
resulted in a structure characterized by unequal
transfer relations. The enormous expansion and un-
folding of productive forces in Europe and the
United States resulted in a corresponding decrease
of the potential for autonomous accumulation and the
retrogression or stagnation of productive forces in
the capitalist periphery."

13. The conclusions summarized in the textual quota-
tions are based upon the following: Bruce M. Russett
and David J. Sylvan, "The Effects of Arms Transfers
on Developing Countries"; Marga Institute, "Armaments Culture and the Diffusion of the Values of
Militarization"; Herbert Wulf, Michael Brzoska and
Peter Lock, "Transnational Transfer of Arms Production Technology"; Raimo Vayrynen, "Industrialization, Economic Development and the World Military
Order"; Harvey Brooks, "Technology, Evolution and

102

Purpose", UNSG, 1982:86-87.

14. Thompson's (1973:44) analysis of coup grievances during 1946-70 revealed that less than one-fifth could be classified as "strikingly reformist". His more recent reanalysis (1980) of the data indicated also that in a substantial majority of all coups, the motives were "subcorporate" in nature; that is, factional, ethnic, personalist, etc. My own classification of military dominant regimes in September 1982 reveals no more than ten or one-quarter of the total could be depicted as reformist or non-capitalist, and this would necessitate inclusion of such marginal cases as North Yemen and Mali.

15. He emphasizes that longitudinal data "for an individual country reflect a variety of political and economic factors: cyclical variations in their utilization; the ability of workers to resist reductions in their share of consumption; trends in the size of government sector and in international competitiveness, etc.".

16. As for Khrushchev, Becker quotes the following from his posthumously published memoirs (1974:535, 540): "When I was the leader of the Party and the government, I, too, realized that we had to economize drastically in the buildup of homes, the construction of communal services, and the development of agriculture in order to build up our defenses. I went so far as to suspend the construction of subways in Kiev, Baku and Tbilisi so that we could redirect these funds into strengthening our defense and counterattack forces. We also built fewer athletic stadiums, swimming pools, and cultural facilities." Khrushchev's sensitivity to these costs was also highlighted by his demobilization of nearly a quarter million army men in the early 1960s so that these rather than socioeconomic investment funds could be employed to reach strategic parity in missiles with the United States following the apparently successful intimidation by Kennedy during the "missile crisis" in Cuba.

17. The implications of such studies for conversion are highlighted by Whynes' (1979:124-5) observation that "the report of the UK Labour Party Defence Study Group is of general interest as it pays attention to our two 'optimistic contributions', namely, the economic viability of armaments reduction and the need for rational planning. A belief in the

necessity for weapons reduction has a long history in the UK Labour Party, based upon the notion that the very existence of armaments constitutes a serious threat to world peace and also 'socially desirable' production. These factors played a key part in LPDSG's policy analysis, the main recommendation of which was the reduction of the UK defence burden to a level commensurate with that of European NATO allies by means of the rigorous application of cost effective analysis of weapons systems. Based upon a substantial volume of empirical data, a variety of resource-saving options were presented (e.g. running down the nuclear submarine fleet, or the air force) these options representing an average saving of some 20 per cent on projected defence budgets. In parallel, studies were also carried out which convinced LPDSG that the necessary adjustments to the economy (to redirect activity away from defence production towards civil manufacturing industry) were entirely feasible."

18. Such inflationary consequences derive not only from the oligopolistic cost-plus military firms, preference for ultra-sophisticated weapons systems and non-competitive procurement practices (Fallows, 1981; Rickover, 1982; "Defending America", 1982), but also from the unwillingness to finance such outlays through taxation as opposed to debt creation. Hence, depending upon the financing variable - military expenditures generate inflation and/or unemployment - both of which are detrimental to mass welfare. These consequences are also underscored by the recent report of the UN Group of Governmental Experts on the Relationship between Disarmament and Development (UNSG, 1982:76-80). They take pains to emphasize (71) that "the poorer sections of society, whether concentrated in small pockets in the generally well-off developed world or more broadly scattered among the developing countries, are more vulnerable to the inflationary pressures than their better-off counterparts".

19. "It needs to be emphasized that military R and D is competing with civilian R and D. The direct opportunity costs of military R and D are the lost opportunities in the civil research projects. Also, there is a lot of dissipation of resources in the military R and D. Many prototypes of weapon systems involving a high R and D component never become operational. Military R and D is extremely labour-intensive when it comes to highly qualified scienti-

fic and technical personnel. As a consequence, in the Group's opinion, the arguments in favour of civilian spin-offs of military R and D are out-weighed by its diversion and displacement of human and technological resources from comparable civilian research. Bearing in mind the enormous technological input required to accelerate the developmental pro-cess, particularly for the benefit of developing countries, the enormous asymmetry between the mili-tary and civilian R and D becomes all the more con-spicuous." These conclusions are premised upon the following studies: Dan Smith and Ron Smith, "Mili-tary Expenditure, Resources and Development'; Mary Kaldor, "The Role of Military Technology in Indus-trial Development"; and UNSG (1978). Reference is also made to a study by Jacques Fontanel, "Formal-ized Studies and Econometric Analyses of the Rela-tionship between Military Expenditure and Economic Development. Examples: France and Morocco".

20. Russett (1970:128-30) notes that because of the paucity of stock and real property ownership or the absence of union protection through cost of living clauses, that "White-collar workers and especially pensioners and poor unorganized laborers have the most nearly fixed income and the greatest vulnera-bility." Similarly, "even within industry and em-ployment groups, defense spending makes the rich richer. The reason is the need in most weapons manu-facture for a highly skilled and therefore expensive labor force." More generally, The Washington Specta-tor (15 January 1980, p. 3) reported that "John C. Davis, former member of the President's Council of Economic Advisors, says: 'Since defense spending is the most inflationary of all government expendi-tures, there is almost no possibility that we shall stop our inflationary price spiral until the arms race is brought under control.'" He is wrong of course. Reagan has demonstrated that such inflation can be reduced through forcing high unemployment, direct curtailment of social welfare measures, dete-rioration of transport and other infrastructure, accelerating urban decay, etc.

21. Klaus Engelhardt, "Effects of the Arms Race and Disarmament on the Labour Situation in Countries of Different Social Systems". Other research referred to in the textual quotation includes: Seymour Melman, "Barriers to Conversion from Military to

Civilian Industry - in Market, Planned and Developing Economies"; Roger H. Bezdek, "The 1980 Economic
Impact - Regional and Occupational - of Compensated
Skills in Defense Spending", Journal of Regional
Science, vol. 15, no. 2 (1975:183-98); Alexander
Krusky and Mikhail Khlusov, "Post-War Economic Re-
construction in the USSR", in Socio-Economic Prob-
lems of Disarmament by the Soviet Peace Committee,
International Institute for Peace, Vienna, pp. 21-
31; Marion Anderson, The Empty Pork Barrel: Unem-
ployment and the Pentagon Budget (Lansing, PILGRIM,
April 1975); Chase Econometrics Associates, Economic
Impact of the B-1 Program on the U.S. Economy and
Comparative Case Studies (Cynnyd, Pennsylvania,
1975); Institute for United States and Canadian
Affairs, USSR Academy of Sciences, Urgent Political,
Social and Economic Problems of the Present Stage of
the Development of Mankind and Practical Ways of
Diverting to Development Needs the Resources Now Absorbed by the Arms Race; Institute of World Economics and International Relations of the USSR Academy
of Sciences, Economic and Social Effects of a Continuing Arms Race and of the Implementation of Disarmament Measures; Polish Institute of International
Affairs, Arms Race and Global Problems of International Economic Relations (reports prepared for the
Group).

22. Military capabilities have also been reduced because of excessive costs due to procurement corruption waste and the military-industrial complex's
ability to induce military purchases of breakdown-
prone, high cost and difficult to maintain "gold
plated" weapons systems - now much in demand by
Third World officers. See: Kaldor (1981); Fallows
(1981); "Defending America" (1982:12-38), and for an
incisive critique from an "insider" with decades of
experience, Rickover (1982:12-14).

23. A less determinative conclusion was reached by
Robert Jackman (1976:1078-97) after a statistical
reanalysis of Nordlinger's data and additional indicators from the 1960s. In sum, "military intervention in the politics of the Third World has no
unique effects on social change, regardless either
of the level of economic development or geographical
region".

24. Finer (1975:234-8) also reports that "In those
Latin American states (1950-1967) whose military
were not politically involved, the average propor-

tion of defence expenditure to the central government's expenditure was 9.3 per cent; from those with
intermittent military involvement, it was 14.1 per
cent; for those ruled by the military circa 1960, it
was 18.5 per cent. In between 1960-1965 the first
group of states increased their military expenditure
by 2.8 per cent annually, the second group by 3.3
per cent but the third group increased it by 14 per
cent. What applied to Latin America, applied, in a
broad sense, to a sample of seventy-four states (including Latin American ones). The proportion of
G.N.P. devoted to defence was almost twice as large
in countries ruled by the military 1957-62, as in
countries whose military were not politically involved."

25. Other distinctions that have been suggested
(Ravenhill, 1980:99-126) to further refine our comparisons are those which acknowledge different types
of civilian and military regimes. Thus Ravenhill reports his "study of the performance of 50 regimes in
sub-Saharan Africa in the period 1960-73, utilizing
an analysis of variance and covariance design, finds
no statistically significant difference between the
two regime types. But this type of research design,
by aggregating the performance data for all 'military' regimes, obscures the substantial differences
in performance between regimes classified within
either the civilian or military groupings." In Chapter 5 which follows, I employ such controls. An
earlier (Wolpin, 1977:128-9) comparison of cost/
benefit performances for leftist and rightist military regimes during 1965-74 concluded that:

"The open door military regime distinguished itself
in a more ominous way on the cost indicators. It
ranked highest by far on more costs than any other
regime type: government sanctions; political deten-
tions; disappearances and executions; torture; increase in size of the armed forces; consumer price
inflation; and the rise in indirect taxes. As for
benefits, it ranked highest only on gross fixed
capital formation. Military "moderates" did manage
to rank lowest on one cost indicator - change in per
capita military expenditures though as pointed out
previously such items may have been concealed under
other budgetary classifications. Admittedly, they
did not rank lowest upon any benefit measures.

Left wing officers distinguished themselves by ranking lowest on only one cost indicator - rise in in-

direct taxes. The importance of this to the masses
and the fact that the only benefit for which they
scored highest was the restriction of food price
increases suggest that their populist commitments
have a real substantive rather than rhetorical
basis. While increasing the external debt burden was
the only cost upon which they ranked highest, the
fact that radical officers turned in the worst performance on five benefit indicators implies that
despite the greater stability of their regimes, they
may be if anything less capable of overcoming the
development challenge than are civilian radicals.
These five benefit areas were: rise in manufacturing
output and employment; gross fixed capital formation; teacher/student ratios; and per capita food
production.In sum while right wing officers do stimulate somewhat higher production than their radical
counterparts, it is at a cost which is incomparably
higher to the little people or 'citizens'."

26. "Over the past fifteen years, total military expenditures made by developing nations have been much
greater than all nonmilitary official development
aid and have been even greater than total net capital inflows to these countries. When official development aid is aggregated from 1965 through 1973,
the total is about $50 billion; total net transfers
for this period amount to approximately $134 billion
(in current dollars). However, total military expenditures for the period exceeded this inclusive inflow figure. If the net capital transfer figures are
converted into a constant 1970 dollar basis and the
world price deflator provided by the International
Monetary Fund is used, the constant dollar value is
about $137 billion, while constant dollar military
expenditures were $140 billion. Even more signifi-
cant is the fact that the compounded growth rate of
military expenditures (10 per cent) is greater than
the growth rate of net capital transfers (in constant dollar terms increasing only 4.5 per cent).
While aid and capital transfers have grown both in
absolute and constant dollar values, military expenditures during the same period grew at more than
double that rate."

27. Those referred to respectively in the quoted
section are: Lance Taylor, "Defense Spending, Economic Structure and Growth: Evidence Among Countries
and Over Time"; Bruce M. Russett and David J.
Sylvan, "The Effects of Arms Transfers on Developing
Countries"; and James Fontanel, "Formalized Studies

and Econometric Analyses of the Relationship between Military Expenditure and Economic Development. Examples: France and Morocco".

28. The studies referred to are the ones by: Fontanel (see preceding note); Lance Taylor, "Defense Spending, Economic Structure and Growth: Evidence Among Countries and Over Time"; Dan Smith and Ron Smith, "Military Expenditure, Resources and Development"; Jose Antonio Encinas del Pando, "Declaration of Ayacucho: Analysis and Quantification of a Possible Agreement on Limitation of Military Expenditures in South America".

29. Findings mentioned at the beginning of the quoted paragraph are by: Smith and Smith (see preceding note); Encinas del Pando (see preceding note); Seymour Melman, "Barriers to Conversion from Military to Civilian Industry in Market, Planned and Developing Countries"; Mary Kaldor, "The Role of Military Technology in Industrial Development".

30. This is partially explained by methodological differences with respect to statistical techniques, years encompassed, variables selected, nations included, data sources, etc.

31. Even these I concede are at best imperfect and frequently indirect indicators of progress toward mass socio-political well-being. Thus their validity remains partial as important dimensions cannot be quantified or fairly portrayed by available data. Further, data is sometimes missing and often inaccurate due to error or the type of bias discussed in the text of this chapter.

32. The following are also excluded: Austria, Japan, Angola, Mozambique, Kampuchea, Laos, Vietnam, Guinea-Bissau and Fiji. All data is available from the International Peace Research Institute, Oslo (PRIO) Data Bank. In Appendix A, a complete list of countries with PRIO Nation Code numbers appears. Appendix B records the abridged titles and variable acronyms for quick reference. Their sources as well as fuller explanations where necessary appear in Appendix C.

33. To be classified as military ruled, the Chief Executive must be either designated or subject to military command veto for at least two-thirds of the period in question (1960-7, 1960-78, 1965-78). The

same temporal criterion was employed to classify development strategies as monopoly capitalist or "open door", state capitalist or "state dominant", and state socialist or "centrally planned" (1960-78, 1970-8, 1965-78). A "mixed" category was also used for countries which altered their development approach for more than one-third of the period in question. Appendices D and E provide lists of countries as classified by civilian/military regime type and development strategy respectively.

34. Unrotated loadings for the Military Burden factor (MILSPFAC) were: AFRTIO67 (.750), MXGNP68 (.927), MIXCGE67 (.646); MLXPER68 (.850); USTAFS (-.311); ARMIMT77 (.651). The second factor USTAFFAC which loaded most strongly with the US Military Training impact (USTAFS), explained only 17 per cent of the cumulative variance. Its loadings were: .310, -.031, -.395, .264, .826, .128.

35. Unrotated loadings for the Physical Welfare (PHYSICAL) factor were: CHLPER75 (-.824); PROPER76 (.110); WOMLF77 (-.083); PTRPED77 (-.552); FPRSCH77 (.739); FSCHSCH77 (.864); CALPER77 (.729); LITRCY78 (.937); CHILDM78 (-.955); LIFEXB78 (.962). The second factor (WOMENFAC), which loaded most strongly with women as a percentage of the labour force explained less than 14 per cent of the cumulative variance. Its loadings were: .378, .262, .865, .459, .312, -.015, .248, .087, -.080, .053.

36. For the civilian governments the mean was -.163 with a standard deviation of .888 (N 37), while for the military regimes they were .014 (N 8).

37. On this factor (WOMENFAC), the second referred to above in note 35, the civilian mean was .200, standard deviation .927 (N 50), while for the military regimes they were -1.050, .908 (N 8, R^2 .18).

38. These are designated as the "open door" or monopoly capitalist, the state capitalist and the state socialist orientation or mode of production. All involve extensive state involvement in national economic policy formation. To be so classified, a regime must follow such an orientation for two-thirds of the period in question. Those in the mixed category were "unstable" in that they failed to conform with the two-thirds criterion - thus altering their development policies in midstream so to speak. Appendix D lists all countries as classified.

Under monopoly capitalism, the political and bureaucratic elites "regulate" to enhance the profitabili-
ty of the private corporate sector. Because the latter is dominated by transnational corporations in
most underdeveloped areas, so long as indigenous
officials acquiesce in such relations their domestic
and even foreign policy choices tend to depend upon
favourable reactions by such corporations and associated international financial institutions. "Dependency" then as the sources referred to in notes 7
and 12 above argue, has evolved historically with
the growth and extension of monopoly capitalism into
a world system.

State capitalism involves attempts radically to reduce dependency (enlarging policy alternatives) and
simultaneous promotion of industrial development.
Characteristic of such regimes are state ownership
of most large economic enterprises and diversifica-
tion of economic relations so that major transactions occur with Eastern state socialist systems.
Other policies usually associated with state capitalist regimes are listed in note 7 above.

State socialist systems may be distinguished from
state capitalism in the following ways. First, the
residual sector is being reduced rather than tole-
rated as legitimate. This residual private sector is
also much smaller and generally limited to medium
and more commonly small-scale economic undertakings.
Finally, primary elite roles are those of production
mobilizers rather than bureacratic consumers. Their
socialist orientation is manifested by a distinctive
ethos and style of life.

Many societies are obviously on a continuum, and
neither linearity of movement nor stability of position are ubiquitous. In short, state socialist systems (Yugoslavia) may "degenerate" into state capitalist regimes, while revolutionary elites who seize
monopoly capitalist systems (China) can virtually
telescope the state capitalist phase by moving
quickly on to state socialism. Similarly, state
capitalist regimes like Egypt and Ghana, may revert
in some measure toward monopoly capitalism. Rever-
sion is, however, seldom complete. Chile is excep-
tional in this regard. Thus the consonance of state
capitalist production relations with the neutraliza-
tion of at least some major contradictions in Third
World monopoly capitalism explains why the right
wing coups generally accept enlarged state sectors -

sales of a few enterprises notwithstanding - and
limit themselves to adopting a deferential stance to
foreign investment only in as yet unexploited areas.
Hence the trend in monopoly capitalist systems is an
ineluctable if gradual historical one toward what
might be termed "creeping state capitalism". In
Black Africa today, for example, 18 out of 30 states
have instituted selective or comprehensive national-
izations of foreign investments. And as their technical and managerial skills improve, this will be
extended to modern manufacturing (largely import
assembly plants) operations which as yet are least
affected.

39. Before doing so, however, it might be interesting to briefly picture interrelationships found
among the control variables themselves. One of the
strongest coefficients in Table 11 is between our
two indicators (PRESS67, FREEDM73) of associational
freedom. On the latter low scores mean greater freedom. Weaker (r .40, r -.34) significant associations
appear between both of the aforementioned and our in-
ndustrialization/economic development level variable
(MFGDP70). The latter in turn is negatively (r
-.23) correlated with 1973-75 per capita aid
(AIDPER75) which in turn is more strongly (r .44)
associated with 1978 external debt as a percentage
of GNP (EPDGNP78). Both of these external assistance
measures are positively (r .46, r .53) associated
with 1978 public consumption as a percentage of GDP
(PUCGDP78). Finally, the 1970-7 change in gross
fixed capital formation (CGFCF77) exhibits weak (r
-.28, r -.27) yet significant development (MFGDP70)
as well as state extractive capability (GVTGDP70).

40. The regression coefficient of CGDP70 with
CGDPPC70 is r .72 (p .0005, N 50), with CGFCF70 is r
.61 (p .0005, N 37), and with CGDPPC77 is r .49 (p
.0005, N 55).

41. The first nine of these were among the ten from
which PHYSICAL was extracted - see note 35 above.
With the exception of FSCSCH for which there was a
paucity in 1970 for many countries, then, all are
used. I have added five others which are specifical-
ly designed to measure changes in prices, food production and employment, all of which directly reflect physical welfare at the mass level.

42. The militarization indicators in Table 33 are
calculated from the following variables whose sour-

ces are listed in Appendix C: CMILEX70; CAF70; AFSIZE (AFSIZE77/AFSIZE61); MILEX (MILEX77/MILEX68); CAFR6779; CMCG6778; MXGNP77/MXGNP61).

43. Yet there are very strong regression coefficients between AFSIZE and both ARMIMT77 (r .77, p .001, n 82) and AFSIZE77 (r .90, p .001, n 85). As for expenditures, MXGNP61 varies as follows: MXGNP70 (r .56, p .001, n 90); MXGNP77 (r .47, p .001, n. 89); ARMIMT77 (r .78, p 001, n 87); AFSIZE77 (r .87, p .001, n 90). On the other hand both AFSIZE61 as well as MXGNP61 were negatively correlated with CAF70 (r -.60, and r -.42) both significant at the .001 level (n 72). Thus the greatest armed forces expansion during the 1960s occurred in countries with the smaller military establishments. These also tended to be the most socially impoverished as the following regression coeffients with CAF70 for various 1960 physical welfare indicators reveal: child mortality (r .50, p .001, n 73); infant mortality (r .49, p .002, n 32); protein supply per capita (r -.32, p .007, n 59); life expectancy at birth (r -.47, p .001, n 69); literacy (r -.48, p .001, n 54); female primary school enrolment ratio (r -.40, p .001, n 68); female secondary school enrolment ratio (r -.49, p .001, n 66); child labour (r .43, p .001, n 72). The above are Spearman rank order correlations for 1960 indicators. They are not employed in succeeding portions of this analysis.

44. Unrotated loadings for the financial militarization or ME factor (MXCGFAC) were: MILEX (.85); CMCG6778 (.73); MXGNP (.50); CMILEX (.45).

45. This was also the case for FREEDM82 and both USTAFS and MILSPAC. The latter approached the .20 confidence level with means for the "more free" of -.172 (SD .791, n 29) and for the "less free" of .205 (SD 1.240, n 21).

46. USTAFFAC was even more strongly negatively associated with the PHYSICAL welfare factor.

47. An earlier economic and welfare performance analysis which yielded similar conclusions was published by Wolpin (1977).

48. Despite continuous journalistic exposures of military waste and the assumption of a linkage between efficiency and both competitiveness and functional specialization, this particular rela-

tionship has to my knowledge not been systematically examined. How much more cost effective are civilian educational, construction, health and similar programmes? Other research suggested by this inquiry pertains to the existence and strength of association between prior militarization and subsequent military dominance of Third World politics. A third investigation might assess whether the incidence of domestic and external war in the South has risen in the 1970s as compared with the 1960s when the current militarization and arms transfer escalation began. And finally, there is an obvious need for systematic study of regime type and data bias. To what extent, if at all, do military regimes, heavy militarizers and/or poor social welfare performers understate military burdens and overstate socio-economic welfare performance more than better performing regimes?

49. Thus, Tuomi and Väyrynen (1980:239) warn those endeavouring to create or expand indigenous arms industries against "the disproportionate allocation of resources to the military R&D, which prevents the development of science- and technology-related components in the civilian industry. This is in fact detrimental in the long run even for the military industry because its technology base is much more dependent on a healthy civilian technology than vice versa."

50. Those engaging in torture, executions and political disappearances were superior on the PHYSICAL welfare factor in both years, while regimes not so classified scored higher on the WOMEN factor only in 1975. There was no difference on this in 1979. Country classification on these controls appears in Appendix F.

51. The socialists did particularly well on the welfare factors, reduction of child labour and increasing female secondary school enrolments. State capitalist regimes were most outstanding on raising average protein intake and increasing female primary school enrolment ratios.

52. The "less free" were also somewhat lower on economic growth during the 1960s, per capita income and industrialization.

53. It should also be borne in mind that as I stressed in Chapter 5, statistical significance is

Notes

based upon normal distributions characteristic of sampling probabilities. Here we have compared differences among the universe of countries rather than a sample. Thus where they appear, such differences have been genuine in an empirical sense, rather than a consequence of sampling error. At most, then, failure to attain customary p = .05 significance reveals the degree of dispersion or the meaningfulness of observed differences.

54. The UN Group of Experts (UNSG, 1982:88) also recognizes this:

"Attributing their under-development to their military spending seems to ignore the fact that quite a few among them continue to experience low or negligible rates of economic growth simultaneously with extremely low or negligible allocations to their military sector. Quite a few of the better economic performers among them also make sizeable allocations to the military sector although in these cases their social development performance may be affected. What is even more important, to over-emphasize the developing countries' responsibility in this sphere, would be to lose all sense of proportion. While resources redirected from their own military spending might be expected to be more directly available for development purposes, it must be recalled that they account for a total of 16 per cent of world military spending, a major portion of which is concentrated in only one region. Thus the developed countries are responsible for the lion's share of the more than $500 billion annually now poured into military expenditures, precisely the kinds of sum required to make a substantial impact on the global problems of under-development."

How much difference even a major increase in aid would make - without internal political transformations - is an open question. That some amelioration of mass welfare would indeed occur seems less problematic from our findings.

Afghanistan 302
Albania 401
Algeria 101
Angola 102
Argentina 202
Bangladesh 321
Benin 113
Bolivia 207
Botswana 104
Brazil 208
Bulgaria 405
Burma 307
Burundi 105
Cameroon 106
Cent.Af.Rep. 108
Chad 109
Chile 212
China 301
Colombia 213
Congo 111
Costa Rica 214
Cuba 215
Cyprus 311
Dominican Republic 217
Ecuador 218
Egypt 155
El Salvador 219
Ethiopia 114
Fiji 506
Gabon 115
Gambia 116
Ghana 117
Greece 414
Guatemala 224
Guinea 118
Guyana 225
Haiti 227
Honduras 228
India 313
Indonesia 314
Iran 315
Iraq 316
Ivory Coast 122
Jamaica 229
Jordan 320
Kampuchea 308
Kenya 123
N. Korea 322
S. Korea 323
Laos 225

Lebanon 326
Lesotho 103
Liberia 124
Madagascar 126
Malawi 127
Malaysia 328
Mali 128
Mauritania 129
Mexico 231
Mongolia 330
Morocco 131
Mozambique 132
Nepal 332
Nicaragua 234
Niger 133
Nigeria 134
Oman 331
Pakistan 333
Panama 235
Paraguay 236
Peru 237
Philippines 335
Portugal 426
Romania 427
Rwanda 137
Senegal 140
Sierra Leone 142
Singapore 341
Somalia 143
South Africa 145
Sri Lanka 309
Sudan 149
Syria 342
Tanzania 151
Thailand 344
Togo 152
Trinidad & Tobago 244
Tunisia 153
Turkey 346
Uganda 154
Upper Volta 156
Uruguay 247
Venezuela 248
Vietnam 347
N. Yemen 349
S. Yemen 301
Yugoslavia 436
Zaire 112
Zambia 157
Zimbabwe 136
Taiwan 343

PRIONU	PRIO nation code, ident. nos. for nations
ACRMAA68	Accident rate in manufacturing
ACRMAA77	Accident rate in manufacturing
AFRTIO67	Armed forces per 1,000 1967
AFRTIO68	Armed forces per 1000 persons
AFSIZE61	Armed forces, thousands
AFSIZE68	Armed forces in thousands
AFSIZE70	Armed forces, thousands
AFSIZE77	Armed forces in thousands
AIDPER75	Per capita foreign aid: 1973-1975
AIDTOT70	Foreign aid received in millions
AIDTOT75	Foreign aid total: 1973-1975
ARMIMT77	Average 1968-1977 arms imports as % tot.
CAF70	Increase in size of armed forces
CAFR6779	Per cent change in armed forces ratios
CALPER60	Calorie supply per capita: daily ave.
CALPER70	Calorie supply per capita: daily ave.
CALPER77	Calorie supply per capita: daily ave.
CFOODP68	Food production: 1967-1968 average
CFOODP78	Food production: 1977-1978 average
CGDP70	GDP: Average annual growth rate: 1960-1970
CGDPPC70	GDP average annual per capita growth
CGDPPC77	GDP average annual per capita growth
CGFCF70	Gross fixed capital formation growth
CGFCF77	Gross fixed capital formation growth
CHILDM60	Child death rate: 1-4 yrs
CHILDM70	Child death rate: 1-4 yrs
CHILDM78	Child death rate: 1-4 yrs
CHLPER60	Children in the labour force
CHLPER70	Children in the labour force
CHLPER75	Children in the labour force
CIVLIB75	Pol. Repr. Indic. 67-75
CIVLIB79	Polit Repr Inds 1976-9
CIVMIL67	Civilian vs. military rule: 1960-1967
CIVMIL78	Civilian vs. military rule: 1960-1978
CMCG6778	Change 1967 to 1978 in mil. expendit.
CMILEX70	% change in military expenditures
CVML6578	Civilian vs. military rule: 1965-78
DEMSYS66	"Democratic systems", 1=yes, 2=no
DEMSYS68	Fully inclusive polyarchies
DEVSTR78	Regime class. by dev. strat.
DSTRAT69	Regime classification by dev. strat.
DSTRAT78	Regime class. by dev. strat.
DVST6578	Regime classification by dev. strat.
EDGP7078	Total external public debt as % exps.
EMPLOY60	General employment level
EMPLOY68	General employment level, 1963=100
EMPLOY78	General employment level, 1970=100
EPDGNP70	External public debt as % of GNP

EPDGNP78	Total external public debt as % GNP
EPDIMP79	Ratio of public debt to imps.
EXILE79	Polit repr inds 1976-9
FOODIN69	Inflation: rise in food prices
FOODIN78	Inflation: rise in food prices
FPRSCH60	Female primary school enrolment
FPRSCH70	Female primary school enrolment
FPRSCH77	Female primary school enrolment
FREEDM73	Status of freedom ranking
FREEDM79	Status of freedom ranking
FREEDM82	Status of freedom ranking
FSCSCH60	Female secondary school enrolment
FSCSCH70	Female secondary school enrolment
FSCSCH77	Female secondary school enrolment
GVTGDP60	Central government revenue as % GDP
GVTGDP70	Central government revenue as % GDP
INDLAB60	Industrial percentage of the labour force
INDLAB78	Industrial percentage of the labour force
INFL6078	Inflation: per cent change 1960-1970
INFLAA70	Inflation: average rate, 1960-1970
INFLAA78	Inflation: average rate, 1970-1978
LABORF60	Labour force size in 1960
LABORF78	Labour force size in 1978
LEGOPP77	Legisl. opposition index
LIFEXB60	Life expectancy at birth
LIFEXB70	Life expectancy at birth
LIFEXB78	Life expectancy at birth
LITRCY52	Percentage literate of population
LITRCY60	Percentage literate of population
LITRCY70	Percentage literate of population
LITRCY75	Percentage literate of population
LITRCY78	Percentage literate of population
LOAN7078	Ratio of 78 net inflow of pub. & private loans to 1970
MFGDP60	Manufacturing as a per cent of GDP
MFGDP70	Manufacturing as a per cent of GDP
MFGDP78	Manufacturing as a per cent of GDP
MILEX53	Military expenditures in constant $
MILEX60	Military expenditures in constant $
MILEX68	Military expenditures in constant $
MILEX70	Military expenditures in constant $
MILEX75	Military expenditures in constant $
MILEX77	Military expenditures in constant $
MIXCGE67	Military expenditures as % of cent. govt. expenditure
MLXPER68	Military expenditures per capita
MXGNP61	Military expenditures as a % of GNP
MXGNP68	Military expenditures as a % of GNP

MXGNP70	Military expenditures as a % of GNP
MXGNP77	Military expenditures as a % of GNP
NAIPER63	Per capita national income
NEWSPR60	Daily general interest newspaper circulation
NEWSPR70	Daily general interest newspaper circulation
IRREG67	Electoral irregularities: 1959-1967
PARTY68	Party fractionalization: 1962-1968
PRESS67	Press freedom index: 1961-1967
PRISON75	Polit repr. inds 1967-75 prison mistreatment
PRISON79	Polit repr. inds 1976-9: prison mistreatment
PROPER60	Protein supply per capita: average
PROPER70	Protein supply per capita: average
PROPER76	Protein supply per capita: average
PRVPER76	Public revenues per capita
PTRPED60	Pupil teacher ratios in primary ed.
PTRPED70	Pupil teacher ratios in primary ed.
PTRPED77	Pupil teacher ratios in primary ed.
PUCGDP60	Public consumption as a percent of GDP
PUCGDP78	Public consumption as a percent of GDP
TORTUR75	Polit. repr. inds.: 1967-75 executions
TORTUR79	Polit. repr. inds.: 1976-79 executions
UNEMAV69	Unemployment level average percentage
UNEMAV77	Unemployment level average percentage
USMAID69	US military aid, in 100 000 US $
USMAID76	US military aid, in 100 000 US $
USTRNG76	U.S. training of foreign military
VOTERS67	Voters as a percent of electorate
WKRSID68	Workers involved in industrial disputes
WKRSID77	Workers involved in industrial disputes
WKRSID79	Workers involved in industrial disputes
WOMLF60	Women as a percent of total labour force
WOMLF70	Women as a percent of total labour force
WOMLF77	Women as a percent of total labour force

APPENDIX C: FULL VARIABLE TITLES AND SOURCES

PRIONU: PRIO Nation Code, (ID Nos. for Nations).
            Source: International Peace Research
            Institute, Oslo

ACRMAA68:   Accident Rate in Manufacturing.
            Source: Yearbook of Labour Statistics
            1978, pp. 607-9.

ACRMAA77:   Accident rate in manufacturing.
            Source: Yearbook of Labour Statistics
            1978. pp. 607-9:

AFRTI067:   Armed Forces per Thousand 1967.
            Source: USACDA: World Military Expendi-
            tures and Arms Transfers 1967-1976,
            Washington.

AFRTI068:   Armed Forces per 1000 Persons.
            Source: World Military Expenditures and
            Arms Transfers: 1968-1977, USACDA.

AFSIZE61:   Armed Forces, Thousands.
            Source: World Military Expenditures 1971,
            USACDA.

AFSIZE68:   Armed Forces in Thousands.
            Source: World Military Expenditures and
            Arms Transfers: 1968-1977, USACDA.

AFSIZE70:   Armed Forces, Thousands.
            Source: World Military Expenditures: 1971,
            USACDA.

AFSIZE77:   Armed Forces in Thousands.
            Source: World Military Expenditures and
            Arms Transfers, 1968-1977, USACDA.

AIDPER75:   Per Capita Foreign Aid: 1973-1975.
            Source: UN Statistical Yearbook: 1977 in
            G.T. Kurian, The Book of World Rankings,
            NY: Facts on File, 1979.

AIDTOT70:   Foreign Aid Received in Millions of Cur-
            rent Dollars: 1961-1970 Total.
            Source: USACDA. World Military Expendi-
            tures 1971, Washington.

AIDTOT75:   Foreign aid total: 1973-1975.
            Source: UN Statistical Yearbook: 1977, in
            G.T.Kurian, The Book of World Rankings,
            NY: Facts on File, 1979.

Appendix C

ARMIMT77: Average 1968–1977 Arms Imports as a
Percentage of Total Imports 1968–1977.
Source: World Military Expenditures and
Arms Transfers: 1968–1977, USACDA.

CAF70: Increase in Size of Armed Forces (%):
1961–1970.
Source: World Military Expenditures: 1971,
USACDA.

CAFR6779: Per Cent Change in Armed Forces per 1000:
1967 to 1979.
Source: USACDA: World Military Expenditures and Arms Transfers 1967–76,
1970–79.

CALPER60: Calorie Supply Per Capita: Daily Average
Per Cent of Requirements.
Source: World Tables 1976. World Bank. pp.
518–521.

CALPER70: Calorie Supply Per Capita: Daily Average
Per Cent of Requirements.
Source: World Tables 1976. World Bank. pp.
518–521.

CALPER77: Calorie Supply Per Capita: Daily Average
Per Cent of Requirements.
Source: World Development Report 1980.
World Bank. pp. 152–153.

CFOODP68: Food Production: 1967–1968 Average
(1963=100).
Source: UN Statistical Yearbook 1969. pp.
90–91.

CFOODP78: Food Production: 1977–1978 Average.
(1969–1971=100)
Source: UN Statistical Yearbook 1978.

CGDP70: GDP: Average Annual Growth Rate:
1960–1970.
Source: World Development Report 1980.
World Bank. pp. 112–113.

CGDPPC70: GDP Average Annual Per Capita Growth Rate:
1960–1970. Source: UN Statistical
Yearbook 1978.

Appendix C

CGDPPC77: GDP Average Annual Per Capita Growth Rate:
1970-1977.
Source: UN Statistical Yearbook 1978.

CGFCF70: Gross Fixed Capital Formation Growth Rate:
1960-1970.
Source: UN Statistical Yearbook 1978.

CGFCF77: Gross Fixed Capital Formation Growth Rate:
1970-1977.
Source: UN Statistical Yearbook 1978.

CHILDM60: Child Death Rate: 1-4 Yrs.
Source: World Development Report 1980.
World Bank. pp. 150-151.

CHILDM70: Child Death Rate: 1-4 Yrs.
Source: World Atlas of the Child. World
Bank. 1979.

CHILDM78: Child Death Rate: 1-4 Yrs.
Source: World Development Report 1980.
World Bank. pp. 150-151.

CHLPER60: Children in the Labour Force Per One
Thousand Population. Source: World Atlas
of the Child. World Bank. 1979.

CHLPER70: Children in the Labour Force Per One
Thousand Population. Source: World Atlas
of the Child. World Bank. 1979.

CHLPER75: Children in the Labour Force Per One
Thousand Population. Source: World Atlas
of the Child. World Bank. 1979.

CIVLIB75: Pol. Repression Indic. 67-75: Subst.
Restr. on Civil Liber., Due Process 1=Yes,
2=No.
Source: Amn)∅|& u<|)`<d a)?_`| < h_`|/`)e
B973. Amnesty Intern. Report: 1975-76.

CIVLIB79: Polit Repr Inds: 1976-9: Subst Restr upon
Civ Libert or Due Process: 1=Yes, 2=No.
Source: Amnesty Internat. Repts on Torture
1979. US State Dept Rept on Human Rights:
1979.

CIVMIL67: Civilian vs. Military Rule: 1960-1967.
(1=Civilian, 2=Military) Min. 5 Years.
Source: M. Wolpin, Militarism & Soc.Revol.
in the Thirld World. NJ: Allanheld, Osmun
Co, 81.

CMCG6778: Change 1967 to 1978 in Mil. Expenses as a
Per Cent of Central Government Expenditures.
Source: USACDA, World Military Expenditures and Arms Transfers 1967-76, &
70-79.

CMILEX70: Per Cent Change in Military Expenditures
(current $): 1961-1970.
Source: World Military Expenditures: 1971,
USACDA.

CVML6578: Civilian vs. Military Rule: 1965-78
(1=Civ, 2=Mil, 3=Mix) Min. 9 Years.
Source: MD Wolpin: Militarism & Social
Revolution in the Third World. NJ:
Allanheld Osmun.

DEMSYS66: "Democratic Systems", 1=Yes, 2=No.
Source: Dankwart, A. Rustow, A World of
Nations. Wash.: Brookings Institution,
1967.

DEMSYS68: Fully Inclusive Polyarchies: December
1968.
Source: R. Dahl, Polyarchy: Particip. and
Opposition. New Haven: Yale Univ. Pr.
1971.

DEVSTR78: Regime Classification by Dev. Strat.: 1.
MC, 2. SC, 3. SS, 4. Mixed. 1960-78.
Source: Miles D. Wolpin, SUNY, Potsdam,
NY USA.

DSTRAT69: Regime Classification by Development
Strategy: 1960-69.
Source: Miles D. Wolpin, SUNY, Potsdam,
NY, USA.

DSTRAT78: Regime Classification by Dev. Strat.: 1.
MC, 2. SC, 3. SS, 4. Mixed. 1970-78.
Source: Miles D. Wolpin, SUNY, Potsdam,
NY, USA.

DVST6578: Regime Classification by Development
Strategy 65-75. 1=mc, 2=sc, 3=ss, 4mix.
Source: M D Wolpin: Militarism & Social
Revolution in the Third World. NJ:
Allanheld Osmun.

EDGP7078: Total External Public Debt as a Percent of
GNP in Mill. $ - % change 70-78.
Source: USACDA: World Milit. Expen. & Arms
Trans: 1970-78; World Devt Rept World
Bank, 1980.

EMPLOY60: General Employment Level.
Source: Yearbook of Labour Statistics:
1970. pp. 333-5.

EMPLOY68: General Employment Level, 1963=100.
Source: Yearbook of Labour Statistics:
1970. pp. 333-4.

EMPLOY78: General Employment Level, 1970=100.
Source: Yearbook of Labour Statistics:
1979. pp. 202-4.

EPDGNP70: External Public Debt Outstanding (Total
and Disbursed) as a Percent of GNP.
Source: World Development Report 1980.
World Bank. pp. 138-9.

EPDGNP78: Total External Public Debt as a Percent of
GNP (1978) in Mill US $.
Source: USACDA: World Mil. Expen. & Arms
Trans.: 1970-78; World Dev. Rep. World
Bank 1980.

EPDIMP79: Ratio of 12/31/79 Outst. Disb. Ext. Pub.
Debts US$ to 1978 Imp. in Curr. $.
Source: USACDA: World Mil. Expend. & Arms
Transfers 1970-79: World Bank Annual
Report: 1981.

EXILE79: Polit. Repr. Inds.: 1976-79: Good Prison,
Forced Exile, Econ. Sanct: 1=Yes, 2=No.
Source: Amnesty Internat. Repts on Torture:
1979. US State Dept. Rept. on Human Rights:
1979.

FOODIN69: Inflation: Rise in Food Prices,
1968-1969. (1963=100).
Source: Yearbook of Labour Statistics
1978.

Appendix C

FOODIN78: Inflation: Rise in Food Prices,
1968-1978. (1970=100).
Source: Yearbook of Labour Statistics
1978.

FPRSCH60: Female Primary School Enrolment Ratio.
Source: World Atlas of the Child. World
Bank, 1979.

FPRSCH70: Female Primary School Enrolment Ratio.
Source: World Atlas of the Child. World
Bank, 1979.

FPRSCH77: Female Primary School Enrolment Ratio.
Source: World Atlas of the Child. World
Bank, 1979.

FREEDM73: Status of Freedom Ranking: Political and
Civil Rights (1-7:High-Low).
Source: Raymond Gastil, "Comparative
Survey of Freedom", Freedom at Issue, No.
17 (1973):4.

FREEDM79: Status of Freedom Ranking: Political &
Civil Rights 1979. (1-7: High-Low).
Source: R. Gastil, "Comparative Survey of
Freedom", Freedom at Issue, N. 49
(Jan.-Feb 1979):7.

FREEDM82: Status of Freedom Ranking: Political &
Civil Rights,1982. Values: 1 (high) - 7
(low).
Source: R. Gastil, "Comparative Survey of
Freedom", Freedom at Issue no. 64 (1982):
8-9.

FSCSCH60: Female Secondary School Enrolment Ratio.
Source: Atlas of the Child. World Bank,
1979. UNESCO Stat. Yearbook: 1978/79. pp.
125-203.

FSCSCH70: Female Secondary School Enrolment Ratio.
Source: World Atlas of the Child. World
Bank, 1979. UNESCO Stat. Yrbk.: 1978/79.
pp. 125-203.

FSCSCH77: Female Secondary School Enrolment Ratio.
Source: UNESCO Statistical Yearbook:
1978-1979. pp. 125-203.

Appendix C

GVTGDP60: Central Government Revenue as a Percent of
GDP.
Source: World Tables: 1976, World Bank.

GVTGDP70 Central Government Revenue as a Percent of
GDP.
Source: World Tables: 1976, World Bank.

INDLAB60: Industrial Percentage of the Labour Force.
Source: World Development Report: 1980.
World Bank, pp. 146-7.

INDLAB78: Industrial Percentage of the Labour Force.
Source: World Development Report: 1980.
World Bank, pp. 146-7.

INFL6078: Inflation: Percent Change 1960-1970 to
1970-1978, Average Annual Rate.
Source: World Development Report: 1980.
World Bank.

INFLAA70: Inflation: Average Annual Rate
(1960-1970).
Source: World Development Report: 1980.
pp. 110-11.

INFLAA78: Inflation: Average Inflation Rate
(1970-1978).
Source: World Development Report: 1980.
pp. 110-11.

LABORF60: Labour Force Size in 1960.
Source: Yearbook of Labour Statistics:
1965. pp. 10-38.

LABORF78: Labour Force Size in 1978.
Source: Yearbook of Labour Statistics
1978.

LEGOPP77: Legisl. Opposition Index. Ratio of Total
Seats to Those Held by Majority Party.
Source: Thomas Kurian, The Book of World
Rankings. NY: Facts on File, 1979.

LIFEXB60: Life Expectancy at Birth.
Source: World Development Report: 1980.
World Bank, pp. 150-1.

LIFEXB70: Life Expectancy at Birth.
Source: World Atlas of the Child. World
Bank, 1979.

LIFEXB78: Life Expectancy at Birth.
Source: World Development Report: 1980.
World Bank, pp. 150-1.

LITRCY52: Percentage Literate of Population Aged 15
and Over.
Source: B. Russett et al: World Handbook
of Political and Social Indicators, 1964.

LITRCY60: Adult Literacy Rate.
Source: World Development Report: 1980.
World Bank, pp. 154-5.

LITRCY70: Adult Literacy Rate.
Source: UNESCO Statistical Yearbook: 1977.
pp. 42-50. World Tables 1976. World Bank.

LITRCY75: Adult Literacy Rate.
Source: World Development Report: 1980.
World Bank, pp. 154-155.

LITRCY78: Literacy Rate for Adults, 1978.
Source: Ruth Leger Sivard: World Military
and Social Expenditures: 1981.

LOAN7078: Ratio of 78 Net Inflow of Public &
Publicly Guaran. Med. $ Long Term Loans to
1970.
Source: World Bank Development Report:
1980.

MFGDP60: Manufacture as a Percent of Gross Domestic
Product: 1960.
Source: World Development Report: 1980,
pp. 114-5.

MFGDP70: Manufacturing as a Percent of Gross
Domestic Product.
Source: UN Statistical Yearbook: 1978. pp.
724-37.

MFGDP78: Manufacturing as a Percent of Gross
Domestic Product.
Source: World Development Report: 1980.
pp. 114-5.

MILEX53: Military Expenditures in Constant Dollars
1953.
Source: World Armaments and Disarmament:
1974. App. 6B. Reprinted SIPRI Yearbook:
1975.

MILEX60:   Military Expenditures in Constant
            Dollars.
            Source: World Armaments and Disarmament,
            1974. Reprinted from SIPRI Yearbook: 1975.

MILEX68:   Military Expenditures in Constant $.
            Source: World Military Expenditures and
            Arms Transfers: 1968-1977. USACDA.

MILEX70:   Military Expenditures in Constant Dollars.
            Source: SIPRI. World Armaments and
            Disarmament: 1974. Reprinted from SIPRI
            Yearbook: 1975.

MILEX75:   Military Expenditures: 1973-1975.
            Source: UN Stat. Yrbk.: 1977, in G.T.
            Kurian, The Book of World Rankings. NY:
            Facts on File, 1979.

MILEX77:   Military Expenditures in Constant
            Dollars.
            Source: World Military Expenditure and
            Arms Transfer, 1968-1977. USACDA.

MIXCGE67:   Military Expenditures as a Percent of
            Central Government Expenditures 1967.
            Source: USACDA: World Mil. Expenditures &
            Arms Transfers: 1967-76.

MLXPER68:   Military Expenditures per capita in
            Millions of Current Dollars.
            Source: USACDA. World Military Expendi-
            tures and Arms Transfers: 1968-1977.

MXGNP61:   Military Expenditures in Current Dollars.
            Source: USACDA: World Military Expendi-
            tures: 1971.

MXGNP68:   Military Expenditures as a Percentage of
            GNP.
            Source: USACDA. World Military Expendi-
            tures and Arms Transfers: 1968-1977.

MXGNP70:   Military Expenditures as a Percent of GNP
            (Current $).
            Source: USACDA: World Military Expendi-
            tures: 1971.

MXGNP77:   Military Expenditures as a Percent of GNP.
            Source: USACDA. World Military Expenditure
            and Arms Transfers: 1968-1977.

NAIPER63: Per Capita National Income, ($Market Prices).
Source: UN Statistical Yearbook: 1972. pp. 621-6.

NEWSPR60: Daily General Interest Newspaper Circulation Per 1000 Inhabitants.
Source: UNESCO Statistical Yearbook: 1964.

NEWSPR70: Daily General Interest Newspaper Circulation Per 1000 Inhabitants.
Source: UNESCO Statistical Yearbook: 1976.

IRREG67: Electoral Irregularities: 1959-1967.
1=Free, Competitive; 2=Not Free or None.
Source: C.L. Taylor, M.C. Hudson. World Handb. of Political & Social Indicators. N. Haven: Yale Univ. Pr. 1979.

PARTY68: Party Fractionalization: 1962-1968. Seats.
Source: C.L. Taylor, M.C. Hudson. World Handb. of Political & Social Indic. N. Haven: Yale Univ. Pr.,1979.

PRESS67: Press Freedom Index: 1961-1967, (Maximum 4.00, Minimum -4.00).
Source: C.L. Taylor, M.C. Hudson. W. Handb. of Political & Social Indicators. N. Haven: Yale Univ. Pr., 1979.

PRISON75: Polit. Repr. Indicators 1967-75: Prison Mistreatment and/or Political Detention 1=Yes, 2=No.
Source: Amnesty International Rept. on Torture 1973. Amnesty International Report: 1975-76.

PRISON79: Polit. Repress. Inds. 1976-79: Prison Mistreatment and/or Political Detention, 1=Yes, 2=No.
Source: Amnesty Internat. Report on Torture: 1979. US State Dept. Report on Human Rights: 1979.

PROPER60: Protein Supply Per Capita: Average Grams Daily.
Source: World Tables: 1976. World Bank, pp. 518-21.

Appendix C

PROPER70: Protein Supply Per Capita: Average Grams
           Daily.
           Source: World Tables: 1976. World Bank,
           pp. 518-521.

PROPER76: Protein Supply Per Capita: Average Grams
           Daily.
           Source: R. Sivard. World Military and
           Social Expenditures 1979. pp. 29-33.

PRVPER76: Public Revenues Per Capita: Average Grams
           Daily.
           Source: George Thomas Kurian. The Book of
           World Rankings. N.Y.: Facts on File,
           1979.

PTRPED60: Pupil Teacher Ratios in Primary
           Education.
           Source: World Atlas of the Child. World
           Bank, 1979.

PTRPED70: Pupil Teacher Ratios in Primary Education.
           Source: World Atlas of the Child. World
           Bank, 1979.

PTRPED77: Pupil Teacher Ratios in Primary
           Education.
           Source: UNESCO Statistical Yearbook:
           1978-1979. pp. 226-250.

PUCGDP60: Public Consumption as a Percent of GDP.
           Source: World Development Report: 1980.
           World Bank, pp. 118-119.

PUCGDP78: Public Consumption as a Percent of GDP.
           Source: World Development Report: 1980.
           World Bank, pp. 118-119.

TORTUR75: Political Repression Indicators: 1967-75.
           Executions, Disappearances or Torture:
           1=Yes, 2=No.
           Source: Amnesty International Report on
           Torture: 1973.

TORTUR79: Political Repression indicators: 1976-9.
           Executions, Disappearances or Torture.
           1=Yes, 2=No.
           Source: Amnesty International Report on
           Torture: 1979. US State Dept. Report on
           Human Rights: 1979.

Appendix C

UNEMAV69: Unemployment, (Average Percentage):
1968-1969.
Source: UN Statistical Yearbook: 1978.

UNEMAV77: Unemployment (Average Percentage):
1976-1977.
Source: UN Statistical Yearbook: 1978.

USMAID69: US Military Aid (Millions of Dollars).
Source: Stephen P. Gilbert:
Soviet-American Military Aid Competition
in the Third World. Orbis (Winter 1974).

USMAID76: US Military Assistance Program Total:
1946-1976 (Million Current Dollars by
Fiscal Year).
Source: M.T. Klare, Supplying Repression.
NY: The Field Foundation, 1977. pp. 31-3.

USTRNG76: U.S. Training of Foreign Military
Personnel: Fiscal Years 1950-1976
(Number).
Source: US Defense Security Assistance
Agency. Foreign Military Sales and
Military Assistance Facts. Washington,
1977. pp.36-7.

VOTERS67: Voters as a Percent of Electorate:
1960-1967.
Source: C.L. Taylor, M.C. Hudson, World
Handbook of Political & Social Indicators.
N. Haven: Yale Univ. Pr. 1979.

WKRSID68: Workers Involved in Industrial Disputes:
1960-1968.
Source: Yearbook of Labour Statistics:
1969. pp. 758-61.

WKRSID77: Workers Involved in Industrial Disputes:
1968-1977.
Source: Yearbook of Labour Statistics:
1978.

WKRSID79: Workers Involved in Industrial Disputes:
1971-1979.
Source: Yearbook of Labour Statistics:
1981. pp 605-12.

WOMLF60: Women as a Percent of Total Labour Force.

Source: World Tables: 1980. World Bank,
pp. 460-4.

Appendix C

WOMLF70:   Women as a Percent of Total Labour Force.
             Source: World Tables: 1980. World Bank,
             pp. 460-4.

WOMLF77:   Women as a Percent of Total Labour Force
             (1977, Most Recent Estimate).
             Source: World Tables: 1980. World Bank,
             pp. 460-4.

APPENDIX D: CIVILIAN AND MILITARY NATION LIST

1. CIVMIL67

   a. <u>Civilian</u>

Albania	Nigeria
Argentina	North Korea
Bangladesh	Panama
Benin	Peru
Bulgaria	Philippines
Burundi	Romania
Cameroon	Rwanda
Central Africa	Senegal
Chad	Sierra Leone
Chile	Singapore
China	Somalia
Colombia	South Africa
Congo	South Yemen
Costa Rica	Sri Lanka
Cuba	Tanzania
Cyprus	Thailand
Dominican Rep.	Trinidad
Ethiopia	Tunisia
Gabon	Turkey
Gambia	Uganda
Ghana	Upper Volta
Greece	Uruguay
Guinea	Venezuela
Guyana	Yugoslavia
Haiti	Zaire
India	Zambia
Indonesia	Zimbabwe
Iran	
Ivory Coast	
Jamaica	b. <u>Military</u>
Jordan	
Kenya	Burma
Lebanon	Egypt
Lesotho	Guatemala
Liberia	Iraq
Madagascar	Nicaragua
Malawi	Pakistan
Malaysia	Paraguay
Mali	South Korea
Mauritania	Syria
Mauritius	Taiwan
Mexico	Yemen
Mongolia	
Morocco	
Nepal	
Niger	

Appendix D

2. CIVMIL78

a. Civilian

Albania
Bangladesh
Bulgaria
Cameroon
Chad
Chile
China
Colombia
Costa Rica
Cuba
Cyprus
Dominican Rep.
Ethiopia
Gabon
Gambia
Greece
Guinea
Guyana
Haiti
India
Iran
Ivory Coast
Jamaica
Jordan
Kenya
Lebanon
Lesotho
Liberia
Madagascar
Malawi
Malaysia
Mauritania
Mauritius
Mexico
Mongolia
Morocco
Nepal
Niger
North Korea
Philippines
Romania
Rwanda
Senegal
Sierra Leone
Singapore
South Africa

South Yemen
Sri Lanka
Tanzania
Trinidad
Tunisia
Turkey
Uruguay
Venezuela
Yugoslavia
Zambia
Zimbabwe

b. Military

Algeria
Argentina
Benin
Bolivia
Brazil
Burma
Congo
Ecuador
Egypt
El Salvador
Ghana
Guatemala
Honduras
Indonesia
Iraq
Nicaragua
Nigeria
Pakistan
Paraguay
South Korea
Sudan
Syria
Taiwan
Thailand
Togo
Upper Volta
Yemen
Zaire

Appendix D

3. CIVMIL6578

a. Civilian   b. Military

Albania   Tanzania   Algeria
Bulgaria   Trinidad   Argentina
Burundi   Tunisia   Benin
Cameroon   Turkey   Bolivia
Chad   Venezuela   Botswana
China   Yugoslavia   Brazil
Colombia   Zambia   Burma
Costa Rica   Zimbabwe   Central Afr. Rep.
Cuba   Chile
Cyprus   Congo
Dominican Rep.   Ecuador
Ethiopia   Egypt
Fiji   El Salvador
Gabon   Ghana
Gambia   Guatemala
Guinea   Honduras
Guyana   Indonesia
Haiti   Iraq
India   Kampuchea
Iran   Laos
Ivory Coast   Madagascar
Jamaica   Mali
Jordan   Nigeria
Kenya   Pakistan
Lebanon   Panama
Lesotho   Paraguay
Liberia   Peru
Malawi   Somalia
Malaysia   South Korea
Mauritania   Sudan
Mauritius   Syria
Mexico   Taiwan
Mongolia   Thailand
Morocco   Togo
Mozambique   Upper Volta
Nepal   Yemen
Nicaragua   Zaire
Niger
North Korea
Philippines   c. Mixed
Romania   Angola
Senegal   Bangladesh
Sierra Leone   Greece
Singapore   Rwanda
South Africa   Uganda
South Yemen   Uruguay
Sri Lanka   Vietnam

APPENDIX E: DEVELOPMENT STRATEGY NATION LIST

1. DEVSTR78

a. Open Door

Argentina	Niger	
Bangladesh	Nigeria	
Benin	Pakistan	
Bolivia	Panama	
Botswana	Paraguay	
Brazil	Philippines	
Burundi	Rwanda	
Cameroon	Senegal	
Cent. Afr. Rep.	Sierra Leone	
Chad	Singapore	
Chile	South Africa	
Colombia	South Korea	
Costa Rica	Sudan	
Cyprus	Taiwan	
Dominican Rep.	Thailand	
Ecuador	Togo	
El Salvador	Trinidad	
Ethiopia	Tunisia	
Gabon	Turkey	
Gambia	Upper Volta	
Ghana	Uruguay	
Greece	Venezuela	
Guatemala	Yemen	
Guyana	Zaire	
Haiti	Zambia	
Honduras	Zimbabwe	
India		
Indonesia		
Iran		
Ivory Coast		
Jamaica		
Jordan		
Kenya		
Lebanon		
Lesotho		
Liberia		
Madagascar		
Malawi		
Malaysia		
Mali		
Mauritania		
Mauritius		
Mexico		
Morocco		
Nepal		
Nicaragua		

b. State Capitalist

Algeria
Burma
Guinea
Iraq

c. State Socialist

Albania
Bulgaria
Cuba
Mongolia
North Korea
Romania
Yugoslavia

d. Mixed

China
Congo
Egypt
Peru
Somalia
South Yemen
Sri Lanka
Syria
Tanzania
Uganda

Appendix E

2. DSTRAT69

a. <u>Open door</u>   b. <u>State</u>
                                                       <u>capitalist</u>

Argentina   Panama
Bangladesh   Paraguay   Algeria
Benin   Philippines   Burma
Bolivia   Rwanda   Egypt
Botswana   Senegal   Guinea
Cameroon   Sierra Leone   Iraq
Cent. Afr. Rep.   Singapore
Chad   Somalia
Chile   South Africa
Colombia   South Korea   c. <u>State</u>
Congo   South Yemen   <u>socialist</u>
Costa Rica   Sri Lanka
Cyprus   Sudan   Albania
Dominican Rep.   Syria   Bulgaria
Ecuador   Taiwan   China
El Salvador   Tanzania   Cuba
Ethiopia   Thailand   North Korea
Gabon   Togo   Romania
Gambia   Trinidad   Yugoslavia
Greece   Tunisia
Guatemala   Uganda
Guyana   Upper Volta
Haiti   Uruguay   d. <u>Mixed</u>
Honduras   Venezuela
India   Zaire   Brazil
Indonesia   Zambia   Ghana
Iran   Zimbabwe   Turkey
Jordan   Yemen
Kenya
Lebanon
Lesotho
Liberia
Madagascar
Malawi
Malaysia
Mali
Mauritania
Mauritius
Mexico
Mongolia
Morocco
Nepal
Nicaragua
Niger
Nigeria
Pakistan

3. DSTRAT78

a. Open door

Argentina	Panama
Bangladesh	Paraguay
Bolivia	Philippines
Botswana	Rwanda
Brazil	Senegal
Burundi	Sierra Leone
Cameroon	Singapore
Cent. Afr. Rep.	South Africa
Chad	South Korea
Chile	Sudan
Colombia	Taiwan
Costa Rica	Thailand
Cyprus	Togo
Dominican Rep.	Trinidad
Ecuador	Tunisia
Egypt	Turkey
El Salvador	Upper Volta
Ethiopia	Uruguay
Gabon	Venezuela
Gambia	Yemen
Ghana	Zaire
Greece	Zambia
Guatemala	Zimbabwe
Haiti	
Honduras	
India	
Indonesia	
Iran	
Ivory Coast	
Jordan	
Kenya	
Lebanon	
Lesotho	
Liberia	
Malawi	
Malaysia	
Mali	
Mauritania	
Mauritius	
Mexico	
Morocco	
Nepal	
Nicaragua	
Niger	
Nigeria	
Pakistan	

b. State capitalist

Algeria
Benin
Burma
Congo
China
Guinea
Iraq
Jamaica
Madagascar
Peru
Somalia
South Yemen
Sri Lanka
Syria
Tanzania
Uganda

c. State socialist

Albania
Bulgaria
Cuba
Mongolia
North Korea
Romania
Yugoslavia

d. Mixed

Guyana

4. DVST6578

a. Open door

a. Open door		b. State capitalist
Angola	Pakistan	Algeria
Argentina	Panama	Burma
Bangladesh	Paraguay	Congo
Benin	Philippines	Guinea
Bolivia	Rwanda	Iraq
Botswana	Senegal	Mali
Brazil	Sierra Leone	Somalia
Burundi	Singapore	South Yemen
Cameroon	South Africa	Syria
Central Africa	South Korea	Tanzania
Chad	Sudan	Yugoslavia
Chile	Taiwan	Zambia
Colombia	Thailand	
Costa Rica	Togo	
Cyprus	Trinidad	c. State
Dominican Rep.	Tunisia	socialist
Ecuador	Turkey	
El Salvador	Uganda	Albania
Ethiopia	Upper Volta	Bulgaria
Fiji	Uruguay	China
Gabon	Venezuela	Cuba
Gambia	Zaire	Mongolia
Ghana	Zimbabwe	North Korea
Greece		Romania
Guatemala		
Haiti		
Honduras		
India		d. Mixed
Indonesia		
Iran		Egypt
Ivory Coast		Guyana
Jordan		Jamaica
Kampuchea		Madagascar
Kenya		Peru
Laos		Sri Lanka
Lebanon		Vietnam
Lesotho		Yemen
Liberia		
Malawi		
Malaysia		
Mauritania		
Mauritius		
Mexico		
Morocco		

APPENDIX F: REPRESSION AND TORTURE NATION LIST

1. TORTUR75

    a. <u>Yes</u>

		b. <u>No</u>
Albania	Taiwan	Algeria
Argentina	Togo	Angola
Bangladesh	Tunisia	Benin
Bolivia	Turkey	Botswana
Brazil	Uganda	Burma
Bulgaria	Uruguay	Cent. Afr. Rep.
Burundi	Venezuela	China
Cameroon	Vietnam	Congo
Chad	Yemen	Costa Rica
Chile	Zambia	Gabon
Colombia	Zimbabwe	Guinea
Cuba		Guyana
Cyprus		Ivory Coast
Dominican Rep.		Jamaica
Ecuador		Kenya
Egypt		Laos
El Salvador		Lesotho
Ethiopia		Madagascar
Ghana		Malawi
Greece		Malaysia
Guatemala		Mali
Haiti		Mozambique
Honduras		Nepal
India		Romania
Indonesia		Somalia
Iran		Tanzania
Iraq		Thailand
Jordan		Yugoslavia
Kampuchea		Zaire
Mauritania		
Mexico		
Morocco		
Nicaragua		
Niger		
Nigeria		
Pakistan		
Panama		
Paraguay		
Peru		
Philippines		
Sierra Leone		
South Africa		
South Korea		
South Yemen		
Sri Lanka		
Sudan		
Syria		

2. TORTUR79

a. <u>Yes</u>   b. <u>No</u>

Angola	Venezuela	Algeria
Argentina	Yemen	Benin
Bangladesh	Zaire	Bolivia
Brazil	Zambia	Botswana
Cent. Afr. Rep.	Zimbabwe	Burma
Chad		Burundi
Chile		Cameroon
China		Costa Rica
Colombia		Cuba
Congo		Dominican Rep.
Cyprus		Ecuador
El Salvador		Egypt
Ethiopia		Fiji
Greece		Gabon
Guatemala		Gambia
Guinea		Ghana
Haiti		Guyana
India		Honduras
Indonesia		Iraq
Iran		Ivory Coast
Jordan		Jamaica
Malaysia		Kampuchea
Mexico		Kenya
Mozambique		Laos
Nicaragua		Lebanon
Pakistan		Lesotho
Paraguay		Liberia
Peru		Madagascar
Philippines		Malawi
Senegal		Mali
Sierra Leone		Mauritania
Singapore		Mauritius
Somalia		Morocco
South Africa		Nepal
South Korea		Niger
South Yemen		Nigeria
Sudan		North Korea
Syria		Panama
Taiwan		Rwanda
Tanzania		Sri Lanka
Thailand	c. <u>Indeter-</u>	Trinidad
Togo	<u>minate</u>	Vietnam
Tunisia		
Turkey	Albania	
Uganda	Bulgaria	
Upper Volta	Romania	
Uruguay	Yugoslavia	

3. FREEDM73

a. More free

Argentina	Venezuela	
Bangladesh	Yemen	
Bolivia	Zambia	
Botswana	Zimbabwe	
Brazil		
Cameroon		
Chile		
Colombia		
Costa Rica		
Cyprus		
Dominican Rep.		
Ecuador		
El Salvador		
Ethiopia		
Fiji		
Gambia		
Guatemala		
Guyana		
Honduras		
India		
Indonesia		
Iran		
Jamaica		
Kampuchea		
Kenya		
Laos		
Lebanon		
Lesotho		
Madagascar		
Malaysia		
Mauritius		
Mexico		
Morocco		
Nepal		
Nicaragua		
Nigeria		
Pakistan		
Paraguay		
Philippines		
Sierra Leone		
South Africa		
South Korea		
Sri Lanka		
Taiwan		
Trinidad		
Tunisia		
Turkey		
Upper Volta		
Uruguay		

b. Less free

Albania
Algeria
Angola
Benin
Bulgaria
Burma
Burundi
Cent. Afr. Rep.
Chad
China
Congo
Cuba
Egypt
Gabon
Ghana
Greece
Guinea
Haiti
Iraq
Ivory Coast
Jordan
Liberia
Malawi
Mali
Mauritania
Mongolia
Mozambique
Niger
North Korea
Panama
Peru
Romania
Rwanda
Senegal
Singapore
Somalia
South Yemen
Sudan
Syria
Tanzania
Thailand
Togo
Uganda
Vietnam
Yugoslavia
Zaire

4. FREEDM82

a. <u>More free</u>

Bangladesh
Botswana
Brazil
Colombia
Costa Rica
Cyprus
Dominican Rep.
Ecuador
El Salvador
Fiji
Gambia
Ghana
Greece
Guyana
Honduras
India
Indonesia
Ivory Coast
Jamaica
Kenya
Lebanon
Lesotho
Malaysia
Mauritius
Mexico
Morocco
Nepal
Nigeria
Panama
Paraguay
Peru
Philippines
Senegal
Sierra Leone
Singapore
South Korea
Sri Lanka
Taiwan
Thailand
Trinidad
Tunisia
Turkey
Uganda
Uruguay
Venezuela
Zimbabwe

b. <u>Less free</u>

Albania
Algeria
Angola
Argentina
Benin
Bolivia
Bulgaria
Burma
Burundi
Cameroon
Cent. Afr. Rep.
Chad
Chile
China
Congo
Cuba
Egypt
Ethiopia
Gabon
Guatemala
Guinea
Haiti
Iran
Iraq
Jordan
Kampuchea
Laos
Liberia
Madagascar
Malawi
Mali
Mauritania
Mongolia
Mozambique
Nicaragua
Niger
North Korea
Pakistan
Romania
Rwanda
Somalia
South Africa
South Yemen
Sudan
Syria
Tanzania
Togo

Upper Volta
Vietnam
Yemen
Yugoslavia
Zaire
Zambia

5. PRESS67

    a. **More free**   b. **Less free**

More free	Less free	
Argentina	Albania	Paraguay
Bolivia	Algeria	Romania
Brazil	Angola	Rwanda
Chad	Bangladesh	Senegal
Chile	Benin	Sierra Leone
Colombia	Bonin Island	Somalia
Costa Rica	Botswana	South Korea
Cyprus	Burma	South Yemen
Dominican Rep.	Burundi	Sudan
Ecuador	Cameroon	Syria
El Salvador	Cent. Afr. Rep.	Taiwan
Greece	China	Thailand
India	Congo	Togo
Jamaica	Cuba	Trinidad
Kenya	Egypt	Tunisia
Lebanon	Ethiopia	Uganda
Malaysia	Fiji	Upper Volta
Mexico	Gabon	Vietnam
Morocco	Gambia	Yemen
Panama	Ghana	Yugoslavia
Peru	Guatemala	Zaire
Philippines	Guinea	
Singapore	Guyana	
South Africa	Haiti	
Sri Lanka	Honduras	
Tanzania	Indonesia	
Turkey	Iran	
Uruguay	Iraq	
Venezuela	Ivory Coast	
Zambia	Jordan	
Zimbabwe	Kampuchea	
	Laos	
	Lesotho	
	Liberia	
	Madagascar	
	Malawi	
	Mali	
	Malta	
	Mauritania	
	Mauritius	
	Mongolia	
	Mozambique	
	Nepal	
	Nicaragua	
	Niger	
	Nigeria	
	North Korea	
	Pakistan	

Table 1: The Widening Gap between Rich and Poor
         Nations

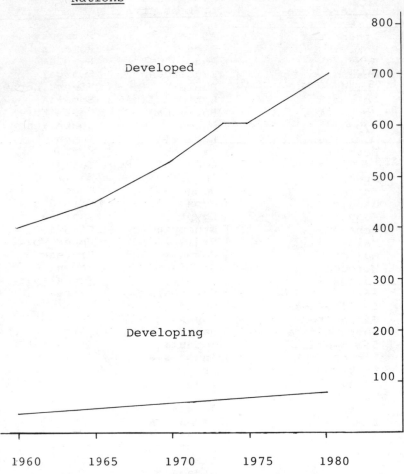

Source: Ruth Leger Sivard. World Military and Social
Expenditures, Leesburg, VA: World Priorities, 1981,
p.18.

   GNP Per Capita.   1978 Dollars.

Table 2: The Inequality of Global Violence

A. Estimated World Totals, 1965 Deaths from:
   International Violence   11 500-23 000
   Civil Violence   92 000
   Structural Violence   14 000 000-18 000 000

B. Distribution of Violent Deaths, 1965 (World =
   100% in each Category)

Affluent 'North'	population	30.6%
	international violence	9.1%
	civil violence	.1%
	structural violence	4.2%
Poor 'South'	population	69.4%
	international violence	90.9%
	civil violence	99.9%
	structural violence	95.8%

Source: Gernot Kohler and Norman Alcock, "An Empirical Table of Structural Violence", Journal of
Peace Research 12:4 (1976):345-349, as reproduced
by Kohler, Global Apartheid. New York: Institute
for World Order, 1978, p. 8.

Table 3: Estimates of Employment Generated by $1 Billion Federal Spending in Various Activities

Program	Jobs
B-1 Bomber	58,000
Army Corps of Engineers	69,000
Law Enforcement	75,000
Sanitation	78,000
Mass Transit Construction	83,000
Public Housing	84,000
Highway Construction	84,000
Conservation and Recreation	88,000
Welfare Payments	99,000
Social Security	108,000
Education	118,000

Source: Gordon Adams. The B-1 Bomber: An Analysis of Its Strategic Utility, Cost, Constituency and Economic Impact New York: Council of Economic Priorities, 1976. As reproduced by Seymour Melman. "Inflation and Unemployment as Products of War Economy," Bulletin of Peace Proposals, v.n. 4(1979):364.

Table 4: Military Burdens, Civil Expenditures and Economic Indicators for Advanced Capitalist States: 1960-1979

	Military Spending/GDP|		
	1960-1979	1970-1979	1960 1969
Civil Government/GDP	-.19	-.10	-.17
Wages	.21	.23	.32
GDP Growth	-.58||	-.49	-.53
Productivity Growth	-.66	-.43	-.75
Investment/GDP	-.52	-.61	-.42
Private Consumption/GDP	.29	.26	.17

Source: Robert DeGrasse Jr. with Paul Murphy and William Ragen, The Costs and Consequences of Reagan's Military Buildup. New York: Council on Economic Priorities, 1982. p. 53.

| Spearman Rank Correlation Coefficients

|| Correlations underlined are significant at .05 or less.

Table 5: <u>Military Burden Indicators</u>

	AFRTIO67	MXGNP68	MIXCGE67	MLXPER68	USTAFS	ARMIMT77
AFRTIO67	1.000	.632	.290	.647	-.087	.324
	94	88	87	85	56	85
		.000	.003	.000	.263	.001
MXGNP68	.632	1.000	.672	.739	-.230	.497
	88	92	84	89	57	87
	.000		.000	.000	.043	.000
MIXCGE67	.290	.672	1.000	.328	-.235	.233
	87	84	90	81	53	80
	.003	.000		.001	.045	.019
MLXPER68	.647	.739	.328	1.000	-.134	.531
	85	89	81	89	55	85
	.000	.000	.001		.165	.000
USTAFS	-.087	-.230	-.235	-.134	1.000	-.158
	56	57	53	55	57	55
	.263	.043	.045	.165		.125
ARMIMT77	.324	.497	.233	.531	-.158	1.000
	85	87	80	85	55	88
	.001	.000	.019	.000	.125	

Source: PRIO Data Bank; Appendix C.

Table 6: Physical Welfare Indicators: 1976–1978

	CHLPER75	PROPER76	WOMLF77	PTRPED77	FPRSCH77	FSCSCH77	CALPER77	LITRCY78	CHILDM78
PROPER76	-.009 90 .466								
WOMLF77	.394 91 .000	.034 90 .376							
PTRPED77	.503 82 .000	.015 81 .446	.212 82 .028						
FPRSCH77	-.517 90 .000	.015 85 .446	.097 86 .188	-.090 80 .213					
FSCSCH77	-.703 87 .000	.043 81 .352	-.041 81 .357	-.466 78 .000	.584 83 .000				
CALPER77	-.504 86 .000	.118 84 .143	.158 85 .075	-.355 77 .001	.449 81 .000	.583 75 .000			
LITRCY78	-.727 96 .000	.164 90 .061	-.029 91 .392	-.434 82 .000	.720 89 .000	.788 85 .000	.621 86 .000		
CHILDM78	.710 91 .000	-.109 85 .160	.025 86 .408	.481 78 .000	-.728 85 .000	-.768 80 .000	-.666 86 .000	-.906 90 .000	
LIFEXB78	-.743 93 .000	.115 85 .148	-.040 86 .357	-.500 78 .000	.715 86 .000	.782 82 .060	.669 86 .000	.898 91 .000	-.975 92 .000

Source: Appendix C.
Brief variable titles for this and succeeding tables appear in Appendix B.

Table 7: <u>Military Burdens, Civilian vs Military Rule and</u>
<u>Development Strategy: 1965–1978</u>

	MXGNP68 Breakdown			
CVML6578	<u>Civilian</u>	<u>Military</u>	<u>Mixed</u>	<u>Total</u>
Mean	3.260	3.389	2.550	3.278
SD	4.010	2.934	1.396	3.530
N	52	35	4	91
$\mid R^2$.001				

DVST6578	<u>Open door</u>	State <u>capitalist</u>	State <u>socialist</u>	<u>Mixed</u>	<u>Total</u>
Mean	2.388	4.975	10.300	2.743	3.278
SD	2.618	3.576	4.467	2.905	3.530
N	66	12	6	7	91
$\mid R^2$.34					

Source: Appendix C.
$\mid$ Eta on this and succeeding breakdowns. Total R^2.3718

Table 8. Civilian vs Military Rule and Development Strategy
(1965–1978) with Military Burdens

	MXGNP68 Breakdown			
DVST6578				
	Civilian	Military	Mixed	Total
Open door				
Mean	2.261	2.562	2.550	2.388
SD	2.969	2.207	1.396	2.618
N	38	24	4	66
State capitalist				
Mean	3.920	5.729		4.975
SD	3.063	3.950		3.576
N	5	7	0	6
Mixed				
Mean	.733	4.250		2.743
SD	.252	3.125		2.905
N	6	4	0	6
Total				
Mean	3.260	3.389	2.550	3.278
SD	4.010	2.934	1.396	3.530
N	52	35	4	91

Source: Appendix C.
| DVST6578 R^2.34; CVML6578 R^2.001; Total $R^2$37

Table 9: Civilian vs Military Rule and Development Strategy Controls (1965-1978), with U.S. Military Training

	USTAFS (USTRNG76 as a % of AFSIZE77) Breakdown				
CVML6578|		DVST6578|			
	Open door	State capitalist	State socialist	Mixed	Total
Civilian					
Mean	9.123	.176	.261	.658	7.617
SD	17.859	.192	.000	.624	16.532
N	24	2	1	2	29
Military					
Mean	9.544	.419		2.902	7.552
SD	13.701	.397		4.041	12.446
N	19	4	0	2	25
Mixed					
Mean	7.471				7.471
SD	3.610				3.610
N	2	0	0	0	2
Total					
Mean	9.227	.338	.261	1.780	7.583
SD	15.621	.343	.000	2.693	14.387
N	45	6	1	4	56

Source: Appendix C.
\|DVST6578 R^2.05; CVML6578 R^2.001; Total R^2.06

Table 10: Civilian vs Military Rule and Development Strategy Controls (1965-1978) with Child Mortality (1978) and Women in the Labour Force (1977)

DVST6578	CHILDM78 Breakdown CVML6578				WOMLF77 Breakdown CVML6578			
	Civilian	Military	Mixed	Total	Civilian	Military	Mixed	Total
Open door								
Mean	17.600	16.292	17.500	17.108	28.916	30.665	31.980	29.758
SD	10.207	10.157	13.233	10.320	11.662	13.358	11.172	12.107
N	35	24	6	65	38	23	5	66
State capitalist								
Mean	22.200	21.714		21.917	30.040	24.329		26.708
SD	12.892	7.952		9.746	14.253	17.328		15.694
N	5	7	0	12	5	7	0	12
State socialist								
Mean	2.286			2.286	40.917			40.917
SD	1.890			1.890	4.600			4.600
N	7	0	0	7	6	0	0	6
Mixed								
Mean	2.000	23.000	6.000	14.571	30.433	19.950		24.443
SD	1.414	7.165	.000	11.759	7.197	18.972		15.121
N	2	4	1	7	3	4	0	7
Total								
Mean	15.245	18.143	15.857	16.407	50.496	28.100	31.980	29.682
SD	11.359	9.659	12.838	10.816	11.548	14.897	11.172	12.811
N	49	35	7	91	52	34	5	91

Source: Appendix C.
| CVML6578 R^2 .02; DVST6578 R^2 .17; Total R^2 .24
|| CVML6578 R^2 .01; DVST5678 R^2 .07; Total R^2 .10

Table 11: Economic and Political Control Variables

	PUCGDP78	MFGDP70	GVTGDP70	CGFCF77	AIDPER75	EPDGNP78	PRESS67	FREEDM73
PUCGDP78	1.000 73	-.133 57 .163	.130 69 .143	-.135 40 .204	.460 66 .000	.528 71 .000	-.218 48 .068	.369 73 .001
MFGDP70	-.133 57 .163	1.000 68	.150 67 .112	-.282 42 .035	-.226 62 .039	.004 62 .487	.395 48 .003	-.335 68 .003
GVTGDP70	.130 69 .143	.150 67 .112	1.000 83	-.266 44 .041	.053 76 .324	.139 73 .121	.059 54 .335	-.038 83 .368
CGFCF77	-.135 40 .204	-.282 42 .035	-.266 44 .041	1.000 46	.066 40 .343	-.139 42 .189	-.141 37 .202	.187 46 .107
AIDPER75	.460 66 .000	-.226 62 .039	.053 76 .324	.066 40 .343	1.000 85	.441 70 .000	-.108 48 .232	.115 85 .147
EPDGNP78	.528 71 .000	.004 62 .487	.139 73 .121	-.139 42 .189	.441 70 .000	1.000 77	-.100 52 .241	.219 77 .028
PRESS67	-.218 48 .068	.395 48 .003	.059 54 .335	-.141 37 .202	-.108 48 .232	-.100 52 .241	1.000 60	-.524 60 .000
FREEDM73	.369 73 .001	-.335 68 .003	-.038 83 .368	.187 46 .107	.115 85 .147	.219 77 .028	-.524 60 .000	1.000 100

Sources: Appendix C.

Table 12: Foreign Aid Variables – Economic and Military

	AIDPER75	AIDMIL75	USMIL75	LOAN7078	EPDGNP78	EDGP7078	EPDIMP79	USTAFS
AIDPER75	1.000 85	.148 77 .099	.284 46 .028	-.062 71 .303	.441 70 .000	-.022 67 .429	.047 77 .342	.208 51 .071
AIDMIL75	.148 77 .099	1.000 77	-.063 46 .338	-.081 70 .251	.075 69 .271	.064 66 .305	-.101 73 .198	-.081 51 .287
USMIL75	.284 46 .028	-.063 46 .338	1.000 47	.004 45 .489	-.008 45 .479	-.164 42 .150	-.107 45 .242	.170 43 .138
LOAN7078	-.062 71 .303	-.081 70 .251	.004 45 .489	1.000 78	.072 76 .268	.198 73 .047	-.108 75 .179	-.083 54 .275
EPDGNP78	.441 70 .000	.075 69 .271	-.008 45 .479	.072 76 .268	1.000 77	.121 74 .153	.472 74 .000	.353 53 .005
EDGP7078	-.022 67 .429	.064 67 .305	-.164 42 .150	.198 73 .047	.121 74 .153	1.000 74	-.054 71 .326	.027 50 .426
EPDIMP79	.047 77 .342	-.101 73 .198	-.107 45 .242	-.108 75 .179	.472 74 .000	-.054 71 .326	1.000 83	-.045 53 .375
USTAFS	.208 51 .071	-.081 51 .287	.170 43 .138	-.083 54 .275	.353 53 .005	.027 50 .426	-.045 53 .375	1.000 57

Source: Appendix C.

Table 13: Aid Per Capita (1973–1975) Control with Military
         Burden and Welfare Factors

AIDPER75 Breakdown

Above Median

	MILSPFAC	USTAFFAC	PHYSICAL	WOMENFAC
MILSPFAC	1.000	-.246	.284	-.686
	16	16	13	13
		.180	.173	.005
USTAFFAC	-.246	1.000	-.627	.233
	16	16	13	13
	.180		.011	.222
PHYSICAL	.284	-.627	1.000	-.117
	13	13	31	31
	.173	.011		.265
WOMENFAC	-.686	.233	-.117	1.000
	13	13	31	31
	.005	.222	.265	

Below Median

	MILSPFAC	USTAFFAC	PHYSICAL	WOMENFAC
MILSPFAC	1.000	.188	.072	-.573
	28	28	23	23
		.169	.372	.002
USTAFFAC	.188	1.000	-.323	-.205
	28	28	23	23
	.169		.066	.175
PHYSICAL	.072	-.323	1.000	.308
	23	23	29	29
	.372	.066		.052
WOMENFAC	-.573	-.205	.308	1.000
	23	23	29	29
	.002	.175	.052	

Sources: PRIO Data Bank; Appendix C.

158

Table 14: External Public Debt as Per Cent of GNP (1978)
Control with Military Burden and Welfare Factors

EPDGNP78 Breakdown

Above Median

	MILSPFAC	USTAFFAC	PHYSICAL	WOMENFAC
MILSPFAC	1.000	-.101	.198	-.662
	21	21	17	17
		.332	.223	.002
USTAFFAC	-.101	1.000	-.467	.050
	21	21	17	17
	.332		.029	.424
PHYSICAL	.198	-.467	1.000	-.128
	17	17	32	32
	.223	.029		.242
WOMENFAC	-.662	.050	-.128	1.000
	17	17	32	32
	.002	.424	.242	

Below Median

	MILSPFAC	USTAFFAC	PHYSICAL	WOMENFAC
MILSPFAC	1.000	.045	.355	-.227
	28	28	22	22
		.410	.053	.155
USTAFFAC	.045	1.000	-.411	.011
	28	28	22	22
	.410		.029	.480
PHYSICAL	.355	-.411	1.000	-.042
	22	22	30	30
	.053	.029		.414
WOMENFAC	-.227	.011	-.042	1.000
	22	22	30	30
	.155	.480	.414	

Sources: PRIO Data Bank; Appendix C.

Table 15: Government Expenditures as per cent of GDP (1970) and Public Consumption as per cent of GDP (1978) Controls with Military Burden Factor

GVTGDP70 Breakdown

Military burden

MILSPFAC	Above	Median	Below	Total
Mean	.181	.107	-.174	-.014
SD	1.176	.960	.875	1.010
N	21	2	27	50
R^2.03				

PUCGDP78 Breakdown

MILSPFAC	Above	Median	Below	Total
Mean	.267	.398	-.316	-.014
SD	1.308	1.458	.448	1.010
N	21	4	25	50
R^2.09				

Sources: PRIO Data Bank; Appendix C.

Table 16: Government Expenditures as per cent of GDP (1970) Control with Military Burden and Welfare Factors

GVTGDP70 Breakdown

Above Median

	MILSPFAC	USTAFFAC	PHYSICAL	WOMENFAC
MILSPFAC	1.000	.013	.132	-.304
	21	21	14	14
		.478	.327	.145
USTAFFAC	.013	1.000	-.492	-.024
	21	21	14	14
	.478		.037	.468
PHYSICAL	.132	-.492	1.000	-.095
	14	14	27	27
	.327	.037		.319
WOMENFAC	-.304	-.024	-.095	1.000
	14	14	27	27
	.145	.468	.319	

Below Median

	MILSPFAC	USTAFFAC	PHYSICAL	WOMENFAC
MILSPFAC	1.000	-.089	.273	-.593
	27	27	25	25
		.330	.094	.001
USTAFFAC	-.089	1.000	-.326	.082
	27	27	25	25
	.330		.056	.349
PHYSICAL	.273	-.326	1.000	-.267
	25	25	35	35
	.094	.056		.061
WOMENFAC	-.593	.082	-.267	1.000
	25	25	35	35
	.001	.349	.061	

Sources: PRIO Data Bank; Appendix C.

Table 17: Public Consumption as a per cent of GDP (1978) Control with Military Burden and Welfare Factors

PUCGDP78 Breakdown

Above Median

	MILSPFAC	USTAFFAC	PHYSICAL	WOMENFAC
MILSPFAC	1.000	.065	.297	-.579
	21	21	15	15
		.390	.141	.012
USTAFFAC	.065	1.000	-.442	.011
	21	21	15	15
	.390		.049	.484
PHYSICAL	.297	-.442	1.000	-.113
	15	15	29	29
	.141	.049		.280
WOMENFAC	-.579	.011	-.113	1.000
	15	15	29	29
	.012	.484	.280	

Below Median

	MILSPFAC	USTAFFAC	PHYSICAL	WOMENFAC
MILSPFAC	1.000	-.479	.401	.033
	25	25	22	22
		.008	.032	.442
USTAFFAC	-.479	1.000	-.412	.178
	25	25	22	22
	.008		.028	.214
PHYSICAL	.401	-.412	1.000	-.034
	22	22	30	30
	.032	.028		.430
WOMENFAC	.033	.178	-.034	1.000
	22	22	30	30
	.442	.214	.430	

Sources: PRIO Data Bank; Appendix C.

Table 18: Manufacturing as a per cent of GDP (1970) Control with Military Burden and Welfare Factors

MFGDP70 Breakdown

Above Median

	MILSPFAC	USTAFFAC	PHYSICAL	WOMENFAC
MILSPFAC	1.000	.019	.038	-.028
	22	22	20	20
		.467	.437	.453
USTAFFAC	.019	1.000	-.267	-.015
	22	22	20	20
	.467		.128	.474
PHYSICAL	.038	-.267	1.000	.537
	20	20	27	27
	.437	.128		.002
WOMENFAC	-.028	-.015	.537	1.000
	20	20	27	27
	.453	.474	.002	

Below Median

	MILSPFAC	USTAFFAC	PHYSICAL	WOMENFAC
MILSPFAC	1.000	.151	.646	-.714
	20	20	14	14
		.262	.006	.002
USTAFFAC	.151	1.000	.120	-.106
	20	20	14	14
	.262		.341	.360
PHYSICAL	.646	.120	1.000	-.290
	14	14	25	25
	.006	.341		.080
WOMENFAC	-.714	-.106	-.290	1.000
	14	14	25	25
	.002	.360	.080	

Sources: PRIO Data Bank; Appendix C.

Gross Domestic Product Average Annual Growth Rate (1960-1970) Control with Military Burden and Welfare Factors

CGDP70 Breakdown

Above Median

	MILSPFAC	USTAFFAC	PHYSICAL	WOMENFAC
MILSPFAC	1.000 25	.095 25 .326	.219 19 .183	-.390 19 .049
USTAFFAC	.095 25 .326	1.000 25	-.320 19 .091	.037 19 .440
PHYSICAL	.219 19 .183	-.320 19 .091	1.000 31	.041 31 .414
WOMENFAC	-.390 19 .049	.037 19 .440	.041 31 .414	1.000 31

Below Median

	MILSPFAC	USTAFFAC	PHYSICAL	WOMENFAC
MILSPFAC	1.000 23	-.202 23 .178	.613 18 .003	-.341 18 .083
USTAFFAC	-.202 23 .178	1.000 23	-.533 18 .011	.110 18 .332
PHYSICAL	.613 18 .003	-.533 18 .011	1.000 31	-.148 31 .213
WOMENFAC	-.341 18 .083	.110 18 .332	-.148 31 .213	1.000 31

Sources: PRIO Data Bank; Appendix C.

Table 20: Press Freedom Control with Military Burden
and Welfare Factors (1961-1967)

PRESS67 Breakdown

More Free - Above Median

	MILSPFAC	USTAFFAC	PHYSICAL	WOMENFAC
MILSPFAC	1.000	-.157	.187	.247
	22	22	19	19
		.242	.222	.154
USTAFFAC	-.157	1.000	-.169	.261
	22	22	19	19
	.242		.245	.140
PHYSICAL	.187	-.169	1.000	.044
	19	19	25	25
	.222	.245		.417
WOMENFAC	.247	.261	.044	1.000
	19	19	25	25
	.154	.140	.417	

Less Free - Below Median|

	MILSPFAC	USTAFFAC	PHYSICAL	WOMENFAC
MILSPFAC	1.000	-.043	.521	-.655
	28	28	20	20
		.414	.009	.001
USTAFFAC	-.043	1.000	-.235	-.062
	28	28	20	20
	.414		.160	.397
PHYSICAL	.521	-.235	1.000	.011
	20	20	40	40
	.009	.160		.474
WOMENFAC	-.655	-.062	.011	1.000
	20	20	40	40
	.001	.397	.474	

Sources: PRIO Data Bank; Appendix C.

| .87 = Median (+4.0 - -4.0)

Table 21: <u>Political and Civil Rights (1973) Control</u>
<u>with Military Burden and Welfare Factors</u>

FREEDM73 Breakdown

Less Free - Above Median|

	MILSPFAC	USTAFFAC	PHYSICAL	WOMENFAC
MILSPFAC	1.000	.059	<u>.553</u>	<u>-.578</u>
	23	23	16	16
		.394	.013	.010
USTAFFAC	.059	1.000	<u>-.564</u>	-.115
	23	23	16	16
	.394		.011	.336
PHYSICAL	<u>.553</u>	<u>-.564</u>	1.000	.015
	16	16	33	33
	.013	.011		.467
WOMENFAC	<u>-.578</u>	-.115	.015	1.000
	16	16	33	33
	.010	.336	.467	

More Free - Below Median|

	MILSPFAC	USTAFFAC	PHYSICAL	WOMENFAC
MILSPFAC	1.000	<u>-.440</u>	.132	-.189
	27	27	23	23
		.011	.274	.194
USTAFFAC	<u>-.440</u>	1.000	-.281	.278
	27	27	23	23
	.011		.097	.100
PHYSICAL	.132	-.281	1.000	.004
	23	23	32	32
	.274	.097		.492
WOMENFAC	-.189	.278	.004	1.000
	23	23	32	32
	.194	.100	.492	

Sources: PRIO Data Bank; Appendix C.

| 5.50 (1-7, more to less free)

Table 22: Physical Indicators of Welfare Change: 1970 - 1978

	CHLPER	PROPER	WOMLF	PTRPED	FPRSCH	FSCSCH
CHLPER	1.000 99	.036 76 .378	-.009 89 .468	.116 80 .153	.178 87 .049	-.115 80 .154
PROPER	.036 76 .378	1.000 77	-.061 76 .299	.085 72 .240	.137 74 .121	-.139 72 .123
WOMLF	-.009 89 .468	-.061 76 .299	1.000 90	.098 79 .195	-.131 82 .120	-.111 78 .167
PTRPED	.116 80 .153	.085 72 .240	.098 79 .195	1.000 81	.206 78 .035	-.011 76 .461
FPRSCH	.178 87 .049	.137 74 .121	-.131 82 .120	.206 78 .035	1.000 88	-.116 77 .157
FSCSCH	-.115 80 .154	-.139 72 .123	-.111 78 .167	-.011 76 .461	-.116 77 .157	1.000 81
CALPER	-.028 72 .409	.245 70 .021	.072 71 .276	-.080 68 .259	-.032 70 .397	-.258 66 .018
CFOODP78	-.162 60 .109	-.041 48 .391	.082 55 .275	.056 51 .349	-.319 54 .009	-.240 51 .045
INFLAA78	.152 75 .096	-.023 65 .427	.017 72 .443	-.167 67 .089	-.085 70 .241	-.089 66 .239
FOODIN78	.127 72 .143	-.021 65 .433	.052 72 .332	-.101 68 .205	-.037 70 .380	-.074 68 .274
LITRCY	.062 92 .280	.466 76 .000	-.085 88 .216	.056 78 .312	-.002 83 .492	.137 78 .117
CHILDM	.108 35 .268	.096 33 .298	.006 35 .487	-.327 33 .031	.444 33 .005	.044 34 .403
LIFEXB	.149 92 .079	.247 71 .019	-.323 83 .001	.059 75 .307	.054 82 .315	.153 74 .097
INFL6078	-.087 74 .232	.037 63 .388	.057 71 .319	-.064 66 .306	-.017 69 .444	-.058 65 .323
EMPLOY78	.165 25 .216	-.094 23 .335	.032 24 .441	-.131 24 .271	.028 26 .447	-.121 25 .282

	CALPER	CFOODP78	INFLAA78	FOODIN78	LITRCY	CHILDM
CHLPER	-.028	-.162	.152	.127	.062	.108
	72	60	75	72	92	35
	.409	.109	.096	.143	.280	.268
PROPER	.245	-.041	-.023	-.021	.466	.096
	70	48	65	65	76	33
	.021	.391	.427	.433	.000	.298
WOMLF	.072	.082	.017	.052	-.085	.006
	71	55	72	72	88	35
	.276	.275	.443	.332	.216	.487
PTRPED	-.080	.056	-.167	-.101	.056	-.327
	68	51	67	68	78	33
	.259	.349	.089	.205	.312	.031
FPRSCH	-.032	-.319	-.085	-.037	-.002	.444
	70	54	70	70	83	33
	.397	.009	.241	.380	.492	.005
FSCSCH	-.258	-.240	-.089	-.074	.137	.044
	66	51	66	68	78	34
	.018	.045	.239	.274	.117	.403
CALPER	1.000	.350	.043	.035	.080	-.019
	73	47	65	61	72	35
		.008	.366	.395	.252	.456
CFOODP78	.350	1.000	-.113	-.177	-.096	-.025
	47	61	48	46	55	30
	.008		.223	.119	.243	.447
INFLAA78	.043	-.113	1.000	.883	-.074	-.036
	65	48	76	63	73	30
	.366	.223		.000	.267	.425
FOODIN78	.035	-.177	.883	1.000	-.068	-.032
	61	46	63	73	73	30
	.395	.119	.000		.285	.434
LITRCY	.080	-.096	-.074	-.068	1.000	.163
	72	55	73	73	93	36
	.252	.243	.267	.285		.172
CHILDM	-.019	-.025	-.036	-.032	.163	1.000
	35	30	30	30	36	36
	.456	.447	.425	.434	.172	
LIFEXB	-.119	-.142	-.080	.016	.322	.166
	72	59	76	67	87	36
	.160	.141	.246	.450	.001	.167
INFL6078	.483	.127	.021	-.014	.144	-.120
	64	47	73	63	73	31
	.000	.197	.431	.457	.112	.259
EMPLOY78	-.015	-.333	.992	.990	-.063	-.063
	22	19	19	24	25	16
	.474	.082	.000	.000	.382	.408

	LIFEXB	INFL6078	EMPLOY78
CHLPER	.149	-.087	.165
	92	74	25
	.079	.232	.216
PROPER	.247	.037	-.094
	71	63	23
	.019	.388	.335
WOMLF	-.323	.057	.032
	83	71	24
	.001	.319	.441
PTRPED	.059	-.064	-.131
	75	66	24
	.307	.306	.271
FPRSCH	.054	-.017	.028
	82	69	26
	.315	.444	.447
FSCSCH	.153	-.058	-.121
	74	65	25
	.097	.323	.282
CALPER	-.119	.483	-.015
	72	64	22
	.160	.000	.474
CFOODP78	-.142	.127	-.333
	59	47	19
	.141	.197	.082
INFLAA78	-.080	.021	.992
	76	73	19
	.246	.431	.000
FOODIN78	.016	-.014	.990
	67	63	24
	.450	.457	.000
LITRCY	.322	.144	-.063
	87	73	25
	.001	.112	.382
CHILDM	.166	-.120	-.063
	36	31	16
	.167	.259	.408
LIFEXB	1.000	-.046	.150
	93	75	23
		.347	.248
INFL6078	-.046	1.000	.063
	75	75	20
	.347		.396
EMPLOY78	.150	.063	1.000
	23	20	26
	.248	.396	

Sources: PRIO Data Bank, Appendix C.

Table 23: Aid Per Capita (1973–1975) Control with
Military Burden and Welfare Change
Indicators (1970–1978)

AIDPER 75

Above Median   Below Median

MILSPFAC|

  CHLPER -.53 (p .02, N 15)   CHILDM .80 (p .01, N 15)
  CALPER -.55 (p .02, N 16)

USTAFFAC|

  FPRSCH .52 (p .03, N 15)   WOMLF -.46 (p .01, N 28)

   Sources: PRIO Data Bank; Appendix C.
   | Regression coefficients lacking significance
    for other welfare change indicators excluded.

Table 24: External Public Debt as a percent of GNP (1978)
Control with Military Burden and Welfare Change
Indicators (1970–1978)

EPDGNP78

Above Median		Below Median	

MILSPFAC |

CALPER	−.47 (p .02, N 21)	CHLPER	.51 (p .01, N 28)
CFOODP78	−.60 (p .02, N 14)	PROPER	.50 (p .01, N 25)
		CALPER	.44 (p .01, N 28)

USTAFFAC |

FPRSCH	.55 (p .01, N 20)	WOMLF	−.57 (p .001, N 27)
		CFOODP78	−.45 (p .02, N 23)
		LIFEXB	.43 (p .02, N 28)

Sources: PRIO Data Bank; Appendix C.
| Regression coefficients lacking significance for other
welfare change indicators excluded.

Table 25: Gross Domestic Product Average Annual Growth
Rate (1960–1970) Control with Military Burden
and Welfare Change Indicators (1970–1978)

CGDP70

Above Median   Below Median

MILSPFAC|

CHLPER −.48 (p .008, N 25)   FPRSCH −.37 (p .04, N 22)
PROPER   .41 (p .03, N 23)
CALPER   .37 (p .03, N 25)

USTAFFAC|

FPRSCH   .43 (p .02, N 23)   WOMLF −.37 (p .04, N 23)
                                  LITRCY .37 (p .04, N 23)

Sources: PRIO Data Bank; Appendix C.
| Regression coefficients lacking significance for other
welfare change indicators excluded.

Table 26: Manufacturing as a percent of GDP (1970) Control with Military Burden and Welfare Change Indicators (1970-1978)

MFGDP70

Above Median   Below Median

MILSPFAC|

CHLPER -.40 (p .04, N 20)   CALPER   -.39 (p .05, N 20)
PROPER   .37 (p .04, N 22)   CFOODP78 -.58 (p .02, N 13)
CALPER   .52 (p .01, N 22)
LITRCY   .51 (p .01, N 22)
CHILDM   .45 (p .04, N 17)

USTAFFAC|

FPRSCH   .54 (p .006, N 21)   PROPER   -.41 (p .05, N 19)
                                     CALPER   -.38 (p .05, N 20)

Sources: PRIO Data Bank; Appendix C.
| Regression coefficients lacking significance for other welfare change indicators excluded.

Table 27: Government Expenditures as a percent of GDP (1970) Control with Military Burden and Welfare Change Indicators (1970-1978)

GVTGDP70

	Above Median	Below Median
MILSPFAC	CHLPER -.40 (p .04, N 20)	PTRPED -.33 (p .05, N 26) CALPER -.36 (p .03, N 27) CFOODP78 -.52 (p .02, N 18) CHILDM .79 (p .001, N 15)
USTAFFAC		CFOODP78 -.42 (p .05, N 18)

Sources: PRIO Data Bank; Appendix C.
| Regression coefficients lacking significance for other
  welfare change indicators excluded.

Table 28: Public Consumption as a percent of GDP (1978)
Control with Military Burden and Welfare
Change Indicators (1970-1978)

PUCGDP78

Above Median	Below Median
MILSPFAC	
CHLPER -.59 (p .01, N 20)	
USTAFFAC	
FPRSCH .58 (p .01, N 20)	CHILDM -.51 (p .03, N 15)

Sources: PRIO Data Bank; Appendix C.
Regression coefficients lacking significance for other
welfare change indicators excluded.

Table 29: Press Freedom (1961–1967) Control with Military
Burden and Welfare Change Indicators (1970–1978)

PRESS67

Above Median| Below Median|

MILSPFAC||

CHLPER −.53 (p .01, N 27)
WOMLF   .66 (p .01, N 26)

Sources: PRIO Data Bank; Appendix C.
| Median .87.
|| Regression coefficients lacking significance for other
welfare change indicators excluded.

Table 30: Political and Civil Rights (1973) Control with
Military Burden and Welfare Change Indicators
(1970–1978)

FREEDM73

Above Median| (least free)		Below Median| (most free)	

MILSPFAC\|\|

CHLPER	−.56 (p .01, N 18)	PROPER	.51 (p .01, N 31)
WOMLF	.78 (p .001, N 18)	CALPER	.45 (p .01, N 32)
CHILDM	.80 (p .01, N 8)		

USTAFFAC\|\|

| FPRSCH | .42 (p .05, N 17) |

Sources: PRIO Data Bank; Appendix C.
\| Median 6.0.
\|\| Regression coefficients lacking significance for other
welfare change indicators excluded.

Table 31: Civilian vs Military Rule (1965–1978) Control with Military Burden and Welfare Change Indicators (1970–1978)

CVML6578

	Civilian	Military
MILSPFAC|		
	INFLAA78 .49 (p .01, N 22)	CHLPER −.45 (p .02, N 23)
	FOODIN78 .39 (p .01, N 20)	FPRSCH .42 (p .05, N 22)
USTAFFAC|		
		FPRSCH .51 (p .01, N 22)

Sources: PRIO Data Bank; Appendix C.
| Regression coefficients lacking significance for other welfare change indicators excluded.

Table 32: Development Strategy (1965-1978) Control with
Military Burden and Welfare Change Indicators
(1970-1978)|

DVST6578

	Open Door	State Capitalist

MILSPFAC||

	Open Door	State Capitalist
CHLPER78	-.40 (p .01, N 41)	WOMLF77 .93 (p .01, N 5)
PROPER78	.30 (p .03, N 41)	CHILDM78 1.00 (p .001, N 2)
EMPLOY78	-.64 (p .05, N 8)	EMPLOY78 -1.00 (p .001, N 2)

USTAFFAC||

	Open Door	State Capitalist
FPRSCH77	.28 (p .05, N 39)	CHILDM78 1.00 (p .001, N 2)
		EMPLOY78 -1.00 (p .001, N 2)

Sources: PRIO Data Bank; Appendix C.
| State socialist countries excluded due to paucity of
data.
|| Regression coefficients lacking significance for
other welfare change indicators excluded.

Table 33: Militarization Indicators – Financial and Armed Forces Expansion

	CMILEX70	CAF70	AFSIZE	MILEX	CAFR6779	CMCG6778	MXGNP
CMILEX70	1.000 80	.291 61 .012	.278 71 .009	.177 76 .063	.307 50 .015	.162 71 .088	.091 80 .212
CAF70	.291 61 .012	1.000 63	.857 61 .000	.186 61 .075	.285 39 .039	.010 59 .470	.046 63 .360
AFSIZE	.278 71 .009	.857 61 .000	1.000 75	.436 73 .000	.292 46 .024	.256 67 .018	.044 75 .354
MILEX	.177 76 .063	.186 61 .075	.436 73 .000	1.000 86	.333 52 .008	.492 78 .000	.321 86 .001
CAFR6779	.307 50 .015	.285 39 .039	.292 46 .024	.333 52 .008	1.000 64	.344 53 .006	-.005 64 .484
CMCG6778	.162 71 .088	.010 59 .470	.256 67 .018	.492 78 .000	.344 53 .006	1.000 85	.052 85 .318
MXGNP	.091 80 .212	.046 63 .360	.044 75 .354	.321 86 .001	-.005 64 .484	.052 85 .318	1.000 101

Sources: PRIO Data Bank; Appendix C.

Table 34: Militarization Indicators with Military Burden and Welfare Factors

	MXCGFAC	CAF70	AFSIZE	CAFR6779	MILSPFAC	USTAFFAC	PHYSICAL	WOMENFAC
MXCGFAC	1.000 69	.208 56 .062	.474 63 .000	.379 42 .007	-.091 44 .279	-.029 44 .425	-.296 51 .017	.215 51 .065
CAF70	.208 56 .062	1.000 63	.857 61 .000	.285 39 .039	-.067 0 .340	.269 40 .046	-.195 44 .102	.062 44 .345
AFSIZE	.474 63 .000	.857 61 .000	1.000 75	.292 46 .024	-.061 47 .341	.300 47 .020	-.355 51 .005	.054 51 .353
CAFR6779	.379 42 .007	.285 39 .039	.292 46 .024	1.000 64	-.280 29 .071	.072 29 .356	-.152 38 .182	.195 38 .121
MILSPFAC	-.091 44 .279	-.067 40 .340	-.061 47 .341	-.280 29 .071	1.100 50	-.031 50 .416	.271 39 .048	-.475 39 .001
USTAFFAC	-.029 44 .425	.269 40 .046	.300 47 .020	.072 29 .356	-.031 50 .416	1.000 50	-.423 39 .004	.035 39 .417
PHYSICAL	-.296 .904 .867	-.195	-.355	-.152	.271	-.423	1.000	-.034
WOMENFAC	.215 51 .065	.062 44 .345	.054 51 .353	.195 38 .121	-.475 39 .001	.035 39 .417	-.034 65 .396	1.000 65

Source PRIO Data Bank; Appendix C.

Table 35: Militarization and Welfare Change Indicators (1970 - 1978)

	CHLPER	PROPER	WOMLF	PTRPED	FPRSCH	FSCSCH	CALPER	CRGODP78	INFLAA78
MXCGFAC	.200 68 .051	.598 59 .000	-.092 67 .230	.276 62 .015	.216 63 .045	-.195 60 .068	.195 58 .071	.071 43 .324	-.158 54 .128
AFSIZE	.038 74 .373	.428 61 .000	-.179 71 .068	-.029 63 .411	.348 65 .002	-.141 64 .134	-.041 60 .142	-.154 51 .141	-.033 58 .404
MILEX	.110 85 .158	.346 73 .001	.099 83 .188	.394 76 .000	.237 77 .019	-.265 73 .012	.204 71 .044	.233 52 .048	-.141 67 .128
MXGNP	-.026 99 .400	.023 77 .422	-.008 90 .471	-.021 81 .425	.057 88 .298	.125 81 .133	.109 73 .180	.085 61 .256	.068 74 .283

	FOODIN78	CHILLM	LIFEXB	INFL6078	EMPLOY78
MXCGFAC	-.147 55 .142	.291 28 .067	.131 65 .149	.088 54 .264	-.327 17 .100
AFSIZE	-.082 57 .272	.119 32 .258	.402 72 .000	.033 57 .404	-.171 19 .242
MILEX	-.121 66 .167	.174 34 .162	.036 81 .376	.088 66 .241	.295 24 .081
MXGNP	.031 72 .397	.018 36 .460	-.087 93 .205	.064 73 .297	.186 25 .186

Source: PRIO Data Bank; Appendix C.

Table 36: Development Strategy (1965 - 1978)
Control with Militarization Indicators

DVST6578 Breakdown

	Open Door	State Capitalist	State Socialist	Mixed	Total
MXCGFAC					
Mean	-.078	.223	-.501	.412	-.023
SD	.598	1.080	.217	.617	.689
N	50	10	4	5	69
R^2 .08					
CAF70					
Mean	127.093	173.190	8.943	236.800	128.266
SD	558.005	279.984	25.928	377.386	474.923
N	41	10	7	4	62
R^2 .01					
AFSIZE					
Mean	364.104	797.184	121.418	887.790	455.062
SD	735.337	966.016	43.225	404.193	835.113
N	49	11	7	7	74
R^2 .07					
CAFR6779					
Mean	74.302	49.200	8.000	43.400	61.750
SD	134.761	82.880	30.646	51.651	117.331
N	43	10	6	5	64
R^2 .03					

Sources: PRIO Data Bank; Appendix C.

Table 37: Civilian vs Military Rule and Development Strategy Controls 1960–1978), with Armed Forces Expansion (1961–1970)

CAF70 Breakdown|

	Open Door	State Capitalist	State Socialist	Mixed	Total
Civilian					
Mean	51.892		3.500	470.450	66.550
SD	82.315		21.766	607.475	164.589
N	25	0	7	2	34
Military					
Mean	261.953	31.500		57.700	209.788
SD	828.475	25.343		36.685	723.853
N	19	3	0	3	25
Total					
Mean	142.600	31.500	3.500	222.800	127.244
SD	549.707	25.343	21.766	379.524	487.157
N	44	3	7	5	59

Source: Appendix C.
|DEVSTR78 R^2 .01, p .86; CIVMIL78 R^2 .02, p .27; Total R^2 .06.

Table 38: Civilian vs Military Rule and Development Strategy Controls (1960-1978), with Change in Armed Forces Ratios (1967-1979)

CAFR6779 Breakdown|

	Open Door	State Capitalist	State Socialist	Mixed	Total
Civilian					
Mean	83.783	50.000	-3.000	63.333	65.121
SD	151.787	.000	31.705	124.307	134.499
N	23	1	6	3	33
Military					
Mean	38.800	14.500		53.000	37.737
SD	68.299	44.548		94.752	65.757
N	15	2	0	2	19
Total					
Mean	66.026	26.333	-3.000	59.200	55.115
SD	126.335	37.581	31.705	100.013	114.254
N	38	3	6	5	52

Source: Appendix C.
|DEVSTR78 R^2 .04, p .57; CIVMIL78 R^2 .01, p .41; Total R^2 .07.

Table 39: Civilian vs Military Rule and Development
Strategy Controls (1960–1978), with
Militarization Factor

MXCGFAC Breakdown|

	Open Door	State Capitalist	State Socialist	Mixed	Total
Civilian					
Mean	-.028		-.400	1.174	-.004
SD	.594		.196	2.629	.760
N	32	0	4	2	38
Military					
Mean	-.056	-.470		-.023	-.100
SD	.648	.231		.101	.586
N	20	3	0	3	26
Total					
Mean	-.039	-.470	-.400	.456	-.043
SD	.609	.231	.196	1.471	.691
N	52	3	4	5	64

Source: PRIO Data Bank; Appendix C.
|DEVSTR78 R^2 .08, p .19; CIVMIL78 R^2 .001,
p .59; Total R^2 .13.

Table 40: Civilian vs Military Rule and Development
Strategy Controls (1965-1978) with
Militarization Factor

MXCGFAC Breakdown|

	Civilian	Military	Mixed	Total
Open Door				
Mean	-.064	-.154	.309	.078
SD	.603	.552	.919	.598
N	27	20	3	50
State Capitalist				
Mean	1.222	-.205		.223
SD	1.679	.313		1.080
N	3	7	0	10
State Socialist				
Mean	-.501			-.501
SD	.217			.217
N	4	0	0	4
Mixed				
Mean	.605	.364		.412
SD	.000	.702		.617
N	1	4	0	5
Total				
Mean	.015	-.099	.309	-.023
SD	.790	.543	.919	.689
N	35	31	3	69

Source: PRIO Data Bank; Appendix C.
| CVML6578 R^2 .02, p .56; DVST6578 R^2 .08,
p .14; Total R^2 .23.

Table 41: Civilian vs Military Rule and Development
Strategy Controls (1965-1978) with Armed
Forces Expansion (1961-1977)

AFSIZE Breakdown|

	Civilian	Military	Mixed	Total
Open Door				
Mean	294.341	443.296	490.417	364.104
SD	335.622	1107.400	571.588	735.337
N	27	19	3	49
State Capitalist				
Mean	1352.000	480.147		797.184
SD	1454.882	417.722		966.016
N	4	7	0	11
State Socialist				
Mean	121.418			121.418
SD	43.225			43.225
N	7	0	0	7
Mixed				
Mean	310.000	1321.132		887.790
SD	343.948	1811.195		404.193
N	3	4	0	7
Total				
Mean	369.000	568.939	490.417	455.062
SD	591.222	1107.663	571.588	835.113
N	41	30	3	74

Source: PRIO Data Bank; Appendix C.
| CVML6578 R^2 .01, p .61; DVST6578 R^2 .07,
p .14; Total R^2 .15.

Table 42: Economic and Political Controls with
          Militarization Indicators

Economic/ Political Controls	Militarization Indicators			
	MXCGFAC	CAF70	AFSIZE	CAFR6779
PUCGDP78	.216	.018	.083	-.123
	57	50	60	46
	.053	.451	.265	.208
MFGDP70	-.065	-.259	-.321	-.103
	51	42	53	39
	.326	.049	.010	.266
GVTGDP70	-.038	-.047	.015	-.023
	63	54	65	48
	.383	.368	.452	.439
CGFCF77	.182	-.284	-.413	.018
	37	32	39	31
	.141	.058	.004	.463
AIDPER75	.004	.048	.076	.338
	57	51	62	53
	.489	.369	.277	.007
EPDGNP78	.295	-.128	-.023	.061
	61	54	62	45
	.011	.178	.430	.346
PRESS67	.130	.061	.071	.260
	51	47	54	35
	.182	.343	.304	.066
FREEDM73	.094	-.015	.005	.010
	69	63	75	64
	.221	.452	.485	.470

Sources: PRIO Data Bank; Appendix C.

Table 43: Press Freedom (1961-1967) and Political/Civil Rights (1979) Controls with Militarization Indicators

| | PRESS67 | | | | | |
| | (CAFR6779) | | | (AFSIZE) | | |
FREEDM79	More Free	Less Free	Total	More Free	Less Free	Total
More Free						
Mean	19.500	25.286	21.632	325.902	708.952	438.564
SD	62.867	73.792	65.104	493.193	1524.141	913.489
N	12	7	19	24	10	34
Less Free						
Mean	131.000	17.636	53.063	226.495	411.179	392.711
SD	210.771	69.122	134.078	63.985	713.395	677.353
N	5	11	16	2	18	20
Total						
Mean	52.294	20.611	36.000	318.255	517.527	421.581
SD	128.708	68.899	102.114	473.997	1056.355	827.374
N	17	18	35	26	28	54

| | (MXCGFAC) | | | (CAF70) | | |
FREEDM79	More Free	Less Free	Total	More Free	Less Free	Total
More Free						
Mean	-.110	-.039	-.085	46.847	388.280	173.304
SD	.502	.410	.466	96.541	1129.048	689.366
N	20	11	31	17	10	27
Less Free						
Mean	-.059	-.108	-.101	4.050	93.022	84.125
SD	.133	.980	.901	6.576	208.592	199.205
N	3	17	20	2	18	20
Total						
Mean	-.103	-.081	-.091	42.342	198.471	135.355
SD	.469	.795	.662	92.028	687.028	535.708
N	23	28	51	19	28	47

Sources: PRIO Data Bank; Appendix C.
| PRESS67 R^2.02, p .37; FREEDM79 R^2.02, p .37; Total R^2 .15.
‖ R^2.01, p .38; R^2.001, p .85; Total R^2 .03.
‖‖ R^2.001, p .91; R^2.001, p .93; Total R^2 .001.
‖‖‖‖ R^2.02, p .33; R^2.01, p .58; Total R^2 .06.

Table 44: Foreign Aid Controls with Militarization Indicators

EPDGNP78

	(CAFR6779)			(MKCGFAC)		
	Above Median	Below Median	Total	Above Median	Below Median	Total
Above Median						
Mean	64.438	22.250	50.375	.338	-.225	.137
SD	74.165	69.207	73.876	.961	.234	.828
N	16	8	24	18	10	28
Below Median						
Mean	150.000	72.818	96.938	-.062	-.096	-.088
SD	206.155	120.120	149.391	.502	.686	.639
N	5	11	16	6	20	26
Total						
Mean	84.810	51.526	69.000	.238	-.139	.029
SD	118.405	102.648	111.068	.877	.582	.745
N	21	19	40	24	30	54

AIDPER75

	(AFSIZE)			(CAF70)		
	Above Median	Below Median	Total	Above Median	Below Median	Total
Above Median						
Mean	577.058	236.690	436.216	128.447	43.500	94.468
SD	824.882	105.105	649.818	235.163	36.377	185.902
N	17	12	29	15	10	25
Below Median						
Mean	415.570	426.713	424.998	67.020	83.018	79.382
SD	324.405	836.255	774.646	56.985	193.255	170.648
N	4	22	26	5	17	22
Total						
Mean	546.298	359.646	430.913	113.090	68.381	87.406
SD	751.234	676.167	704.838	205.371	154.335	177.153
N	21	34	55	20	27	47

Sources: PRIO Data Bank; Appendix C.

| | AIDPER75 R^2 .02, p.35; EPDGNP78 R^2 .04, p .20; Total R^2 .11.
| || R^2 .02, p.34; R^2 .001, p .95; Total R^2 .03.
| ||| R^2 .06, p.06; R^2 .02, p .27; Total R^2 .09.
| |||| R^2 .02, p.40; R^2 .002, p .77; Total R^2 .03.

Table 45: Government Expenditures as a percent of GDP (1970) and Public Consumption as a percent of GDP (1978) with Militarization Indicators

PUCGDP78

	(CAFR6779)			GVTGDP70 (AFSIZE)		
	Above Median	Below Median	Total	Above Median	Below Median	Total
Above Median						
Mean	52.412	59.444	54.846	499.755	814.416	588.254
SD	68.802	66.312	66.696	728.239	1572.847	1017.565
N	17	9	26	23	9	32
Below Median						
Mean	92.333	41.400	60.500	199.774	218.833	212.734
SD	207.053	76.040	135.677	80.190	181.000	154.268
N	6	10	16	8	17	25
Total						
Mean	62.826	49.947	57.000	422.341	424.996	423.552
SD	116.221	70.221	97.236	638.917	946.622	786.594
N	23	19	42	31	26	57

	(MXCGFPAC)			(CAF70)		
	Above Median	Below Median	Total	Above Median	Below Median	Total
Above Median						
Mean	.171	-.001	.115	111.589	460.489	223.736
SD	.757	.764	.751	210.773	1177.850	684.260
N	21	10	31	19	9	28
Below Median						
Mean	-.111	-.168	-.154	7.967	32.636	25.235
SD	.374	.639	.577	15.932	43.288	38.516
N	6	18	24	6	14	20
Total						
Mean	.108	-.108	-.002	86.720	200.057	141.027
SD	.694	.677	.688	188.181	742.412	528.539
N	27	28	55	25	23	48

Sources: PRIO Data Bank; Appendix C.

GVTGDP70

| R^2 .005, p .67; PUCGDP78 R^2 .001, p .86; Total R^2 .03.

|| R^2 .001, p .99; R^2 .06, p .07; Total R^2 .08.

R^2 .03, p .25; R^2 .04, p .15; Total R^2 .05.

||| R^2 .01, p .46; R^2 .04, p .20; Total R^2 .09.

Table 46: Gross Domestic Product Average Annual Growth Rate (1960-1970) and Manufacturing as a percent of GDP (1970) Controls with Militarization Indicators

	MFGDP70			CGDP70		
	Above Median	Below Median	Total	Above Median	Below Median	Total
(CAFR6779)				**(AFSIZE)**		
Above Median						
Mean	83.091	-8.429	47.500	202.399	149.922	181.019
SD	148.534	55.800	127.218	88.638	78.780	87.237
N	11	7	18	16	11	27
Below Median						
Mean	62.400	79.455	74.125	604.861	643.999	629.767
SD	34.732	125.592	104.422	647.398	1276.671	1071.942
N	5	11	16	8	14	22
Total						
Mean	76.625	45.278	60.029	336.553	426.605	382.498
SD	122.996	111.000	116.085	412.605	973.703	746.788
N	16	18	34	24	25	49
(MXCGFPAC)				**(CAF70)**		
Above Median						
Mean	-.054	-.222	-.117	21.743	11.229	18.238
SD	.483	.320	.430	21.204	29.981	24.243
N	15	9	24	14	7	21
Below Median						
Mean	.470	-.258	-.026	111.986	359.708	268.442
SD	.822	.421	.657	145.857	1021.085	811.984
N	7	15	22	7	12	19
Total						
Mean	.113	-.244	-.074	51.824	231.321	137.085
SD	.641	.379	.546	92.600	816.872	566.228
N	22	24	46	21	19	40

Sources: PRIO Data Bank; Appendix C.

CGDP70 R^2 .02, p .44; MFGDP70 R^2 .01, p .51; Total R^2 .10.

|| R^2 .001, p .66; R^2 .09, p .04; R^2 .09.

|| R^2 .11, p .03; R^2 .01, p .58; R^2 .21.

|||| R^2 .03, p .32; R^2 .05, p .17; R^2 .07.

Table 47: Militarization Indicators with Welfare Factors and Welfare Change Indicators: 1970-1978

	PHYSICAL	WOMENFAC	CHLPER	PROPER	WQMLF	PTRPED	FPRSCH	FSCSCH	CALPER
MXCGFAC	-.296 51 .017	.215 51 .065	.200 68 .051	.598 59 .000	-.092 67 .230	.276 62 .015	.216 63 .045	-.195 60 .068	.195 58 .071
CAF70	-.195 44 .102	.062 44 .345	.004 62 .487	.196 51 .084	-.159 59 .114	.052 54 .354	.124 56 .182	.033 54 .408	-.174 52 .109
AFSIZE	-.355 51 .005	.054 51 .353	.038 74 .373	.428 61 .000	-.179 71 .068	-.029 63 .411	.348 65 .002	-.141 64 .134	-.141 60 .142
CAFR6779	-.152 38 .182	.195 38 .121	.240 63 .029	.168 45 .136	.091 55 .255	.133 48 .184	.123 54 .187	-.003 49 .492	.193 43 .107

	FOODIN78	LITRCY	CHILDM	LIFEXB	INFL6078	EMPLOY78	CFOODP78	INFLAA78
MXCGFAC	-.147 55 .142	.184 68 .067	.291 28 .067	.131 65 .149	.088 54 .264	-.327 17 .100	.071 43 .324	-.158 54 .128
CAF70	-.047 47 .377	.316 60 .007	.199 27 .160	.398 62 .001	.079 48 .296	-.361 16 .085	-.117 41 .233	.027 48 .428
AFSIZE	-.082 57 .272	.350 72 .001	.119 32 .258	.402 72 .000	.033 57 .404	-.171 19 .242	-.154 51 .141	-.033 58 .404
CAFR6779	-.122 41 .223	.042 58 .377	-.213 24 .158	-.005 59 .486	-.021 42 .447	.424 14 .065	.037 39 .412	-.076 41 .318

Sources: PRIO Data Bank; Appendix C.

Table 48: AID Per Capita (1973-1975) Control with Militarization and Welfare Change Indicators (1970-1978)

AIDPER75 – Above Median

	PHYSICAL	WOMENFAC	CHLPER	PROPER	WOMLF	PTTRED	FPRSCH	FSCSCH	CALPER
MXCGFAC	-.062 / 20 / .398	.271 / 20 / .124	.152 / 25 / .234	.662 / 25 / .000	-.174 / 25 / .203	.448 / 25 / .012	.145 / 25 / .244	-.021 / 25 / .461	.263 / 23 / .113
CAF70	-.117 / 16 / .332	-.535 / 16 / .016	.200 / 19 / .206	.893 / 20 / .000	-.258 / 19 / .143	.353 / 19 / .069	.161 / 19 / .255	-.174 / 20 / .231	.273 / 19 / .129
AFSIZE	-.231 / 17 / .186	.431 / 17 / .042	.129 / 21 / .289	.769 / 22 / .000	-.296 / 21 / .097	.219 / 21 / .170	.375 / 21 / .047	-.229 / 22 / .153	.221 / 20 / .175
CAFR6779	.063 / 18 / .403	.200 / 18 / .213	.449 / 27 / .009	.155 / 23 / .241	.211 / 25 / .155	.193 / 24 / .183	.055 / 26 / .394	.052 / 23 / .407	.353 / 20 / .063

	FOODIN78	LITRCY	CHILDM	LIFEXB	INFL6078	EMPLOY78	CFOODP78	INFLAA78
MXCGFAC	.014 / 20 / .477	.202 / 26 / .162	.452 / 7 / .154	.151 / 24 / .241	.212 / 23 / .166	-.633 / 6 / .089	.002 / 10 / .498	.033 / 23 / .440
CAF70	.011 / 15 / .484	.504 / 20 / .012	.125 / 9 / .374	.429 / 20 / .030	.115 / 19 / .319	-.732 / 5 / .080	-.125 / 10 / .365	-.095 / 19 / .349
AFSIZE	-.169 / 18 / .251	.361 / 22 / .049	-.080 / 9 / .419	.379 / 21 / .045	-.017 / 20 / .472	-.442 / 6 / .190	-.124 / 11 / .358	-.188 / 20 / .213
CAFR6779	-.527 / 20 / .008	.033 / 27 / .436	-.325 / 9 / .197	.146 / 24 / .248	.447 / 19 / .028	.484 / 7 / .136	.186 / 12 / .281	-.321 / 19 / .090

Sources: PRIO Data Bank; Appendix C.

195

Table 48: AID Per Capita (1973-1975) Control with Militarization and Welfare Change Indicators [1970-1978] (cont'd)

AIDPER75 - Below Median

	PHYSICAL	WOMENFAC	CHLPER	PROPER	WOMLF	PTRPED	FPRSCH	FSCSCH	CALPER
MXCGFAC	-.264 26 .097	-.115 26 .287	.092 31 .312	.221 28 .130	-.066 31 .362	-.078 29 .344	.198 31 .143	-.539 28 .002	.239 28 .110
CAF70	-.415 23 .025	-.391 23 .033	.064 31 .365	-.198 26 .166	-.173 29 .185	-.264 28 .087	.405 30 .013	-.317 28 .050	-.327 26 .051
AFSIZE	-.433 29 .010	-.415 29 .013	.084 40 .304	-.177 33 .162	-.111 38 .254	-.248 34 .079	.467 37 .002	-.345 35 .021	-.437 33 .006
CAFR6779	-.102 17 .349	-.266 17 .151	.217 25 .149	.506 19 .014	.046 22 .419	-.102 19 .339	.094 21 .343	-.193 22 .195	.314 18 .102

	FOODIN78	LITRCY	CHILDM	LIFEXB	INFL6078	EMPLOY78	CFOODP78	INFLAA78
MXCGFAC	-.187 26 .181	-.115 30 .273	.120 15 .335	-.165 30 .192	.120 25 .283	.178 8 .337	.225 25 .140	-.150 26 .233
CAF70	-.205 24 .168	.294 28 .064	-.087 12 .394	.229 30 .112	.103 23 .321	-.559 8 .075	.181 23 .205	-.026 24 .452
AFSIZE	-.142 30 .227	.060 37 .363	.436 17 .040	-.004 39 .490	.045 31 .406	.156 10 .334	-.094 31 .307	-.012 33 .473
CAFR6779	-.105 16 .349	-.210 22 .174	-.307 11 .179	.260 24 .110	-.136 18 .296	.321 5 .299	.061 19 .403	.103 18 .342

Sources: PRIO Data Bank; Appendix C.

Table 49: External Public Debt as a percent of GNP (1978) Control with Militarization and Welfare Change Indicators (1970-1978)

EPDGNP78 - Above Median

	PHYSICAL	WOMENFAC	CHLPER	PROPER	WOMLF	PTRPED	FPRSCH	FSCSCH	CALPER
MXCGFAC	-.195 / 24 / .180	.309 / 24 / .071	.233 / 27 / .121	.672 / 27 / .000	-.204 / 27 / .154	.450 / 27 / .009	.188 / 27 / .174	-.116 / 27 / .282	.184 / 26 / .185
CAF70	-.179 / 21 / .219	.618 / 21 / .001	.134 / 24 / .266	.895 / 25 / .000	-.295 / 24 / .081	.365 / 24 / .040	.186 / 24 / .192	-.164 / 25 / .217	.244 / 24 / .125
AFSIZE	-.226 / 24 / .144	.463 / 24 / .011	.133 / 28 / .250	.781 / 29 / .000	-.288 / 28 / .069	.203 / 27 / .155	.421 / 28 / .013	-.205 / 28 / .148	.167 / 28 / .198
CAFR6779	-.597 / 19 / .003	.279 / 19 / .124	.389 / 23 / .033	.432 / 23 / .020	-.311 / 24 / .070	.362 / 23 / .045	.392 / 23 / .032	-.280 / 22 / .103	-.018 / 22 / .468

	FOODIN78	LITRCY	CHILM	LIFEXB	INFL6078	EMPLOY78	CROODP78	INFLAA78
MXCGFAC	-.265 / 23 / .110	.330 / 28 / .043	.330 / / .212	.196 / 28 / .158	.142 / 26 / .245	-.553 / 7 / .099	.104 / 15 / .356	-.238 / 26 / .121
CAF70	-.025 / 21 / .457	.604 / 25 / .001	.148 / 10 / .342	.439 / 25 / .014	.057 / 24 / .396	-.547 / 7 / .102	-.053 / 15 / .426	-.120 / 23 / .293
AFSIZE	-.106 / 25 / .306	.467 / 29 / .005	-.061 / 10 / .434	.404 / 29 / .015	-.051 / 27 / .399	-.253 / 9 / .255	-.073 / 17 / .391	-.218 / 27 / .137
CAFR6779	-.416 / 19 / .038	.063 / 24 / .385	-.531 / 9 / .071	.423 / 24 / .020	.071 / 21 / .380	-.185 / 6 / .363	.092 / 13 / .382	-.452 / 21 / .020

Sources: PRIO Data Bank; Appendix C.

197

Table 49: External Public Debt as a percent of GNP (1978) Control with Militarization and Welfare Change Indicators (1970-1978) (cont'd)

EPDGNP78 - Below Median

	PHYSICAL	WOMENFAC	CHLPER	PROPER	WOMLF	PTRPED	FPRSCH	FSCSCH	CALPER
MXOGFAC	-.238 / 25 / .126	.076 / 25 / .358	.165 / 33 / .180	.280 / 27 / .078	-.095 / 32 / .303	-.038 / 30 / .420	.197 / 31 / .144	-.429 / 28 / .011	.291 / 29 / .063
CAF70	-.242 / 21 / .145	-.074 / 21 / .375	-.070 / 29 / .358	-.205 / 23 / .174	-.224 / 28 / .126	-.004 / 26 / .493	.150 / 27 / .228	.159 / 24 / .229	-.281 / 25 / .087
AFSIZE	-.472 / 24 / .010	-.197 / 24 / .179	.023 / 33 / .451	-.215 / 27 / .141	-.151 / 32 / .205	-.124 / 30 / .257	.350 / 30 / .029	-.052 / 28 / .397	-.323 / 29 / .044
CAFR6779	.141 / 17 / .295	.216 / 17 / .203	.635 / 21 / .001	.422 / 17 / .046	.350 / 20 / .065	-.039 / 20 / .435	-.051 / 19 / .418	.015 / 19 / .476	.349 / 19 / .072

	FODIN78	LITRCY	CHILDM	LIFEXB	NFL6078	EMPLOY78	CPOODP78	INFLAA78
MXOGFAC	-.184 / 27 / .180	-.054 / 32 / .385	.397 / 17 / .057	.049 / 32 / .395	.189 / 28 / .167	.239 / 7 / .303	.204 / 24 / .170	-.079 / 28 / .344
CAF70	-.070 / 24 / .373	.333 / 28 / .042	.234 / 14 / .211	.473 / 28 / .006	.064 / 24 / .384	-.431 / 6 / .197	-.192 / 21 / .203	.015 / 24 / .472
AFSIZE	-.085 / 28 / .333	.312 / 32 / .041	.251 / 19 / .150	.419 / 32 / .009	.064 / 28 / .374	.110 / 7 / .407	-.196 / 26 / .168	.005 / 28 / .489
CAFR6779	-.104 / 17 / .346	-.025 / 20 / .458	-.173 / 13 / .286	-.128 / 20 / .296	.003 / 17 / .496	-.161 / 4 / .420	-.126 / 16 / .321	-.048 / 16 / .431

Sources: PRIO Data Bank; Appendix C.

Table 50: Open Door Development Strategy (1960-1978) with Militarization and Welfare Change Indicators (1970-1978)

	PHYSICAL	WOMENFAC	CHLPER	PROPER	WOMLF	PTRPED	FPRSCH	FSCSCH	CALPER
MXOGFAC	-.309 42 .023	.019 42 .453	.195 53 .081	.052 50 .361	-.052 52 .357	.289 49 .022	.371 50 .004	-.129 49 .188	.108 48 .233
CAF70	-.183 35 .147	-.041 35 .406	-.092 44 .277	-.193 42 .110	-.171 43 .137	.023 40 .444	.181 41 .126	.089 41 .291	-.223 42 .078
AFSIZE	-.337 42 .014	-.138 42 .192	-.082 54 .277	-.179 51 .104	-.158 53 .129	-.080 49 .292	.379 50 .003	-.085 51 .277	-.280 49 .025
CAFR6779	-.062 31 .371	.108 31 .282	.491 41 .001	.226 37 .089	.164 41 .153	.136 37 .211	.141 39 .196	.067 38 .344	.148 35 .198

	FOODIN78	LITRCY	CHILIM	LIFEXB	INFL6078	EMPLOY78	CROODP78	INFLAA78
MXOGFAC	-.201 43 .098	-.210 53 .066	.254 24 .116	-.040 50 .391	-.002 44 .496	-.307 12 .166	.214 34 .112	-.262 45 .041
CAF70	-.053 35 .382	.246 43 .056	.161 23 .232	.388 44 .005	.061 38 .359	-.330 10 .176	-.133 30 .242	.030 39 .427
AFSIZE	-.086 44 .289	.196 53 .080	.050 28 .400	.337 52 .007	-.010 45 .474	-.158 12 .312	-.167 39 .155	-.048 47 .374
CAFR6779	-.141 33 .218	.019 41 .453	-.225 21 .164	-.066 37 .350	.003 32 .493	.506 10 .068	-.054 26 .397	-.061 32 .370

Sources: PRIO Data Bank; Appendix C.

Table 51: Civilian Rule (1960-1978) with Militarization and Welfare Change Indicators: 1970-1978

	PHYSICAL	WOMENFAC	CHILPER	PROPER	WOMLF	PTRPED	FPRSCH	FSCSCH	CALPER
MXCGFAC	-.282 27 .077	.278 27 .080	.263 37 .058	.680 33 .000	-.049 37 .387	.419 33 .008	.360 34 .018	.341 32 .028	.237 32 .096
CAF70	-.260 22 .121	.487 22 .011	.097 33 .295	.888 26 .000	-.157 31 .200	.180 27 .185	.251 29 .094	-.234 28 .115	.052 27 .399
AFSIZE	-.337 28 .040	.494 28 .004	.052 44 .368	.724 35 .000	-.184 42 .122	.098 35 .288	.288 37 .042	-.226 37 .089	-.001 34 .497
CAFR6779	.063 18 .402	.247 18 .162	.260 32 .075	.184 23 .200	.295 31 .054	.144 26 .242	.103 27 .305	.023 25 .457	.260 22 .121

	FOODIN78	LITRCY	CHILDM	LIFEXB	INFL6078	EMPLOY78	CROODP78	INFLAA78
MXCGFAC	-.077 30 .343	.378 38 .010	.293 19 .112	.229 35 .093	.026 28 .448	-.349 12 .133	.001 24 .498	-.104 26 .306
CAF70	-.112 24 .301	.639 32 .000	.226 17 .192	.448 34 .004	.010 23 .481	-.322 11 .167	-.109 22 .314	-.129 22 .283
AFSIZE	-.090 32 .312	.497 43 .000	.074 22 .372	.331 43 .015	-.050 32 .393	-.185 14 .263	-.128 31 .246	-.153 31 .206
CAFR6779	.022 20 .463	.155 32 .198	-.233 15 .202	-.046 30 .405	-.025 20 .459	.454 10 .094	-.021 19 .466	.012 18 .482

Sources: PRIO Data Bank; Appendix C.

Table 51: Military Rule (1960-1978) with Militarization and Welfare Change Indicators: 1970-1978 (cont.)

	PHYSICAL	WOMENFAC	CHILPER	PROPER	WOMLF	PTRPED	FPRSCH	FSCSCH	CALPER
MXCGFAC	-.426 20 .030	.198 20 .201	-.007 26 .486	-.112 23 .305	-.126 25 .274	-.272 24 .100	.591 24 .001	-.176 24 .205	.052 23 .407
CAF70	-.263 19 .138	.061 19 .403	-.121 25 .282	-.357 22 .052	-.243 24 .126	.060 23 .393	.322 23 .067	.063 23 .388	-.482 22 .011
AFSIZE	.452 20 .023	-.122 20 .304	-.048 26 .407	.388 23 .034	-.188 25 .184	-.154 24 .237	.647 24 .000	-.140 24 .257	-.509 23 .007
CAFR6779	-.634 15 .006	-.024 15 .466	.292 19 .113	-.509 17 .018	.090 18 .362	.201 17 .219	.189 17 .234	-.033 18 .448	-.567 17 .009

	FOODIN78	LITRCY	CHILDM	LIFEXB	INFL6078	EMPLOY78	CFOODP78	INFLAA78
MXCGFAC	-.245 20 .149	-.117 25 .289	.399 9 .143	.035 25 .433	.070 21 .382	.147 5 .407	.474 18 .023	-.530 23 .005
CAF70	-.058 19 .407	.299 24 .078	.088 10 .405	.505 24 .006	.189 21 .206	-.930 5 .011	-.205 18 .207	.095 22 .337
AFSIZE	-.075 21 .374	.311 25 .065	.435 10 .104	.490 25 .006	.153 21 .254	-.224 5 .358	-.229 19 .172	.063 23 .388
CAFR6779	-.285 15 .152	.048 18 .425	-.253 8 .273	.256 18 .152	.159 15 .285	-.639 3 .279	-.043 13 .445	-.473 16 .032

Sources: PRIO Data Bank; Appendix C.

201

Table 52: **Development Strategy (1965-1978) Controls with Militarization and Welfare Change Indicators (1970-1978)**

DVST6578 – Open Door

	PHYSICAL	WOMENFAC	CHLPER	PROPER	WOMLF	PTRPED	FPRSCH	FSCSCH	CALPER
MXCGFAC	-.242 38 .072	.118 38 .240	.185 49 .102	.067 46 .329	-.055 48 .355	.352 45 .009	.210 46 .080	-.048 44 .379	.130 45 .197
CAF70	-.155 31 .202	.027 31 .442	-.110 40 .250	-.191 38 .125	-.166 39 .156	.060 36 .363	.098 38 .280	.202 36 .118	-.219 38 .093
AFSIZE	-.225 37 .090	.016 37 .462	-.161 48 .137	-.161 45 .146	-.172 47 .124	.006 43 .486	.114 44 .232	.143 44 .177	-.282 44 .032
CAFR6779	-.069 28 .364	.093 28 .319	.412 42 .003	.225 34 .100	.160 37 .172	.135 33 .227	.139 38 .203	.056 34 .377	.143 33 .214

	FOODIN78	LITRCY	CHILIM	LIFEXB	INFL6078	EMPLOY78	CFOODP78	INFLAA78
MXCGFAC	-.182 40 .131	-.181 50 .104	.262 23 .114	-.137 48 .401	.108 42 .247	-.250 11 .229	.243 33 .086	-.155 43 .160
CAF70	-.051 33 .389	.252 41 .056	.212 22 .171	.396 41 .005	.073 36 .335	-.413 9 .135	-.138 29 .238	.034 36 .421
AFSIZE	-.075 40 .323	.225 49 .060	.216 26 .144	.350 48 .007	.073 42 .322	.196 10 .294	-.177 36 .151	.024 43 .439
CAFR6779	-.143 30 .225	-.027 40 .434	-.222 20 .174	-.031 40 .424	-.032 32 .432	.491 9 .090	.027 29 .445	-.068 32 .355

Sources: PRIO Data Bank; Appendix C.

Table 52: Development Strategy (1965-1978) Controls with Militarization and Welfare Change Indicators (1970-1978) (cont'd)

DVST6578 - State Capitalist

	PHYSICAL	WOMENFAC	CHLPER	PROPER	WOMLF	PTRPED	FPRSCH	FSCSCH	CALPER
MXCGFAC	-.019 7 .484	.792 7 .017	.265 10 .229	.922 8 .001	-.261 10 .233	.365 10 .150	.042 10 .454	-.332 9 .192	.578 9 .052
CAF70	-.001 7 .499	.769 7 .022	.306 10 .195	.906 8 .001	-.317 10 .186	.347 10 .163	.057 10 .438	-.396 9 .145	.578 9 .052
AFSIZE	-.072 7 .439	.693 7 .042	.322 11 .167	.794 8 .009	-.343 11 .151	-.154 10 .335	.295 9 .204	-.532 9 .070	.608 9 .041
CAFR6779	-.532 6 .138	.688 6 .066	.341 10 .168	.655 8 .039	-.452 10 .095	.027 9 .473	.481 9 .095	-.348 8 .199	.690 8 .029

	FOODIN78	LITRCY	CHILLM	LIFEXB	INFL6078	EMPLOY78	CFOODP78	INFLAA78
MXCGFAC	.041 9 .458	.876 10 .000	1.000 2 .000	.732 10 .008	.170 9 .331	-.967 5 .082	.187 5 .381	-.171 8 .343
CAF70	.036 9 .463	.860 10 .001	1.000 2 .000	.750 10 .006	.164 9 .337	-.933 3 .117	.176 5 .389	-.138 8 .373
AFSIZE	-.039 9 .461	.666 11 .013	1.000 2 .000	.657 11 .014	.046 10 .450	-.961 3 .089	.173 5 .390	-.087 9 .412
CAFR6779	-.194 7 .339	.301 10 .199	1.000 2 .000	.847 10 .001	-.011 8 .490	-.988 3 .050	.002 4 .499	.056 7 .453

Sources: PRIO Data Bank; Appendix C.

Table 53: Civilian Rule (1965-1978) with Militarization and Welfare Change Indicators (1965-1978)

	PHYSICAL	WOMENFAC	CHLPER	PROPER	WOMLF	PTRPED	FPRSCH	FSCSCH	CALPER
MXCGFAC	-.269 23 .107	.318 23 .070	.277 34 .056	.679 30 .000	-.047 34 .396	.408 30 .013	.348 30 .030	-.373 29 .023	.258 29 .088
CAF70	-.197 18 .216	.547 18 .009	.116 29 .275	.895 22 .000	-.158 27 .215	.130 23 .277	.223 24 .147	-.266 24 .104	.125 23 .285
AFSIZE	-.300 24 .077	.490 24 .008	.054 40 .371	.732 31 .000	-.180 38 .139	.069 31 .356	.283 32 .058	-.233 33 .096	.028 30 .442
CAFR6779	.146 15 .302	.268 15 .167	.252 32 .082	.181 21 .217	.290 29 .064	.126 24 .279	.058 26 .390	.022 23 .461	.277 20 .118

	FOODIN78	LITRCY	CHILDM	LIFEXB	INFL6078	EMPLOY78	CFOODP78	INFLAA78
MXCGFAC	.007 27 .487	.371 35 .014	.309 16 .122	.224 32 .109	.021 25 .460	-.349 12 .133	-.036 22 .437	-.049 25 .409
CAF70	.054 21 .409	.635 29 .000	.312 14 .138	.445 30 .007	-.001 20 .498	-.322 11 .167	-.171 19 .242	-.081 20 .368
AFSIZE	-.036 29 .427	.502 40 .000	.324 19 .088	.318 39 .024	-.052 29 .394	-.185 14 .263	-.171 28 .193	-.197 29 .153
CAFR6779	-.200 18 .213	.137 31 .231	-.257 12 .210	-.059 30 .379	-.026 19 .457	.454 10 .94	-.126 18 .310	-.053 19 .415

Table 53: Military Rule (1965–1978) with Militarization and Welfare Change Indicators (1965–1978) (cont'd)

	PHYSICAL	WOMENFAC	CHLPER	PROPER	WOMLF	PTRPED	FPRSCH	FSCSCH	CALPER
MXCGFAC	-.355 26 .038	.110 26 .297	-.036 31 .423	-.154 27 .222	-.118 30 .268	-.218 29 .128	.207 30 .137	-.081 29 .338	-.014 27 .473
CAF70	-.214 24 .158	.015 24 .471	-.142 29 .231	-.271 26 .090	-.224 28 .126	.071 27 .363	.098 28 .310	.049 27 .403	-.448 26 .011
AFSIZE	-.411 25 .021	-.098 25 .320	-.042 30 .413	-.190 27 .172	-.202 29 .147	-.157 28 .213	.360 29 .027	-.166 28 .199	-.402 27 .019
CAFR6779	-.680 21 .000	.130 21 .287	.371 27 .028	-.014 22 .476	-.134 24 .267	.108 22 .317	.227 25 .138	.003 24 .494	-.310 21 .086

	FOODIN78	LITRCY	CHILDM	LIFEXB	INFL6078	EMPLOY78	CFOODP78	INFLAA78
MXCGFAC	-.245 25 .119	-.117 30 .269	.374 10 .144	-.002 27 .495	.011 26 .479	.147 5 .407	.410 19 .041	-.493 27 .004
CAF70	-.050 23 .410	.296 28 .063	-.025 11 .471	.464 28 .006	.183 25 .191	-.930 5 .011	-.158 19 .259	.086 25 .341
AFSIZE	-.088 25 .339	.231 29 .114	.106 11 .378	.468 29 .005	.107 25 .306	-.224 5 .358	-.185 20 .217	.017 26 .468
CAFR6779	-.254 21 .134	-.231 25 .133	-.222 10 .269	.392 25 .026	.026 20 .456	-.362 4 .319	.243 17 .174	-.500 20 .012

Sources: PRIO Data Bank; Appendix C.

Table 54: Press Freedom (1961-1967) Control with Militarization and Welfare Change Indicators (1970-1978)

PRESS67 - Above Median

	PHYSICAL	WOMENFAC	CHLPER	PROPER	WOMLF	PTRPED	FPRSCH	FSCSCH	CALPER
MXCGFAC	-.372 19 .058	.324 19 .088	.392 23 .032	.005 22 .490	-.036 23 .435	.531 20 .008	.437 21 .024	.146 20 .270	-.042 21 .429
CAF70	-.519 16 .020	.304 16 .126	.191 19 .217	-.423 18 .040	-.228 19 .174	.274 16 .152	.406 18 .047	.044 17 .433	-.291 18 .121
AFSIZE	-.419 21 .029	.218 21 .172	-.160 26 .217	-.038 24 .431	-.222 26 .137	-.062 21 .394	.345 24 .049	-.016 23 .470	-.245 23 .130
CAFR6779	.198 16 .232	.280 16 .147	.538 17 .013	.622 16 .005	.587 17 .007	.087 15 .380	-.094 17 .360	-.074 15 .396	.493 16 .026

	FOODIN78	LITRCY	CHILDM	LIFEXB	INFL6078	EMPLOY78	CROODP78	INFLAA78
MXCGFAC	-.250 18 .158	-.076 23 .365	.444 14 .056	.212 22 .172	-.090 20 .353	.432 5 .234	.011 19 .482	-.274 18 .136
CAF70	-.180 16 .253	-.138 19 .286	.310 12 .164	.142 19 .282	-.157 17 .273	-.185 5 .383	-.067 16 .403	-.372 15 .086
AFSIZE	-.152 21 .256	-.087 26 .337	.703 16 .001	.074 25 .362	-.188 23 .196	-.020 7 .483	-.122 23 .290	-.230 21 .158
CAFR6779	.020 12 .475	.222 17 .195	-.144 11 .336	-.260 17 .157	-.018 15 .475	.313 5 .304	.197 14 .250	.008 13 .490

Sources: PRIO Data Bank; Appendix C.

206

Table 54: Press Freedom (1961-1967) Control with Militarization and Welfare Change Indicators (1970-1978) (cont'd)

PRESS67 - Below Median

	PHYSICAL	WOMENFAC	CHLPER	PROPER	WOMLF	PTRPED	FPRSCH	FSCSCH	CALPER
MXOGFAC	-.127 18 .308	.565 18 .007	.127 27 .264	.856 21 .000	-.126 26 .270	.077 24 .361	.185 25 .188	-.532 22 .005	.389 23 .033
CAF70	-.128 17 .313	.104 17 .345	.010 27 .480	.166 20 .242	-.176 25 .200	.080 24 .355	.119 25 .285	.044 22 .423	-.185 22 .206
AFSIZE	-.237 17 .180	.274 17 .144	.065 27 .374	.456 20 .022	-.221 25 .144	.111 24 .303	.190 25 .182	-.079 22 .363	-.152 22 .249
CAFR6779	-.581 9 .050	.370 9 .163	.209 17 .210	.658 12 .010	-.156 16 .282	.398 14 .079	.722 15 .001	-.386 14 .086	.003 13 .497

	FOODIN78	LITTRCY	CHILDM	LIFEXB	INFL6078	EMPLOY78	CROODP78	INFLAA78
MXOGFAC	-.256 22 .125	.432 28 .011	.242 9 .265	.204 28 .149	.370 20 .054	-.535 10 .055	.179 18 .239	-.113 21 .313
CAF70	.013 21 .478	.375 27 .027	.248 9 .260	.562 28 .001	.238 20 .156	-.579 11 .031	-.100 18 .347	.108 20 .325
AFSIZE	-.017 22 .470	.529 27 .002	.049 9 .450	.635 28 .000	.421 19 .036	-.140 11 .341	-.136 19 .289	.054 20 .411
CAFR6779	-.264 12 .204	.605 17 .005	-.197 7 .336	.630 18 .003	.584 10 .038	-.431 7 .167	.009 13 .489	-.152 11 .327

Sources: PRIO Data Bank; Appendix C.

Table 55: Political and Civil Rights (1973) Control with Militarization and Welfare Change Indicators (1970-1978)

	FREEDOM73 - More Free								
	PHYSICAL	WOMENFAC	CHLPER	PROPER	WOMLF	PTRPED	PPRSCH	FSCSCH	CALPER
MXCGFAC	-.333 29 .039	-.004 29 .492	.359 37 .014	.258 35 .067	-.096 36 .289	.050 34 .389	.300 34 .043	-.301 34 .042	.195 34 .134
CAF70	-.224 27 .131	-.050 27 .402	-.113 34 .261	-.217 32 .116	-.203 33 .128	.020 31 .458	.176 32 .168	.220 31 .118	-.268 33 .066
AFSIZE	-.444 32 .005	-.167 32 .180	-.053 42 .369	-.194 39 .118	-.200 41 .105	-.126 37 .229	.386 39 .008	-.050 38 .383	-.334 38 .020
CAFR6779	-.251 20 .143	.022 20 .463	.276 30 .070	.057 24 .396	.028 27 .446	.304 24 .074	.103 28 .302	.316 25 .062	-.165 22 .232

	FOODIN78	LITRCY	CHILM	LLIFEXB	INFL6078	EMPLOY78	CFOODP78	INFLAA78
MXCGFAC	-.193 30 .153	-.163 37 .167	.325 35 .076	.036 35 .419	-.013 30 .473	-.057 10 .438	-.043 29 .412	-.133 32 .235
CAF70	-.058 27 .388	.386 33 .013	.240 19 .161	.434 34 .005	.055 29 .388	-.310 9 .208	-.178 25 .197	.034 31 .427
AFSIZE	-.090 34 .306	.320 41 .021	.064 23 .386	.399 40 .005	-.023 34 .450	-.145 12 .326	-.235 34 .090	-.046 37 .393
CAFR6779	-.088 22 .348	-.033 29 .433	-.209 15 .227	.130 27 .259	.010 20 .483	.102 7 .414	.032 22 .444	.253 21 .135

Sources: PRIO Data Bank; Appendix C.

Table 55: Political and Civil Rights (1973) Control with Militarization and Welfare Change Indicators (1970-1978) (cont'd)

FREEDM73 - Less Free

	PHYSICAL	WOMENFAC	CHLPER	PROPER	WOMLF	PTRPED	FPRSCH	FSCSCH	CALPER
MXCGFAC	-.255 22 .126	.306 22 .083	.166 31 .186	.683 24 .000	-.093 31 .310	.391 28 .020	.175 29 .182	-.210 26 .152	.261 24 .109
CAF70	-.207 17 .212	.568 17 .009	.126 28 .261	.973 19 .000	-.186 26 .182	.302 23 .081	.185 24 .193	-.192 23 .190	.315 19 .094
AFSIZE	-.227 19 .174	.466 19 .022	.131 32 .237	.922 22 .000	-.185 30 .164	.212 26 .149	.435 26 .013	-.253 26 .106	.336 22 .063
CAFR6779	-.048 18 .425	.277 18 .133	.268 33 .066	.160 21 .244	.163 28 .203	.054 24 .401	.105 26 .304	-.248 24 .122	.467 21 .016

	FOODIN78	LITRCY	CHILDM	LIFEXB	INFL6078	EMPLOY78	CFOODP78	INFLAA78
MXCGFAC	-.263 25 .102	.291 31 .056	-.015 7 .487	.189 30 .159	.344 24 .050	-.613 7 .072	.163 14 .289	-.196 22 .190
CAF70	-.021 20 .465	.632 27 .000	.302 8 .234	.544 28 .001	.304 19 .103	-.687 7 .044	-.049 16 .428	-.022 17 .467
AFSIZE	-.069 23 .377	.488 31 .003	.680 9 .022	.427 32 .007	.308 23 .077	-.364 7 .211	-.026 17 .460	.027 21 .453
CAFR6779	-.353 19 .069	.033 29 .433	-.382 9 .155	-.084 32 .324	.086 22 .352	.378 7 .202	.176 17 .250	-.280 20 .116

Sources: PRIO Data Bank; Appendix C.

Table 56: Government Expenditure as a percent of GDP (1970) Controls with Militarization and Welfare Change Indicators (1970–1978)

GVTGDP70 – Above Median

	PHYSICAL	WOMENFAC	CHLPER	PROPER	WOMLF	PTRPED	FPRSCH	FSCSCH	CALPER
MXCGFAC	-.257	.542	.223	.828	-.135	.286	.121	-.232	.251
	21	21	31	29	31	28	29	28	28
	.130	.006	.114	.000	.235	.070	.267	.118	.099
CAF70	-.382	.584	.200	.894	-.263	.386	.197	-.174	.199
	19	19	26	24	26	23	25	23	25
	.053	.004	.163	.000	.097	.034	.173	.214	.286
AFSIZE	-.474	.503	.001	.706	-.278	.206	.421	-.221	.063
	23	23	34	30	34	28	31	29	29
	.011	.007	.499	.000	.055	.146	.009	.124	.373
CAFR6779	.010	.186	.455	.205	.272	.144	.150	-.130	.018
	18	18	26	23	26	23	25	24	21
	.484	.230	.010	.174	.089	.256	.237	.272	.305

210

	FOODIN78	LITRCY	CHILDM	LIFEXB	INFL6078	EMPLOY78	CFOODP78	INFLAA78
MXCGFAC	-.135	.538	.450	.314	.022	-.265	-.019	-.177
	28	32	12	29	26	9	23	26
	.247	.001	.071	.049	.458	.245	.465	.193
CAF70	-.136	.710	.343	.467	-.008	-.217	-.063	-.195
	23	27	11	27	24	7	20	24
	.268	.000	.151	.007	.486	.320	.396	.180
AFSIZE	-.134	.459	.043	.419	-.079	-.122	-.088	-.189
	29	35	13	33	30	10	26	30
	.244	.003	.444	.008	.339	.369	.334	.159
CAFR6779	-.016	.155	-.219	.042	.020	.508	.015	-.085
	21	27	10	24	21	8	17	21
	.473	.221	.272	.423	.466	.099	.476	.357

Sources: PRIO Data Bank; Appendix C.

211

Table 57: Public Consumption as a percent of GDP (1978) Control with Militarization and Welfare Change Indicators (1970-1978)

PUCGDP78 - Above Median

	PHYSICAL	WOMENFAC	CHLPER	PROPER	WOMLF	PTRPED	FPRSCH	FSCSCH	CALPER
MXCGFAC	-.245 23 .130	.230 23 .146	.345 31 .029	.717 28 .000	-.122 31 .256	.495 28 .004	.191 30 .156	-.225 28 .124	.181 28 .178
CAF70	-.162 20 .248	.132 20 .290	-.070 28 .362	.169 26 .205	-.197 28 .157	.186 25 .187	.067 27 .371	.093 26 .325	-.248 26 .111
AFSIZE	-.283 23 .095	.285 23 .094	-.040 32 .413	.425 29 .011	-.249 32 .085	.199 28 .155	.278 30 .068	.007 29 .485	-.189 29 .163
CAFR6779	-.653 20 .001	.418 20 .033	.518 27 .003	.449 23 .016	-.396 27 .021	.352 25 .042	.383 26 .027	-.250 23 .125	-.021 24 .462

	FOODIN78	LITRCY	CHILDM	LIFEXB	INFL6078	EMPLOY78	CFOODP78	INFLAA78
MXCGFAC	-.204 27 .153	.286 32 .056	.338 12 .141	.158 32 .193	.032 29 .434	.030 9 .469	.023 18 .463	-.077 28 .349
CAF70	-.052 25 .402	.318 29 .046	.261 12 .206	.503 29 .003	.049 26 .406	-.259 8 .268	-.164 17 .265	.268 25 .098
AFSIZE	-.091 28 .323	.379 33 .015	.069 14 .407	.533 33 .001	-.010 30 .479	-.165 10 .324	-.124 19 .307	.107 29 .289
CAFR6779	-.285 23 .094	.118 28 .275	-.348 11 .147	.415 28 .014	-.045 24 .417	-.806 6 .026	.053 13 .432	-.210 23 .168

Table 57: Public Consumption as a percent of GDP (1978) Control with Militarization and Welfare Change Indicators (1970-1978) (cont'd)

PUCGDP78 - Below Median

	PHYSICAL	WOMENFAC	CHLPER	PROPER	WOMLF	PTRPED	FPRSCH	FSCSCH	CALPER
MXCGFAC	-.263 24 .107	.200 24 .175	-.014 25 .474	.170 24 .213	-.182 24 .197	-.064 25 .381	.526 24 .004	-.100 25 .317	.147 24 .246
CAF70	-.462 20 .020	-.394 21 .043	.184 21 .213	-.507 20 .011	-.203 20 .195	-.298 21 .095	.964 20 .000	-.398 21 .037	-.438 20 .027
AFSIZE	-.487 24 .008	-.449 24 .014	.183 27 .180	-.304 25 .070	-.097 26 .319	-.316 25 .062	.918 25 .000	-.339 26 .045	-.560 25 .002
CAFR6779	.244 16 .181	.083 16 .380	.564 18 .007	.747 16 .000	.398 18 .051	-.001 17 .498	-.007 16 .489	-.041 18 .435	.607 16 .006

	FOODIN78	LITRCY	CHILDM	LIFEXB	INFL6078	EMPLOY78	CFOODP78	INFLAA78
MXCGFAC	-.126 20 .298	-.202 24 .172	.146 13 .317	.017 24 .468	-.009 22 .484	-.352 5 .280	.327 19 .086	-.262 23 .113
CAF70	-.268 17 .149	-.171 20 .236	-.274 12 .194	.146 20 .270	.307 19 .100	-.720 5 .085	.031 17 .453	-.345 19 .074
AFSIZE	-.136 22 .272	-.084 26 .342	-.403 15 .068	-.074 26 .360	-.160 24 .228	-.107 6 .420	-.341 23 .056	-.311 25 .065
CAFR6779	.055 13 .429	-.060 17 .410	-.530 11 .047	-.092 17 .363	.064 16 .407	-.921 4 .040	-.078 16 .388	-.070 16 .398

Sources: PRIO Data Bank; Appendix C.

213

Table 58: Gross Domestic Product Average Annual Growth Rate (1960-1970) Control with Militarization and Welfare Change Indicators (1970-1978)

CGDP70 - Above Median

	PHYSICAL	WOMENFAC	CHLPER	PROPER	WOMLF	PTRPED	FPRSCH	FSCSCH	CALPER
MXCGFAC	-.479 / 24 / .009	.358 / 24 / .043	.351 / 34 / .021	.643 / 27 / .000	-.266 / 32 / .071	.445 / 28 / .009	.634 / 29 / .000	-.058 / 27 / .387	.183 / 29 / .172
CAF70	-.353 / 22 / .054	.570 / 22 / .003	.168 / 33 / .175	.892 / 25 / .000	-.348 / 31 / .027	.283 / 26 / .081	.603 / 27 / .000	-.234 / 25 / .130	.156 / 27 / .219
AFSIZE	-.316 / 25 / .062	.471 / 25 / .009	.176 / 36 / .152	.822 / 28 / .000	-.208 / 34 / .119	.212 / 29 / .134	.535 / 30 / .001	-.179 / 28 / .180	.084 / 30 / .329
CAFR6779	-.073 / 18 / .387	.121 / 18 / .317	.355 / 26 / .038	.261 / 20 / .133	.507 / 25 / .005	.198 / 21 / .195	.228 / 21 / .160	-.235 / 20 / .159	.218 / 22 / .165

	FOODIN78	LITTRCY	CHILDM	LIFEXB	INFL6078	EMPLOY78	CROODP78	INFLAA78
MXCGFAC	.003 / 27 / .493	.416 / 34 / .007	.518 / 19 / .012	.264 / 34 / .065	.039 / 26 / .425	-.261 / 13 / .194	-.162 / 22 / .236	-.161 / 26 / .216
CAF70	-.008 / 26 / .484	.657 / 33 / .000	.212 / 20 / .185	.377 / 33 / .015	.032 / 24 / .441	-.413 / 13 / .080	-.213 / 23 / .164	-.154 / 24 / .237
AFSIZE	.036 / 28 / .428	.619 / 36 / .000	.667 / 21 / .000	.329 / 36 / .025	-.013 / 27 / .475	-.291 / 13 / .167	-.290 / 24 / .085	-.138 / 27 / .246
CAFR6779	-.264 / 18 / .145	.269 / 26 / .092	-.140 / 15 / .309	.097 / 26 / .318	.087 / 19 / .362	-.265 / 10 / .230	.063 / 17 / .406	-.308 / 18 / .107

Table 58: Gross Domestic Product Average Annual Growth Rate (1960–1970) Control with Militarization and Welfare Change Indicators (1970–1978) (cont'd)

CGDP70 – Below Median

	PHYSICAL	WOMENFAC	CHLPER	PROPER	WOMLF	PTRPED	FPRSCH	FSCSCH	CALPER
MXOGFAC	-.304 24 .075	.123 24 .283	-.054 28 .393	-.005 27 .489	.116 29 .275	.022 28 .455	.066 29 .366	-.239 27 .115	.021 26 .459
CAF70	-.078 19 .376	-.009 19 .485	-.277 26 .085	-.247 24 .122	-.144 25 .247	.074 25 .362	.022 26 .458	.124 26 .273	-.335 23 .059
AFSIZE	-.263 23 .113	.053 23 .406	-.183 33 .154	-.175 29 .182	-.177 32 .166	.002 29 .497	.218 31 .119	.111 31 .276	-.344 28 .037
CAFR6779	-.498 17 .021	.313 17 .110	.231 23 .145	.190 22 .225	-.289 22 .096	-.078 20 .371	.378 21 .046	-.049 22 .414	.096 17 .357

	FOODIN78	LITRCY	CHILDM	LIFEXB	INFL6078	EMPLOY78	CROODP78	INFLAA78
MXOGFAC	-.212 24 .160	-.199 29 .151	.214 7 .323	-.125 29 .259	.000 28 .500	.193 3 .438	-.046 17 .430	-.351 27 .036
CAF70	-.091 20 .351	.269 25 .097	.180 5 .386	.556 27 .001	.224 24 .146	-.297 3 .404	-.049 16 .429	.060 23 .393
AFSIZE	-.108 26 .300	.208 32 .126	-.203 9 .301	.528 34 .001	.128 30 .250	-.638 6 .086	-.093 23 .337	.007 30 .486
CAFR6779	-.126 18 .309	-.163 23 .229	-.327 7 .237	.057 24 .396	-.261 21 .127	-1.000 2 .000	-.392 14 .083	.026 20 .456

Sources: PRIO Data Bank; Appendix C.

215

Table 59: Manufacturing as a percent of GDP (1970) Control with Militarization and Welfare Change Indicators (1970-1978)

MFGDP70 - Above Median

	PHYSICAL	WOMENFAC	CHLPER	PROPER	WOMLF	PTRPED	FPRSCH	FSCSCH	CALPER
MXOGFAC	-.116 21 .309	.206 21 .186	.308 25 .067	.539 24 .003	.037 25 .431	.335 24 .055	.042 23 .424	-.026 23 .453	.575 23 .002
CAF70	-.416 18 .043	-.325 18 .094	.117 22 .302	.159 21 .245	.301 22 .086	.201 21 .191	.597 20 .003	.177 20 .227	.070 20 .384
AFSIZE	-.353 24 .046	-.294 24 .082	-.202 28 .152	-.083 26 .344	.064 28 .373	-.013 26 .474	.328 26 .051	.014 26 .473	-.109 25 .302
CAFR6779	.148 16 .292	.109 16 .344	.622 20 .002	.268 19 .133	.282 20 .114	.183 18 .234	.355 19 .068	-.009 19 .486	.351 17 .084

	FOODIN78	LITRCY	CHILDM	LIFEXB	INFL6078	EMPLOY78	CFOODP78	INFLAA78
MXOGFAC	-.222 21 .166	.252 25 .112	.172 16 .262	-.014 25 .474	-.253 23 .123	.595 7 .080	.037 23 .433	-.072 22 .375
CAF70	-.210 19 .195	.187 22 .203	.078 13 .400	.356 22 .052	.264 20 .130	-.564 6 .122	-.137 20 .282	-.391 19 .049
AFSIZE	-.171 23 .217	.048 28 .405	.340 18 .084	.133 28 .250	.160 26 .217	.089 8 .417	.104 26 .306	-.159 25 .224
CAFR6779	-.078 16 .387	-.084 20 .362	-.333 13 .133	-.204 19 .201	.066 17 .400	-.557 6 .125	.139 18 .292	-.017 16 .475

Table 59: Manufacturing as a percent of GDP (1970) Control with Militarization and Welfare Change Indicators (1970-1978) (cont'd)

MFGDP70 - Below Median

	PHYSICAL	WOMENFAC	CHLPER	PROPER	WOMLF	PTRPED	FPRSCH	FSCSCH	CALPER
MXCGFAC	-.356 18 .073	.348 18 .079	-.078 25 .356	-.110 23 .309	-.200 25 .169	.014 24 .474	.027 25 .450	-.063 23 .387	-.007 22 .487
CAF70	.063 15 .412	.039 15 .445	-.357 19 .067	-.231 18 .179	-.174 19 .238	-.010 18 .485	.029 20 .451	.131 18 .302	-.197 19 .210
AFSIZE	-.020 16 .471	.082 16 .382	-.270 24 .101	-.175 23 .212	-.213 24 .159	-.012 22 .479	.010 23 .482	-.029 22 .448	-.239 22 .142
CAFR6779	-.525 14 .027	.431 14 .062	.233 18 .177	.150 17 .283	-.268 19 .134	-.068 18 .394	.065 18 .399	.027 18 .457	.128 16 .318

	FOODIN78	LITTRCY	CHILLM	LIFEXB	INFL6078	EMPLOY78	CFOODP78	INFLAA78
MXCGFAC	-.373 22 .044	-.329 26 .050	.402 4 .299	.042 23 .424	.273 20 .122	-.636 5 .124	.427 13 .073	-.305 21 .090
CAF70	.001 17 .499	.337 20 .073	-.142 6 .394	.534 20 .008	.219 18 .192	-.726 4 .137	-.009 11 .489	.158 18 .265
AFSIZE	-.057 23 .397	.251 25 .114	-.350 6 .248	.483 23 .010	.239 20 .155	-.312 5 .305	-.085 15 .382	.071 21 .379
CAFR6779	-.364 16 .083	-.013 19 .479	-.506 6 .153	.052 17 .422	.293 14 .154	.980 3 .063	-.112 10 .379	-.207 15 .229

Sources: PRIO Data Bank; Appendix C.

217

Table 60: Torture, Execution and Disappearance (1975, 1979) Controls with Military Burden and Militarization Indicators

TORTUR79 Breakdown

TORTUR75

	(MILSPFAC)(a)				(USTAFFAC)(b)			
Yes	Yes	No	Indet.	Total	Yes	No	Indet.	Total
Mean	.292	-.146		.158	-.082	-.127		-.096
SD	1.178	.923		1.112	1.001	1.116		1.021
N	25	11	0	36	25	11	0	36
No								
Mean	-.355	-.722	.786	-.461	.273	.395	.378	.357
SD	.143	.231	.000	.506	.282	.293	.000	.262
N	3	6	1	10	3	6	1	10
Total								
Mean	.222	-.349	.786	.023	-.044	.057	.378	.003
SD	1.130	.793	.000	1.039	.953	.934	.000	.928
N	28	17	1	46	28	17	1	46

	(MXCGFAC)(c)				(AFSIZE)(d)			
Yes	Yes	No	Indet.	Total	Yes	No	Indet.	Total
Mean	.017	-.118	-.551	-.030	454.548	596.947	119.045	473.202
SD	.621	.820	.000	.666	758.459	1461.425	21.277	937.951
N	32	11	1	44	35	11	2	48
No								
Mean	.154	-.042	-.432	-.003	785.243	349.111	89.256	497.578
SD	1.209	.425	.213	.811	1014.366	250.007	26.507	687.547
N	8	10	2	20	8	10	2	20
Total								
Mean	.044	-.082	-.472	-.021	516.073	478.930	104.151	480.372
SD	.756	.647	.165	.708	808.784	1054.559	26.094	866.787
N	40	21	3	64	43	21	4	68

	(CAF70)(e)				(CAFR6779)(f)			
Yes	Yes	No	Indet.	Total	Yes	No	Indet.	Total
Mean	74.461	368.960	16.900	145.207	37.692	51.182	-17.000	38.692
SD	164.125	1135.686	12.587	577.555	95.485	60.455	8.485	84.682
N	28	10	2	40	26	11	2	39
No								
Mean	200.043	61.043	-11.300	112.813	78.400	148.000	-33.000	99.278
SD	310.612	46.855	19.940	215.295	90.728	179.856	.000	134.306
N	7	7	2	16	10	7	1	18
Total								
Mean	99.577	242.171	2.800	135.952	49.000	88.833	-22.333	57.825
SD	202.521	866.445	21.223	499.391	94.716	126.197	11.015	105.590
N	35	17	4	56	36	18	3	57

Sources: PRIO Data Bank; Appendix C.
(a) MILSPFAC: (T79) R^2 .08, p .15; (T75) R^2 .06, p .10; (Total) R^2 .13.
(b) USTAFFAC: (T79) R^2 .01, p .87; (T75) R^2 .04, p .18; (") R^2 .04.
(c) MXCGFAC: (T79) R^2 .03, p .43; (T75) R^2 .001, p .89; (") R^2 .03.
(d) AFSIZE: (T79) R^2 .01, p .67; (T75) R^2 .001, p .92; (") R^2 .03.
(e) CAF70: (T79) R^2 .02, p .55; (T75) R^2 .001, p .83; (") R^2 .06.
(f) CAFR6779: (T79) R^2 .06, p .17; (T75) R^2 .07, p .05; (") R^2 .15.

Table 61: Political and Civil Rights (1973, 1982) Controls with
Military Burden and Militarization Indicators

FREEDM82

FREEDM73 Breakdown

	(MILSPFAC)(a)			(USTAFFAC)(b)		
More Free	More Free	Less Free	Total	More Free	Less Free	Total
Mean	-.216	-.034	-.172	.044	-.300	-.039
SD	.799	.812	.791	.513	1.164	.714
N	22	7	29	22	7	29
Less Free						
Mean	-.005	.396	.205	-.374	.413	.038
SD	.974	1.462	1.240	1.513	.391	1.127
N	10	11	21	10	11	21
Total						
Mean	-.150	.229	-.014	-.086	.136	-.006
SD	.847	1.239	1.010	.939	.834	.901
N	32	18	50	32	18	50

	(MXCGFAC)(c)			(CAF70)(d)		
More Free	More Free	Less Free	Total	More Free	Less Free	Total
Mean	-.131	.017	-.097	199.730	66.983	169.096
SD	.455	.745	.523	801.252	77.967	701.707
N	24	7	31	20	6	26
Less Free						
Mean	.108	-.004	.037	120.350	85.050	98.778
SD	.579	.916	.802	220.242	186.820	198.147
N	14	24	38	14	22	36
Total						
Mean	-.043	.001	-.023	167.044	81.179	128.266
SD	.510	.869	.689	624.756	168.311	474.923
N	38	31	69	34	28	62

	(AFSIZE)(e)			(CAFR6779)(f)		
More Free	More Free	Less Free	Total	More Free	Less Free	Total
Mean	412.486	374.356	405.072	47.571	136.250	61.760
SD	941.279	346.291	854.164	109.729	243.000	136.072
N	29	7	36	21	4	25
Less Free						
Mean	722.924	387.759	502.421	36.200	70.552	61.744
SD	1117.418	621.016	825.278	54.311	117.655	105.496
N	13	25	38	10	29	39
Total						
Mean	508.574	384.827	455.062	43.903	78.515	61.750
SD	995.804	567.289	835.113	94.557	134.619	117.331
N	42	32	74	31	33	64

Sources: PRIO Data Bank; Appendix C.
(a) MILSPFAC: (F73) R2 .03, p .21; (F82) R2 .03, p .20; (Total) R2 .06.
(b) USTAFFAC: (F73) R2 .01, p .41; (F82) R2 .001, p .77; (") R2 .10.
(c) MXCGFAC: (F73) R2 .001, p .79; (F82) R2 .01, p .42; (") R2 .02.
(d) CAF70: (F73) R2 .01, p .48; (F82) R2 .01, p .57; (") R2 .01.
(e) AFSIZE: (F73) R2 .01, p .53; (F82) R2 .001, p .62; (") R2 .02.
(f) CAFR6779: (F73) R2 .02, p .24; (F82) R2 .001, p .99; (") R2 .04.

Table 62: Civilian vs Military Rule (1960-1967, 1965-1978) Controls with Political and Civil Rights (1973, 1982)

FREEDM73 Breakdown|

CVML6578   CIVMIL67

	Civilian	Military	Total
Civilian			
Mean	4.875	5.500	4.887
SD	1.715	.000	1.700
N	52	1	53
Military			
Mean	5.063	5.650	5.288
SD	1.559	.580	1.290
N	16	10	26
Mixed			
Mean	4.200		4.200
SD	1.754		1.754
N	5	0	5
Total			
Mean	4.870	5.636	4.970
SD	1.673	.552	1.591
N	73	11	84

FREEDM82 Breakdown||

CVML6578   CIVMIL67

	Civilian	Military	Total
Civilian			
Mean	4.865	3.500	4.840
SD	1.855	.000	1.847
N	52	1	53
Military			
Mean	5.469	5.250	5.385
SD	1.488	1.419	1.437
N	16	10	26
Mixed			
Mean	5.200		5.200
SD	1.823		1.823
N	5	0	5
Total			
Mean	5.021	5.091	5.030
SD	1.775	1.446	1.727
N	73	11	84

Source: PRIO Data Bank; Appendix C.
| FREEDM73: (CIVMIL67) R^2 .001, p .90; (CVML6578) R^2 .02, p .41; (Total) R^2 .03.
|| FREEDM82: (CIVMIL67) R^2 .03, p .14; (CVML6578) R^2 .03, p .31; (Total) R^2 .04.

Table 63: Civilian vs Military Rule (1960-1967, 1965-1978) Controls with Military Burdens

MILSPFAC Breakdown|

CVML6578   CIVMIL67

Civilian	Civilian	Military	Total
Civilian			
Mean	-.160	.693	-.126
SD	1.018	.000	1.011
N	24	1	25
Military			
Mean	-.319	.946	.173
SD	.324	1.476	1.110
N	11	7	18
Mixed			
Mean	.661		.661
SD	1.358		1.358
N	2	0	2
Total			
Mean	-.163	.914	.028
SD	.888	1.369	1.057
N	37	8	45

USTAFS Breakdown||

CVML6578   CIVMIL67

Civilian	Civilian	Military y	Total
Mean	4813.547	86116.667	7617.103
SD	6860.333	.000	16532.427
N	28	1	29
Military			
Mean	6951.592	5231.776	6263.666
SD	15299.477	8271.208	12707.025
N	12	8	20
Mixed			
Mean	7471.810		7471.810
SD	3610.755		3610.755
N	2	0	2
Total			
Mean	5551.001	14218.987	7080.646
SD	9758.961	28049.791	14666.923
N	42	9	51

Sources: PRIO Data Bank; Appendix C.
| MILSPFAC (CIVMIL67) R^2 .16, p .01; (CVML6578)
  R^2 .04, p .46; (Total) R^2 .19.
|| USTAFS (CIVMIL67) R^2 .05, p .11; (CVML6578)
  R^2 .001, p .95; (Total) R^2 .10.

Table 64: Civilian vs Military Rule (1960-1967, 1965-1978)
Controls with Militarization Indicators

(CVML6578)	MXCGFAC|		Breakdowns (CIVMIL67)	AFSIZE||	
Civilian	Civilian	Military	Total	Civilian	Military	Total
Mean	.020	-.148	.015	375.378	120.000	369.150
SD	.801	.000	.790	597.390	.000	591.222
N	34	1	35	40	1	41
Military						
Mean	-.215	-.078	-.161	763.558	568.765	678.865
SD	.409	.641	.506	1320.596	1210.076	1249.013
N	15	10	25	13	10	23
Mixed						
Mean	.309		.309	490.417		490.417
SD	.919		.919	571.588		571.588
N	3	0	3	3	0	3
Total						
Mean	-.031	-.085	-.041	471.654	527.968	480.900
SD	.716	.609	.694	819.964	1155.926	873.599
N	52	11	63	56	11	67

(CVML6578)	CAF70|||		Breakdowns (CIVMIL67)	CAFR6779||||	
Civilian	Civilian	Military	Total	Civilian	Military	Total
Mean	76.486	20.000	74.603	67.633	20.000	66.097
SD	175.576	.000	172.830	140.314	.000	138.220
N	29	1	30	30	1	31
Military						
Mean	346.431	98.100	238.461	49.818	17.714	37.333
SD	978.478	248.031	750.493	67.370	69.916	68.224
N	13	10	23	11	7	18
Mixed						
Mean	59.800		59.800	47.500		47.500
SD	121.804		121.804	74.246		74.246
N	3	0	3	2	0	2
Total						
Mean	153.358	91.000	141.109	62.140	18.000	55.216
SD	544.895	236.478	498.319	121.973	64.735	115.528
N	45	11	56	43	8	51

Sources: PRIO Data Bank; Appendix C.
MXCGFAC (CIVMIL67) R^2 .001, p .82; (CVML6578) R^2 .03, p .43; (Total) R^2 .03.
AFSIZE   (") R^2 .001, p .85;   (") R^2 .03, p .40;   (") R^2 .03.
CAF70   (") R^2 .001, p .71;   (") R^2 .03, p .48;   (") R^2 .05.
CAFR6779 (") R^2 .02, p .33;   (") R^2 .01, p .71;   (") R^2 .02.

Table 65: Civilian vs Military Rule (1965-1978)
Control with Welfare Factors

(CVML6578)	PHYSICAL			WOMENFAC		
	Civilian	Military	Total	Civilian	Military	Total
Civilian						
Mean	-.076		-.076	.111		.111
SD	1.070		1.070	.924		.924
N	32	0	32	32	0	32
Military						
Mean	-.183	.014	-.111	.359	-1.050	-.153
SD	1.083	.799	.973	.943	.908	1.143
N	14	8	22	14	8	22
Mixed						
Mean	.211		.211	.358		.358
SD	1.547		1.547	1.068		1.068
N	4	0	4	4	0	4
Total						
Mean	-.083	.014	-.070	.200	-1.050	.028
SD	1.091	.799	1.050	.927	.908	1.015
N	50	8	58	50	8	58

Sources: PRIO Data Bank; Appendix C.
| R2 .01, p .86.
|| R2 .02, p .52.

Table 66: Civilian vs Military Rule (1965-1978) and Welfare Change Indicators (1970-1978)

CVML6578	CHLPER	PROPER	WOMLF	PTRPED	FPSCH	FSCSCH	CALPER
Civilian							
Mean	.856	1.284	1.035	.987	1.290	1.535	1.044
SD	.141	1.607	.071	.211	.550	.507	.151
N	52	42	50	43	44	43	39
Military							
Mean	.881	1.016	1.019	.952	1.481	1.885	1.036
SD	.068	.104	.032	.108	1.108	.928	.087
N	26	22	25	24	25	24	23
Mixed							
Mean	.881	.987	1.014	.901	1.015	1.169	1.097
SD	.106	.055	.020	.098	.206	.182	–
N	5	3	5	5	5	4	3
Total							
Mean	.865	1.183	1.029	.969	1.336	1.632	1.044
SD	.120	1.275	.059	.177	.774	.692	.128
N	83	67	80	72	74	71	65
	R^2 .01	R^2 .01	R^2 .02	R^2 .02	R^2 .03	R^2 .08	R^2 .01
	p .65	p .71	p .47	p .50	p .39	p .05	p .75

CVML6578	LIFEXB	CFOODP78	INFLAA78	FOODIN78	INFL6078	EMPLOY78
Civilian						
Mean	1.088	123.033	11.405	233.479	366.514	135.111
SD	.055	16.798	4.803	90.682	385.271	35.041
N	48	30	37	38	37	19
Military						
Mean	1.100	120.800	13.841	683.920	295.591	119.533
SD	.058	13.492	7.202	1440.218	222.858	14.180
N	25	15	22	20	22	6
Mixed						
Mean	1.075	113.333	31.375	1238.860	308.800	–
SD	.044	15.275	23.435	2061.675	321.822	–
N	5	3	4	5	5	–
Total						
Mean	1.091	121.729	13.524	456.268	337.625	131.372
SD	.055	15.624	8.990	1005.641	330.338	31.763
N	78	48	63	63	64	25
	R^2 .02	R^2 .02	R^2 .29	R^2 .10	R^2 .01	R^2 .05
	p .55	p .58	p .001	p .05	p .72	p .30

Sources: PRIO Data Bank; Appendix C.

Table 67: Political and Civil Rights (1973, 1982) Controls with Welfare Change Indicators (1970-1978)

FREEDM73 Breakdowns

(LITRCY)

FREEDM82	More Free	Less Free	Total
More Free			
Mean	1.146	1.155	1.155
SD	.310	.204	.291
N	37	9	46
Less Free			
Mean	1.331	1.490	1.443
SD	.607	.853	.784
N	14	33	47
Total			
Mean	1.197	1.426	1.300
SD	.415	.769	.608
N	51	42	93

(F73) R2 .04, p .07; (F82) R2 .06, p .02 (T) R2 .06

(CHILDM)

FREEDM82	More Free	Less Free	Total
More Free			
Mean	1.815	.839	1.645
SD	2.505	.350	2.301
N	19	4	23
Less Free			
Mean	1.514	1.514	1.514
SD	.960	1.252	1.081
N	6	7	13
Total			
Mean	1.743	1.268	1.598
SD	2.217	1.046	1.932
N	25	11	36

(F73) R2 .01, p .51; (F82) R2 .001, p .85; (T) R2 .03

(CHILPER)

FREEDM82	More Free	Less Free	Total
More Free			
Mean	.857	.904	.867
SD	.071	.099	.078
N	36	9	45
Less Free			
Mean	.900	.857	.870
SD	.050	.157	.135
N	16	37	53
Total			
Mean	.871	.867	.869
SD	.068	.148	.112
N	52	46	98

(F73) R2 .001, p .86; (F82) R2 .001, p. 87; (T) R2 .03.

(PROPER)

FREEDM82	More Free	Less Free	Total
More Free			
Mean	1.027	1.013	1.024
SD	.127	.134	.127
N	32	8	40
Less Free			
Mean	1.062	1.460	1.327
SD	.189	2.121	1.733
N	12	24	36
Total			
Mean	1.036	1.348	1.168
SD	.145	1.838	1.197
N	44	32	76

(F73) R2 .02, p .27; (F82) R2 .27; (T) R2 .03

(WKMLF)

FREEDM82	More Free	Less Free	Total
More Free			
Mean	1.051	1.031	1.047
SD	.088	.079	.086
N	35	9	44
Less Free			
Mean	1.031	1.019	1.019
SD	2.028	.048	.043
N	13	32	45
Total			
Mean	1.045	1.021	1.034
SD	.07	.055	.068
N	48	41	89

(F73) R2 .03, p .09; (F82) R2 .03, p .10; (T) R2 .04

(PTIRPED)

FREEDM82	More Free	Less Free	Total
More Free			
Mean	.967	.903	.952
SD	.166	.190	.172
N	30	9	39
Less Free			
Mean	.923	1.010	.982
SD	.126	.195	.179
N	13	28	41
Total			
Mean	.954	.994	.968
SD	.155	.196	.175
N	43	37	80

(F73) R2 .01, p .44; (F82) R2 .05, .01, p .45; (T) R2

(FPRSCH)

FREEDM82	More Free	Less Free	Total
More Free			
Mean	1.209	1.045	1.175
SD	.532	.133	.481
N	35	9	44
Less Free			
Mean	1.425	1.524	1.494
SD	.542	1.004	.884
N	13	30	43
Total			
Mean	1.267	1.413	1.333
SD	.538	.903	.723
N	48	39	87

(F73) R2 .01, p .35; (F82) R2 .06 .05, p .04; (T) R2 .06

(FSCSCH)

FREEDM82	More Free	Less Free	Total
More Free			
Mean	1.500	1.965	1.591
SD	.466	.939	.603
N	33	8	41
Less Free			
Mean	1.278	1.963	1.752
SD	.470	.915	.860
N	27	12	39
Total			
Mean	1.441	1.963	1.669
SD	.473	.907	.739
N	45	35	80

(F73) R2 .12, p .01; (F82) R2 .13, .01, p .33; (m) R2

(CALPER)

FREEDM82	More Free	Less Free	Total
More Free			
Mean	1.048	1.030	1.044
SD	.105	.137	.111
N	28	8	36
Less Free			
Mean	1.047	1.033	1.037
SD	.166	.123	.136
N	12	24	36
Total			
Mean	1.048	1.032	1.041
SD	.124	.124	.124
N	40	32	72

(F73) R2 .001, p .59; (F82) R2 .001 .001, p .83; (T) R2

225

Table 67: <u>Political and Civil Rights (1973, 1982) Controls with Welfare Change Indicators (1970-1978)</u> (cont'd)

FREEDM73 Breakdowns

FREEDM82

	(LIFEXB)			(CFOODP78)		
More Free	More Free	Less Free	Total	More Free	Less Free	Total
Mean	1.076	1.068	1.074	124.667	123.000	124.364
SD	.059	.055	.057	15.325	15.849	15.182
N	32	9	41	27	6	33
Less Free						
Mean	1.094	1.115	1.109	115.818	111.438	113.222
SD	.066	.093	.086	24.437	19.541	21.326
N	15	36	51	11	16	27
Total						
Mean	1.081	1.105	1.093	122.105	114.591	119.350
SD	.061	.088	.076	18.519	18.983	18.886
N	47	45	92	38	22	60

(F73) R^2 .03, p .13; (F82) R^2 .05, p .03 (T) R^2 .06

(F73) R^2 .04, p .14; (F82) R^2 .09, p .03; (T) R^2 .09

	(INFLAA78)			(FOODIN78)		
More Free	More Free	Less Free	Total	More Free	Less Free	Total
Mean	15.560	16.250	15.705	410.739	449.963	418.785
SD	11.012	11.006	10.864	843.062	387.744	767.511
N	30	8	38	31	8	39
Less Free						
Mean	12.109	9.983	10.651	874.250	254.291	442.158
SD	6.169	4.775	5.256	2023.743	231.686	1128.045
N	11	24	35	10	23	33
Total						
Mean	14.634	11.550	13.282	523.790	304.787	429.497
SD	9.991	7.202	8.953	1222.772	286.391	942.831
N	41	32	73	41	31	72

(F73) R^2 .03, p .15; (F82) R^2 .08, p .01; (T) R^2 .09

(F73) R^2 .01, p .33; (F82) R^2 .001, p .92; (T) R^2 .04

	(INFL6078)			(EMPLOY78)		
More Free	More Free	Less Free	Total	More Free	Less Free	Total
Mean	393.857	376.333	389.595	122.400	109.400	119.614
SD	451.290	186.898	400.709	19.739	10.762	18.660
N	28	9	37	11	3	14
Less Free						
Mean	369.545	256.400	290.972	129.933	152.488	146.336
SD	260.144	189.143	216.012	23.072	43.283	39.100
N	11	25	36	3	8	11
Total						
Mean	387.000	288.147	340.959	124.014	140.736	131.372
SD	403.286	193.316	324.702	19.797	41.708	31.763
N	39	34	73	14	11	25

(F73) R^2 .02, p .20; (F82) R^2 .02, p .20; (T) R^2 .04

(F73) R^2 .07, p .20; (F82) R^2 .18, p .04 (T) R^2 .24

Sources: PRIO Data Bank; Appendix C.

Table 68: Political and Civil Rights (1973, 1982) Controls with Welfare Factors

FREEDM73 Breakdown

FREEDM82

	(WOMENFAC)			(PHYSICAL)		
	More Free	Less Free	Total	More Free	Less Free	Total
More Free						
Mean	-.097	.231	-.020	.312	.379	.328
SD	.600	.624	.613	.759	1.113	.837
N	26	8	34	26	8	34
Less Free						
Mean	-.195	.045	-.040	-.450	-.571	-.528
SD	1.224	1.409	1.331	1.036	1.022	1.011
N	11	20	31	11	20	31
Total						
Mean	-.126	.098	-.030	.085	-.299	-.080
SD	.817	1.227	1.012	.907	1.117	1.013
N	37	28	65	37	28	65

Sources: PRIO Data Bank; Appendix C.
(F73) R2 .01, p .38; (F82) R2 .001, p .93; (T) R2 .02.
(F73).

Table 69: Torture, Execution and Disappearance (1975, 1979) Controls with Welfare Factors

TORTUR79 Breakdown

TORTUR75

	(PHYSICAL)				(WOMENFAC)			
	Yes	No	Indet.	Total	Yes	No	Indet.	Total
Yes								
Mean	.073	-.298	1.988	-.001	-.337	-.731	.661	-.440
SD	.975	.764	.000	.959	.769	.827	.000	.809
N	29	14	1	44	29	14	1	44
No								
Mean	-.268	-.391	1.758	-.198	.973	1.002	.697	.970
SD	.873	1.085	.000	1.076	1.171	.716	.000	.867
N	6	8	1	15	6	8	1	15
Total								
Mean	.015	-.331	1.873	-.051	-.113	-.101	.679	-.081
SD	.955	.869	.163	.984	.969	1.150	.026	1.025
N	35	22	2	59	35	22	2	59

Sources: PRIO Data Bank; Appendix C.
| (T79) R2 .17, p .01; (T75) R2 .01, p .51; (Total) R2 .18.
|| (T79) R2 .02, p .57; (T75) R2 .37, p .001; (") R2 .41.

Table 70: Political and Civil Rights (1982) with Economic and Political Controls

	(AIDPER75)			(EPDGNP78)		
FREEDM82	More Free	Less Free	Total	More Free	Less Free	Total
Mean	10.336	14.543	12.490	22.947	34.744	28.922
SD	10.818	21.187	16.971	16.413	28.484	23.918
N	41	43	84	38	39	77
	(R^2 .02, p .26)			(R^2 .06, p .03)		

	(CGDP70)			(GVTGDP70)		
	More Free	Less Free	Total	More Free	Less Free	Total
Mean	5.231	4.595	4.894	18.111	18.330	18.210
SD	1.896	2.395	2.186	5.629	7.178	6.334
N	39	44	83	45	37	82
	(R^2 .02, p .19)			(R^2 .001, p .88)		

	(MFGDP70)		
	More Free	Less Free	Total
Mean	14.974	12.310	13.838
SD	5.508	6.048	5.853
N	39	29	68
	(R^2 .05, p .06)		

Sources: PRIO Data Bank; Appendix C.

Table 71: Welfare Change Indicators and Factors with Development Strategy Controls (1965-1978)

(WELFARE)	Open Door	State Capitalist	(DVST6578) State Socialist	Mixed	Total	Eta
CHLPER						
Mean	.883	.869	.719	.876	.868	r .38
SD	.069	.060	.329	.095	.117	R^2 .14
N	65	12	7	6	90	p .01
PROPER						
Mean	1.026	2.183	1.098	1.108	1.173	r .31
SD	.138	3.458	.000	.181	1.213	R^2 .10
N	59	9	1	5	74	p .06
WOMLF						
Mean	1.037	1.028	1.002	1.052	1.034	r .14
SD	.071	.068	.007	.078	.069	R^2 .02
N	64	12	5	6	87	p .65
PTRPED						
Mean	.970	.991	.908	.940	.969	r .09
SD	.194	.103	.093	.142	.177	R^2 .01
N	59	11	3	5	78	p .89
FPRSCH						
Mean	1.242	1.936	.951	1.396	1.337	r .34
SD	.451	1.538	.062	.793	.741	R^2 .11
N	61	11	3	6	81	p .03
FSCSCH						
Mean	1.644	1.992	2.037	1.002	1.663	r .29
SD	.682	1.028	.850	.550	.747	R^2 .09
N	60	9	4	5	78	p .08
CALPER						
Mean	1.037	1.050	1.102	1.079	1.042	r .10
SD	.133	.085	.000	.124	.125	R^2 .01
N	55	10	1	4	70	p .88
LIFEXB						
Mean	1.093	1.101	1.068	1.069	1.091	r .16
SD	.060	.048	.059	.041	.057	R^2 .03
N	61	12	7	4	84	p .56
CFOODP78						
Mean	123.805	113.000	127.250	119.250	122.722	r .22
SD	16.328	9.000	19.755	10.720	15.755	R^2 .05
N	41	5	4	4	54	p .46
INFLAA78						
Mean	14.204	10.367	----	11.325	13.536	r .15
SD	9.672	3.036	----	4.203	8.917	R^2 missing
N	56	9	----	4	69	p .43
FOODIN78						
Mean	493.487	238.344	105.350	233.580	431.029	r .12
SD	1081.692	71.234	2.475	68.632	955.718	R^2 .02
N	54	9	2	5	70	p .80
INFL6078						
Mean	363.073	247.300	----	297.750	342.507	r .13
SD	354.690	224.128	----	155.973	330.785	R^2 .02
N	55	10	----	4	69	p .58
EMPLOY78						
Mean	136.244	125.600	132.200	110.333	131.372	r .27
SD	37.882	15.505	12.106	7.220	31.763	R^2 .07
N	16	3	3	3	25	p .64
PHYSICAL						
Mean	-.078	-.518	1.873	-.205	-.073	r .37
SD	.999	.653	.163	1.123	1.019	R^2 .14
N	50	7	2	4	63	p .03
WOMENFAC						
Mean	-.081	.159	.679	-.073	-.029	r .15
SD	.889	1.515	.026	1.937	1.025	R^2 .02
N	50	7	2	4	63	p .73

Sources: PRIO Data Bank; Appendix C.

Table 72: <u>Alternative Security Systems and Doctrines</u>

Dimension	Technocratic army	People's army
Weapons and Equipment	Capital-intensive modern carrier systems: tanks, aircraft, and fighting ships, mobile tank divisions; partly locally built and assembled	Simple: anti-aircraft and anti-tank missiles, light infantry weapons; mainly local production; diversified supply lines; marine equipment for coastal protection
Armed Forces	Professional army: specialized troops in army, navy, air force	Militia system, personnel intensive, new organizational forms geared to serve also economic functions
Mobilization	Permanent mobilization of the professionals, limited reserves	In peacetime limited mobilization; in wartime total mobilization of the population
Command and Structure	Hierarchical, centralized	Democratic, decentralized
Strategy	Defensive and offensive, including potential for pre-emptive strikes	Defensive, reactive, territorial defence to prevent occupations

REFERENCES

Adams, G. (1976) The B-1 Bomber: An Analysis of Its Strategic Utility, Cost, Constituency and Economic Impact. Washington: Council on Economic Priorities.

Adekson, J. Bayo. (1978) "On the Theory of the Modernising Soldier: A Critique." Current Research on Peace and Violence (I): 28-31.

Albrecht, Ulrich, Peter Lock and Herbert Wulf. (1974) "Armaments and Underdevelopment." Bulletin of Peace Proposals, (V): 173- 185.

_____ (1978) "Appendix II: Researching Conversion: A Review of the State of the Art." In A Short Research Guide on Arms and Armed Forces. Ed. by U. Albrecht, Asbjørn Eide, Mary Kaldor, Milton Leitenberg and Julian Perry Robinson. London: Croom Helm.

_____ (1978a) Rustungskonversionsforschung. Eine Literaturstudie mit Forschungsempfelungen. Berlin.

Amnesty International. (1975) Amnesty International Report on Torture. New York: Farrar, Straus and Giroux. 1973 ed.

_____ (1976) Amnesty International Report 1975-1976. London: Amnesty International.

_____ (1979) Amnesty International Report: 1978. London: Amnesty International Publications.

References

_____ (1979a) *Amnesty International Report: 1979*. London: Amnesty International Publications.

Anderson, James R. (1982) *Bankrupting America*. Lansing, MI: Employment Research Association.

Anderson, Marion. (1975) *The Empty Pork Barrel*. Lansing, MI: Public Interest Research Group.

Askari, Hossein and Michael Glover. (1977) *Military Expenditures and the Level of Economic Development*. Austin: University of Texas, Bureau of Business Research.

Aspin, Les. (1976) "Jobs and Military Spending." *Priorities* (June).

Avery, William P. (1978) "Domestic Influences on Latin American Importation of U.S. Armaments." *International Studies Quarterly*, 22 (March): 121-42.

Ball, Nicole. (1981) *The Military in the Development Process*. Clarmont, CA: Regina Books (P.O. Box 280).

_____ (1983) "Defense and Development: A Critique of the Benoit Study". *Economic Development and Cultural Change*, 31:3 (April: 501-40.

Banks, Arthur S. and William Overstreet, eds. (1980) *Political Handbook of the World: 1980*. New York: McGraw Hill.

Becker, Abraham S. (1981) *The Burden of Soviet Defense: A Political-Economic Essay*. Santa Monica, CA: Rand Corp.

Benoit, Emile. (1973) *Defense and Economic Growth in Developing Countries*. Lexington, MA: D.C. Heath.

Bergendorff, Hans and Per Strangert. (1976) "Projections of Soviet Economic Growth and Defense Spending." Prepared statement for *The Soviet Economy in a New Perspective*, Subcommittee on Foreign Economic Policy, Joint Economic Committee, U.S. Congress. Washington, D.C.: U.S. Government Printing Office. Pp. 394-430.

References

Bezdek, Roger H. (1975) "The 1980 Economic Impact - Regional and Occupational - of Compensated Shifts in Defense Spending." Journal of Regional Science, 15 (2): 183-198.

Blechman, Barry M. and Stephen S. Kaplan. (1978) Force without War: U.S. Armed Forces as Political Instruments. Washington: Brookings Institution.

Block, Fred. (1978) "Marxist Theories of the State in World System Analysis". In Social Changes in the Capitalist World Economy. Ed. by Barbara Hockey Kaplan. Beverly Hills, CA: Sage.

Bollen, Kenneth (1983) "World System Position, Dependency, and Demography: The Cross-National Evidence". American Sociological Review, 48 (August):468-79.

Bond, Daniel L. And Herbert S. Levine. (1981) "The 11th Five-Year Plan, 1981-1985." Revised version of a paper prepared for the "Conference on the 26th Congress of the CPSU." Sponsored by the Rand Corporation and Columbia University, April 23-25.

Brzoska, Michael. (1981) "The Reporting of Military Expenditures." Journal of Peace Research, XVIII (3): 261-276.

_____ and Herbert Wulf. (1980) "Rejoinder to Benoit's 'Growth and Defense in Developing Countries' - Misleading Results and Questionable Methods." Hamburg: Institut für Friedensforschung und Sicherheitspolitik an der Universität Hamburg.

Burke, David. (1980) "Defense and Mass Mobilization in Romania." Armed Forces and Society, 7 (Fall): 31-49.

Calmfors, Lars and Jan Rylander. (1976) "Economic Restrictions on Soviet Defense Expenditure - A Model Approach." Prepared statement for The Soviet Economy in a New Perspective, Subcommittee on Foreign Economic Policy, Joint Economic Committee, US Congress. Washington, D.C.: U.S. Government Printing Office. Pp. 377-93.

References

Caputo, David. (1975) "New Perspectives on the Pub-
    lic Policy Implications of Defense and Welfare
    Expenditures in Four Modern Democracies:
    1950-1970." Policy Sciences (6): 423-46.

Chikwendu, Ebitimi. (1977) "Considerations of the
    Freedom Value in a Military Regime: A Decade of
    Military Rule in Nigeria." Verfassung und Recht
    in Übersee. (Hamburg), 10 (4): 531-541.

Chomsky, Noam and Edward S. Herman. (1979) The
    Washington Connection and Third World Fascism.
    Boston: South End Press.

CIA. (1977) Organization and Management in the
    Soviet Economy: The Ceaseless Search for
    Panaceas. ER-77-10769. Washington, DC: CIA.

Cohn, Stanley. (1973) "Economic Burden of Defense
    Expenditures." Prepared statement for Soviet
    Economic Prospects for the Seventies, Subcom-
    mittee on Foreign Economic Policy, Joint Econo-
    mic Committee, U.S Congress. Washington, DC:
    U.S. Government Printing Office. Pp. 147-62.

Cortright, David and Michelle Stone. (1982) Military
    Budget Manual. Washington: SANE.

Cusack, Thomas. (1981) "The Economic Burden of
    Defense: A Research Note."

Dabelko, David and James M. McCormick. (1977) "Op-
    portunity Costs of Defense: Some Cross- Natio-
    nal Evidence." Journal of Peace Research, 14
    (2): 145-54.

Danopoulos, Constantine and Kent Patel. (1980)
    "Military Professionals as Political Governors:
    A Case Study of Contemporary Greece." West
    European Politics, 3:2 (May): 188-202.

DeGrasse, Robert Jr, with Paul Murphy and William
    Ragen. (1982) The Costs and Consequences of
    Reagan's Military Buildup. A Report to the
    International Association of Machinists and
    Aerospace Workers and The Coalition for a New
    Foreign and Military Policy. New York: Council
    on Economic Priorities.

Dickson, Thomas Jr. (1977) "An Economic Output and
    Impact Analysis of Civilian and Military

235

Regimes in Latin America." Development and Change, (8): 325-45.

Dumas, Lloyd J. (1981) "Disarmament and Economy in Advanced Industrialized Countries - The U.S. and the U.S.S.R." Bulletin of Peace Proposals, (1): 1-10.

Eberwein, Wolf-Dieter. (1981) "The Quantitative Study of International Conflict: Quantity and Quality? An Assessment of Empirical Research." Journal of Peace Research, XVII (1): 19-38.

Eide, Asbjørn. (1980) "Militarization with a Global Reach: A Challenge to Sovereignty, Security and the International Legal Order". In Problems of Contemporary Militarism. Ed. by A. Eide and Marek Thee. London: Croom Helm. Pp. 299-322.

Emmanuel, Arghiri (1972) Unequal Exchange. New York: Monthly Review Press.

Fallows, James. (1981) National Defense. New York: Random House.

Farris, Fred. (1982) "Measuring the Quality of Life". International Herald Tribune, November 26. P. 7.

Farsoun, Smith K. and Walter F. Carroll. (1978) "State Capitalism and Counterrevolution in the Middle East: A Thesis". In Social Change in the Capitalist World Economy. Ed. by Barbara Hockey Kaplan. Beverly Hills: CA: Sage.

Finer, S.E. (1975) The Man on Horseback. Harmondsworth, UK: Penguin Bks. 2nd ed.

Fitch, John Samuel. (1979) "The Political Impact of U.S. Military Aid in Latin America." Armed Forces and Society, V (Spring): 360-86.

Frank, André Gunder. (1979) The Arms Economy in the Third World. Norwich, UK: University of East Anglia, School of Development Studies.

Galperin, G. and V. Platov. (1982) "Revolutionary Transformation in Ethiopia." International Affairs, 6 (June): 58-66.

References

Gansler, Jacques S. (1982) The Defense Industry.
    Cambridge, MA: MIT Press.

Gastil, Raymond D. (1973) "The New Criteria of
    Freedom." Freedom at Issue, 17 (January/Feb-
    ruary): 2-5.

_____ (1979) "The Comparative Survey of
    Freedom-IX." Freedom at Issue, 49 (January/
    February): 3-14.

_____ (1982) "The Comparative Survey of
    Freedom - the Tenth Year." Freedom at Issue, 64
    (January - February 1982): 3-14.

Gauhar, Altaf. (1982) "The Cost of a Soldier."
    South, 21 (July): 8-14.

Gottheil, Fred M. (1974) "An Economic Assessment of
    the Military Burden in the Middle East."
    Journal of Conflict Resolution, 18 (September):
    502-13.

Halliday, Fred. (1983) The Making of the Second Cold
    War. London: Verso Editions and NLB.

Hansen, B. (1972) "Economic Development of Egypt."
    In Economic Development and Population Growth
    in the Middle East. Ed. by C. Cooper and S.
    Alexander. New York: American Elsevier.

Hanson, Simon G. (1965) "The Alliance for Progress:
    The Third Year - Military." Inter-American
    Economic Affairs, 18 (Spring): 20-37.

_____ (1968) "The Alliance for Progress. The
    Sixth Year - The Military." Inter-American
    Economic Affairs, 22 (Winter): 75-91.

Hayter, Teresa. (1971) Aid as Imperialism.
    Baltimore, MD: Penguin.

Heeger, Gerald. (1977) "Politics in the Post-Mili-
    tary State: Some Reflections on the Pakistan
    Experience." World Politics, 29 (January):
    242-62.

Herman, Edward. (1982) The Real-Terror Network.
    Boston: South End Press.

References

Hobsbawn, Z.J. (1973) Revolutionaries: Contemporary Essays. New York: Pantheon Books.

Hofferbert, Richard I. (1974) The Study of Public Policy. Indianapolis: Bobbs-Merrill Co.

Hurewitz, J.C. (1969) Middle East Policies: The Military Dimension. New York.

Hveem, Helge and Raino Malnes. (1980) Military Use of Natural Resources: The Case for Conversion and Control. A Report Prepared for the United Nations Group of Governmental Experts on the Relationship between Disarmament and Development. Oslo: PRIO (International Peace Research Institute, Oslo).

ILO. (1978) Yearbook of Labour Statistics: 1978. Geneva: International Labour Office.

International Peace Research Association. (1978) "The Impact of Militarization on Development and Human Rights." Statement by the Study Group on Militarization. Bulletin of Peace Proposals, 9 (2): 170-82.

Jackman, Robert. (1976) "Politicians in Uniform?" American Political Science Review, 70 (December): 1078-97.

Janowitz, Morris. (1964) The Military in the Political Development of New Nations. Chicago: University of Chicago Press.

Johansen, Robert C. (1979) "The Arms Bazaar: SALT was Never Intended to Disarm." Harper's Magazine (May).

Johnson, John J. (1962) The Role of the Military in Under-Developed Countries. Princeton, NJ: Princeton University Press.

_____ (1964) The Military and Society in Latin America. Stanford, CA: Stanford University Press.

Jolly, Richard, ed. (1978) Disarmament and World Development. Oxford: Pergamon Press.

Kaldor, Mary. (1976) "The Military in World Development." World Development, 4 (June).

References

_____ (1978) "The Military in Third World Development." In Disarmament and World Development. Ed. by Richard Jolly. Oxford: Pergamon Press. Pp. 57-82.

_____ (1981) The Baroque Arsenal. New York: Hill and Wang.

Kende, Istvan. (1973) Guerres Locales en Asie, en Afrique et en Amërique Latine. Budapest: Centre pour la Recherche de l'Afro- Asie de l'Acadëmie des Sciences de Hongrie.

Kennedy, Gavin. (1974) The Military and the Third World. New York: Scribners.

Khrushchev, N.S. (1974) Krushchev Remembers: The Last Testament. Edited and Translated by Strobe Talbott. Boston: Little, Brown.

Klare, Michael T. (1977) Supplying Repression. New York: The Field Foundation.

_____ (1981) Resurgent Militarism. Washington: Institute for Policy Studies.

_____ (1982) "The Weinberger Revolution". Inquiry, September, pp. 25-8

Kohler, Gernot. (1978) Global Apartheid. New York: World Policy Institute.

Kolodziej, Edward A. (1982) "French Security Policy: Decisions and Dilemmas". Armed Forces and Society, 8:2 (Winter): 185-221.

Kozyrez, A. (1980) "A Goldmine for the Monopolies." International Affairs, (May): 124-5.

Kurian, George Thomas. (1979) The Book of World Rankings. New York: Facts on File.

Landgren-Backstrøm, Signe. (1974) "The World Arms Trade: The Impact on Development." Bulletin of Peace Proposals, 10 (3): 297-300.

Leitenberg, Milton. (1976) "Notes on the Diversion of Resources for Military Purposes in Developing Nations." Journal of Peace Research, XIII (2): 111-16.

_____ and Nicole Ball. (1980) "The Military Expenditures of Less Developed Nations as a Proportion of Their State Budgets: A Research Note." In Problems of Contemporary Militarism. Ed. by Asbjørn Eide and Marek Thee. London: Croom Helm. Pp. 286-95.

Lider, Julian. (1980) "The Critique of Militarism in Soviet Studies". In Problems of Contemporary Militarism. Ed. by Asbjørn Eide and Marek Thee. London: Croom Helm. Pp. 173-91.

Lindroos, Reijo. (1980) Disarmament and Employment: A Study on the Employment Aspects of Military Spending and on the Possibilities to Convert Arms Production to Civilian Production. Tampere, Finland: Central Organization of Finnish Trade Unions, SAK in Cooperation with Tampere Peace Research Institute (TAPRI).

LPDSG. Labour Party Defence Study Group. (1977) Sense About Defence. London: Quartet.

Lumsden, Malvern. (1980) "Militarism: Cultural Dimensions of Militarisation". In Problems of Contemporary Militarism. Ed. by Asbjørn Eide and Marek Thee. London: Croom Helm.

Marquit, Erwin (1983) The Socialist Countries. Minneapolis: Marxist Educational Press.

McKinlay, R.D. and A.S. Cohan. (1976) "Performance and Instability in Military and Nonmilitary Regime Systems." American Political Science Review, LXX:3 (September): 850-64.

Melman, Seymour. (1974) The Permanent War Economy: American Capitalism in Decline. New York: Simon & Schuster.

_____ (1979) "Inflation and Unemployment as Products of War Economy." Bulletin of Peace Proposals, 9 (4): 359-74.

Midlarski, Manus I. and Stafford T. Thomas. (1975) "Domestic Social Structure and International Warfare." In Martin A. Nettleship, R. Dalegivens and Anderson Nettleship, eds. War, Its Causes and Correlates. The Hague: Mouton. Pp. 531-48.

References

Moll, Randall D. (1980) "Arms Race and Military Ex-
    penditure Models". Journal of Conflict Resolu-
    tion, 24 (March): 153-85.

Monteforte Toledo, Mario. (1970) La solucion a la
    peruana. Mexico: UNAM.

Morrison, D.G. and H.M. Stevenson. (1974) "Social
    Complexity, Economic Development and Military
    Coups d'Etat: Convergence and Divergence of
    Empirical Tests of Theory in Latin America,
    Asia, and Africa." Journal of Peace Research, 2
    (4): 345-47.

Mosley, Hugh G. (1982) Economic and Social Conse-
    quences of the Arms Race. Lexington, MA: D.C.
    Heath & Co.

Murphy, Caryle. (1982) "Military Attachës", Inter-
    national Herald Tribune, 25 November 1982. P.
    24.

Needler, Martin C. (1966) "Political Development and
    Military Intervention in Latin America".
    American Political Science Review, 60 (Septem-
    ber): 616-26.

Neuman, Stephanie. (1978) "Security, Military Ex-
    penditures and Socioeconomic Development:
    Reflections on Iran." Orbis, (Fall): 569-94.

Nordlinger, Eric. (1970) "Soldiers in Mufti: The
    Impact of Military Rule upon Economic and
    Social Change in the Non-Western States."
    American Political Science Review, 64 (Decem-
    ber): 1131-48.

Olorunsola, Victor A. (1977) Soldiers and Power: The
    Development Performance of the Nigerian Mili-
    tary Regime. Stanford, CA: Hoover Institution
    Press.

Payer, Cheryl. (1977) The Debt Trap. New York:
    Monthly Review Press.

Perlmutter, Amos. (1977) The Military and Politics
    in Modern Times: On Professionals, Praetorians,
    and Revolutionary Soldiers. New Haven: Yale
    University Press.

References

Peroff, Kathleen and Margaret Podolak-Warren. (1978) "Does Spending on Defence Cut Spending on Health? A Time-Series of the U.S. Economy 1929-74." British Journal of Political Science, (9): 21-39.

Pfaff, William. (1982) International Herald Tribune.

Pierre, Andrew J., ed. (1979) Arms Transfers and American Foreign Policy. New York.

Powell, J. Bingham Jr. (1982) Contemporary Democracies: Participation, Stability and Violence. Cambridge, MA: Harvard University Press.

Pryor, Frederic L. (1968) Public Expenditures in Communist and Capitalist Nations. London: George Allen and Unwin.

Pye, Lucien. (1962) "Armies in the Process of Political Modernization." In The Role of the Military in Undeveloped Countries. Ed. by John J. Johnson. Princeton, NJ: Princeton University Press.

Randle, Michael. (1980) Militarism and Repression. South Boston, MA: International Seminars on Training for Nonviolent Action (148 'N' Street, zip 02127).

Ravenhill, John. (1980) "Comparing Regime Performance in Africa: The Limitations of Cross-National Aggregate Analysis." Journal of Modern African Studies, XVII:1 (March): 99-126.

Rickover, Hyman G. (1982) "Advice from Admiral Rickover." "Testimony." The New York Review of Books (March 18): 12-14.

Rimland, Bernard and Gerald E. Larson. (1981) "The Manpower Quality Decline: An Ecological Perspective." Armed Forces and Society, 8:1 (May): 21-78.

Russett, Bruce M. (1970) What Price Vigilance: The Burdens of National Defense. New Haven, CT: Yale University Press.

Sarkesian, Sam C. (1978) "A Political Perspective on Military Power in Developing Areas." In The

References

Military and Security in the Third World:
Domestic and International Impacts. Ed. by
Sheldon W. Simon. Boulder, CO: Westview.

Scheer, Robert. (1982) Reagan, Bush and Nuclear War.
New York: Random House.

Schmitter, Philippe C. (1973) "Foreign Military Assistance, National Military Spending and Military Rule in Latin America." In Military Rule
in Latin America: Functions, Consequences and
Perspectives. Ed. by Philippe C. Schmitter.
Beverly Hills: Sage. Pp. 117-87.

Seliktar, Ofira. (1980) "The Cost of Vigilance in
Israel: Linking the Economic and Social Costs
of Defense." Journal of Peace Research, 17 (4):
339-55.

Selser, Gregorio. (1977) "El Pentagono impone las
reglas del juego." Nueva Politica, 2 (abril -
septiembre): 293-316.

Singer, J. David. (1981) "Accounting for International War: The State of the Discipline."
Journal of Peace Research, XVII:1 (1981):
1-18.

_____ and Melvin Small. (1972) The Wages of
War: 1816- 1965. New York: Wiley.

SIPRI. (1973) The Meaning and Measurement of Mili-
tary Expenditure. SIPRI Research Report No. 10.
Stockholm: Stockholm International Peace
Research Institute.

_____ (1980) Armamentos o desarme? Stockholm:
Stockholm International Peace Research
Institute.

_____ (1981) World Armaments and Disarmament:
SIPRI Yearbook, 1981. Stockholm.

Sivard, Ruth Leger. (1979) World Military and Social
Expenditures: 1979. Leesburg, VA: World
Priorities.

_____ (1981) World Military and Social Expenditures, 1981. Leesburg, VA: World Priorities.

References

Skjelsbaek, Kjell (1981). "Militarism. Its Dimen-
    sions and Corollaries: An Attempt at Conceptual
    Clarification." In Problems of Contemporary
    Militarism. Ed. by Asbjørn Eide and Marek Thee.
    London: Croom Helm. Pp. 77-105.

Sklar, Holly. (1980) The Trilateral Commission and
    Elite Planning for World Management. Boston:
    South End Press.

Smith, R.P. (1977) "Military Expenditure and Capi-
    talism." Cambridge Journal of Economics (I):
    61-76.

Stein, Arthur A. (1978) The Nation at War.
    Baltimore: Johns Hopkins University Press.

Szymanski, Albert. (1973) "Military Spending and
    Economic Stagnation." American Journal of
    Sociology, 79 (July): 1-14.

_____ (1981) The Logic of Imperialism. New
York: Praeger.

Tannahill, R. Neal. (1976) "The Performance of Mili-
    tary Governments in South America." Journal of
    Political and Military Sociology, 4 (Fall):
    233-44.

Taylor, Charles Lewis and Michael C. Hudson. (1972)
    World Handbook of Political and Social Indica-
    tors. New Haven, CT: Yale University Press. 2nd
    ed.

Terhal, Peter. (1982) "Foreign Exchange Costs of the
    Indian Military: 1950-1972." Journal of Peace
    Research, XIX (3): 251-59.

Thee, Marek. (1980) "The China-Indochina Conflict:
    Notes on the Background and Conflict - The Case
    of Neutrality." Journal of Peace Research. 17
    (3): 223-33.

_____ (1981) "Scope and Priorities in Peace
    Research." UNESCO Yearbook in Peace and Con-
    flict Studies 1981.

Thompson, William R. (1973) The Grievances of Mili-
    tary Coup-Makers. Beverly Hills, CA: Sage.

References

_____ (1980) "Corporate Coup-Maker Grievances and
Types of Regime Targets." Comparative Political
Studies, 12 (January): 485-96.

Tuomi, Helena and Raino Vayrynen. (1980) Transnatio-
nal Corporations, Armaments and Development: A
Study of Transnational Military Production,
International Transfer of Military Technology
and Their Impact on Development. Tampere,
Finland: Tampere Peace Research Institute.
Report No. 22.

UNSG. (1978) Economic and Social Consequences of the
Arms Race and of Military Expenditures. Revised
Report of the Secretary-General, New York:
United Nations.

_____ (1982) The Relationship between Disarmament and Development. Department of Political
and Security Council Affairs, United Nations
Centre for Disarmament. Report of the Secretary-General. New York: United Nations.

USACDA. (1972) World Military Expenditures: 1971.
Washington: US Arms Control and Disarmament
Agency.

_____ (1978) World Military Expenditure and
Arms Transfers: 1967-1976. Washington: US Arms
Control and Disarmament Agency.

_____ (1979) World Military Expenditure and
Arms Transfers: 1968-1977. Washington: US Arms
Control and Disarmament Agency.

_____ (1982) World Military Expenditure and
Arms Transfers: 1970-1979. Washington: US Arms
Control and Disarmament Agency.

USDL. (1972) Projections of the Post-Vietnam
Economy, 1975. Washington: US Department of
Labor, Bureau of Labor Statistics.

_____ (1976) The Structure of the U.S.
Economy in 1980 and 1985. Washington: US
Department of Labor, Bureau of Labor
Statistics.

USDS. (1979) Report on Human Rights Practices in
Countries Receiving U.S. Aid by the U.S.
Department of State. Submitted to the Committee

References

on Foreign Relations, US Senate, and Committee
on Foreign Affairs, US House of Representa-
tives, 8 February 1979.

Vagts, Alfred. (1967) A History of Militarism. New
York: Free Press 1957 ed. reprinted.

Wangborg, Manne. (1979) "The Use of Resources for
Military Purposes: A Bibliographical Starting
Point". Bulletin of Peace Proposals. 10 (3):
319-31.

Weaver, Jerry L. (1973) "Assessing the Impact of
Military Rule: Alternative Approaches." In
Military Rule in Latin America: Functions, Con-
sequences and Perspectives. Ed. by Philippe C.
Schmitter. Beverly Hills, CA: Sage.

Weede, Erich. (1981) "Income Inequality, Average Income, and Domestic Violence". Journal of Conflict Resolution. 25:4 (December): 639-54.

Whynes, David K. (1979) The Economics of Third World
Military Expenditures. London: Macmillan.

Woddis, Jack. (1977) Armies and Politics. London:
Lawrence & Wishart.

Wolpin, Miles D. (1973) Military Aid and Counterrevolution in the Third World. Lexington, MA:
D.C. Heath.

_____ (1977) "Militarism, Socialism and
Civilian Rule in the Third World: A Comparison
of Development Costs and Benefits". Instant
(Current) Research on Peace and Violence. VIII
(3-4): 105-33.

_____ (1981) (1982) Militarism and Social
Revolution in the Third World. Totowa, NJ:
Alanheld, Osmun & Co.

_____ (1981a) "Military Professionalism and
Leftist Political Movements". Current Research
on Peace and Violence. (1): 33-54.

_____ (1983). State Terrorism in the Third
World. Oslo: International Peace Research
Institute, Oslo.

References

                (1983a) "Socio-Political Radicalism and Military Professionalism in the Third World." Comparative Politics, XV:3 (April).

World Bank. (1976) World Tables: 1976. Baltimore: Johns Hopkins University Press.

                (1979) World Atlas of the Child. Washington: World Bank.

                (1979a) 1978 World Bank Atlas. Washington: World Bank.

                (1980) World Tables: 1980. Baltimore: Johns Hopkins University Press.

                (1980a) World Development Report: 1980. Washington: World Bank.

                (1981) World Bank Annual Report: 1981. Washington: World Bank.

The World in Figures: 1976. London: The Economist. 1976.

Wulf, Herbert. (1979) "Dependent Militarism in the Periphery and Possible Alternative Concepts." In Arms Transfers in the Modern World. Ed. by Stephanie G. Neuman and Robert E. Harkavy. New York: Praeger.